EDITH MARYON

Rudolf Steiner and the Sculpture of Christ in Dornach

Peter Selg

Translated by Matthew Barton

TEMPLE LODGE

Temple Lodge Publishing Ltd.
Hillside House, The Square
Forest Row, RH18 5ES

www.templelodge.com

Published by Temple Lodge 2022

Originally published in German under the title *Edith Maryon, Rudolf Steiner und die Dornacher Christus-Plastik* by Verlag am Goetheanum, Dornach, Switzerland, 2006. This edition is based on the revised second edition, 2018

A CIP catalogue record for this book is available from the British Library

ISBN 978 1 912230 95 2

Cover by Morgan Creative
Typeset by Symbiosys Technologies, Visakhapatnam, India
Printed and bound by 4Edge Ltd., Essex

 PETER SELG, born 1963, is a medical doctor specializing in child and adolescent psychiatry and psychotherapy. He is head of the Ita Wegman Institute for Basic Research into Anthroposophy in Arlesheim, and co-head of the General Anthroposophical Section of the School of Spiritual Science (Goetheanum, Dornach). He teaches medical anthropology and ethics at the University of Witten/ Herdecke and the Alanus University of Arts and Social Sciences in Alfter, Germany. Peter Selg is the author of dozens of books on anthroposophy.

Contents

Edith Maryon was already a pupil on an esoteric path before she identified Rudolf Steiner as her teacher and asked him that she be allowed to offer her life to the tasks of anthroposophy. In a letter from the beginning of her connection with him, she wrote: 'I think the time may have come when I might do something other than simply sit and study for myself; it is also my great wish, if it should be possible, to do something for Theosophy, and not merely for myself alone.' Rudolf Steiner affirmed her in this wish.

It would become apparent that Edith Maryon placed all her gifts and capacities at the service of the world of spirit and in doing so combined her esoteric life with a practical sense for what was necessary on earth. She offered this service in awareness of what is needed in the world at a particular historical moment. Thus, as Rudolf Steiner once expressed it, she did something for the cause of anthroposophy which, 'unburdened by one's personal existence, is the expression of a responsibility that ascends into worlds of spirit'. Here one's own karma can connect with that of others to pursue a common mission.

Hans Müller-Wiedemann[1]

Foreword

The most essential and intrinsic quality of her soul [...] was not a particular branch of human endeavour, not even art; the most salient of her soul tendencies, her soul intentions, was the striving for spirituality [...]. It was also primarily this pursuit of a deepening esotericism which she then continually sought within the Anthroposophical Society for herself and for her soul's striving. At the same time, certainly, she was moved by the far-reaching and encompassing aim of collaborating in our work.

Rudolf Steiner, 3 May 1924[2]

Edith Maryon (1872-1924) was one of Rudolf Steiner's most important colleagues, a close friend and esoteric pupil at his side. Maryon was of key significance for Rudolf Steiner in the last decade of his life and work. With her he created in Dornach the unparalleled sculpture of Christ as well as numerous further works for the emerging Goetheanum. From 1914/15 onward, Edith Maryon accompanied Rudolf Steiner's endeavours with the greatest attentiveness, in the sanctum of the workshop at the Dornach studio and in almost daily correspondence. No one else, apart from Marie Steiner-von Sivers, participated so fully in Steiner's work and circumstances at this time as Edith Maryon. No one else received anything like so many or such detailed letters from Rudolf Steiner between 1918 and 1924 as she did, letters testifying to a great intimacy in which he spoke of his lectures and his personal situation, of the embattled public standing of anthroposophy, of the failings of the Anthroposophical Society and the lack of sufficient numbers of true colleagues. Almost invariably these letters emphasized his longing for the Dornach studio and their shared work—'To be working again in our studio is something I greatly long for. Well, it will happen again soon.'[3]

The circumstances of Edith Maryon's life and destiny did not often allow her to accompany Rudolf Steiner's lecture tours. Her very limited finances (after she had selflessly relinquished her artistic life in England for work in Dornach), her health and also the need to protect the sculptural 'Christ Group' meant that she almost always remained uninterruptedly in Dornach. After her death Daniel von Mutach wrote as follows to Rudolf Steiner:

> During the hot weeks of summer when you were abroad, and almost all our colleagues left Dornach, Miss Maryon always stayed patiently with the Group, airing the studio at night, and keeping the wood damp to ensure that excessively large pieces of the model did not detach themselves and fall off. In this way she spent long years guarding the model.[4]

Although it was hard for Maryon to bear the loneliness during Rudolf Steiner's absence, this 'guardianship' of the developing work stood always at the centre of her life. The windows of her small, modest flat—in the house that she herself had designed together with Rudolf Steiner—all faced the studio and the Goetheanum, as it were in an absolute focus of consciousness. That Edith Maryon was in a sense the personal victim of the destruction of the Goetheanum by fire on New Year's Eve 1922/23—the arson attack on the building and on Rudolf Steiner—is implicit in, and intrinsic to her path, centred as this was on Rudolf Steiner and the 'Building of Humanity'. Her early death on 2 May 1924, after fifteen months of illness, shook Rudolf Steiner to the core. According to Steiner, the second Goetheanum would inevitably lack the spiritual-moral quality bound up with Edith Maryon's being and work:[5] 'With her death, the Anthroposophical Society and the whole of the anthroposophic movement has suffered a great loss.'[6] In the last period of his life and work this 'great loss' was thus also one suffered by Rudolf Steiner himself, who died less than a year after Edith Maryon, on 30 March 1925.

The present volume on Maryon arose as part of preparatory studies for an extensive biography of Rudolf Steiner. It continues the series of monographs on Steiner's esoteric pupils and colleagues, which includes studies already published on Michael Bauer and Marie Steiner-von Sivers.[7] It makes available for the first time papers from the literary estates of Edith Maryon and Ita Wegman (in the latter case documents which Edith Maryon passed to her doctor Ita Wegman) as well as various handwritten manuscripts from the Rudolf Steiner Archive in Dornach. Despite these papers, this study does not significantly extend the biographical survey of Edith Maryon first offered by Rex Raab.[8] Instead, it focuses consistently and exclusively on Edith Maryon's connection and relationship with Rudolf Steiner. The artistic and (art-historical) dimension of their collaboration is not the primary theme of this account either, figuring only in so far as Rudolf Steiner himself refers to this expressly in lectures and addresses. The aim, rather, is to render more clearly visible through the documentation offered here the spiritual signature of Edith Maryon's connection with Rudolf Steiner, anthroposophy and the Christ sculpture, in the context of the whole of Rudolf Steiner's life's work.

Inner engagement with Edith Maryon's life and destiny and her collaboration on the Christ sculpture in Dornach seems to be of key significance for the future of the anthroposophic movement. It leads directly, after all, to Rudolf Steiner's tasks and the underlying foundations of his work, as he clearly expressed them in his cremation address for Edith Maryon. Maryon's destined path by the side of Rudolf Steiner presents us with a singular and lonely grandeur. Invoking this, Rudolf Steiner at the same time pointed to the moral, or indeed spiritual-moral quality necessary for all true collaborative work at the Goetheanum, indirectly highlighting the widespread lack of this especially—but by no means exclusively—amongst the leading personalities of the Anthroposophical Society. The tragic end of Edith Maryon's path is closely associated with the destruction of the first Goetheanum, which—besides the destructive conflict from an increasingly militant opposition—was preceded by grave inner omissions in the public representation and realization of anthroposophy. Painful accounts of this situation were a recurring motif in numerous letters which Steiner wrote to Maryon prior to 31 December 1922.

If we survey the existential nature of these situations it becomes apparent that Edith Maryon's life and work for and with Rudolf Steiner throws up numerous and still highly topical questions: one of these inevitably concerns the future location of the sculptural Group that had been in progress since the autumn of 1914, and survived the fire. In the spring of 1915, Friedrich Rittelmeyer asked Rudolf Steiner if it would not be necessary to disclose to humanity the image of Christ made possible through spiritual-scientific investigation ('Yes, if you know what Christ looked like, should one not in some way make this image of Christ available to humanity?'[9]) Rudolf Steiner agreed and invited Rittelmeyer to Dornach to acquaint himself more closely with the emerging work, which was conceived as the very centre and crowning point of the St John's building. This left a profound and lasting impression on Rittelmeyer—'The wakening call to our era / that speaks from the deeds of these hands / simply cannot be any more powerful and emphatic.'[10] The view that subsequently became the generally accepted— and even partially exploited—tradition, according to which Rudolf Steiner had wanted the sculpture to be housed in its own room in the second Goetheanum, and had spoken out explicitly against it being placed on the stage, was only questioned around 50 years ago by Russian artist Assja Turgenieff, based on documents newly discovered at the time.[11] Turgenieff, who had collaborated closely with Edith Maryon and had accompanied the Group's development, was better placed than almost anyone else to raise questions once again about 'Rudolf Steiner's true intentions'. Through Edith Maryon, Turgenieff knew of Steiner's reticence about placing the almost finished work in the small cupola for what was called the 'opening ceremony' of the first Goetheanum in the autumn of 1920. ('She [Edith Maryon] repeated his words that the time, and the members were not fit yet for this; that one should wait.'[12]) But she also knew of Steiner's future and further intentions relating to the continuing and even increasing need to make the Christ image 'available to humanity', not in a secluded, isolated, catacomb-type room but at a central place in the Goetheanum, the School of Spiritual Science in Dornach. In the context of current endless internal debates about Rudolf Steiner, the supposedly 'trans-Christian' character of his spiritual science, about constitutional and Society matters and also in view of tendencies to self-involvement and self-destruction within the Anthroposophical Society, we can certainly ask whether the times and especially the 'members' are 'fitter' now in the early 21st century than they were in 1920. But at the same time the importance of Rittelmeyer's words and the need for their visible realization in the near future is beyond question, and indeed still more relevant.

I dedicate my study of Edith Maryon, Rudolf Steiner and the Christ sculpture in Dornach to Johannes Wilhelm Gädeke (Stuttgart), with my gratitude.

Peter Selg
Arlesheim, August 2006

I
'Doing what it is my destiny to do'

Edith Maryon's Path to Rudolf Steiner
(1912-1914)

> *Edith Maryon was destined to join*
> *the anthroposophic movement [....]*[13]

Is there anything that can better enable us to understand the Mystery of Golgotha?

Edith Maryon[14]

In 1909, at the age of 36,[15] the English sculptor Edith Louisa Church Maryon became the member of an esoteric order, the 'Hermetic Students of the Golden Dawn'. At her admission, she chose the Latin motto, *'Viam veram guaero'* ('I seek the true path'), and with these words joined a spiritual school whose form was modelled on the ancient Eleusinian mysteries.[16] Robert William Felkin, leader of the London group 'Stella Matutina' which Maryon joined, was a physician pursuing Rosicrucianism who, since 1906, had tried to make contact with Rudolf Steiner, and succeeded in doing so in 1910. That year Neville Meakin, Felkin's deputy leader of the 'Stella Matutina', stayed in Berlin for several months, and there was able to attend Rudolf Steiner's internal lectures and subsequently reported on these back in London. Edith Maryon herself purchased and studied the English translation of essays by Rudolf Steiner on spiritual schooling which had appeared in previous years in the journal *Lucifer-Gnosis*, and were published in 1909 for the first time in book form in Germany under the title *Knowledge of the Higher Worlds*.

1909 and 1910 were key years in the development of Rudolf Steiner's Christological lectures and writings. During 1909 Steiner completed his wide-ranging book on cosmology and Christology, *Occult Science, an Outline*, and published his schooling book *Knowledge of the Higher Worlds*.

On 1 January 1909 he had already started to describe in his lectures the polar anti-Christian, adversarial powers of Lucifer and Ahriman,[17] and to elaborate on these in ever more detailed fashion. In September 1909, in Basel, Rudolf Steiner first disclosed

INITIATION AND ITS RESULTS

A SEQUEL TO
"THE WAY OF INITIATION"

BY

RUDOLF STEINER, Ph.D.

TRANSLATED FROM THE GERMAN BY
CLIFFORD BAX

LONDON
THEOSOPHICAL PUBLISHING SOCIETY
1909

tangible secrets of the being of Jesus, in a course on the Luke
Gospel whose contents, to some degree at least, formed part of
a mode of cognition and dimension of history which he would
later develop further in what he called the 'Fifth Gospel'.[18] The
following year, 1910, in numerous lectures, Rudolf Steiner developed the theme of the future appearance of the Christ being in
the etheric as the key spiritual event of coming times, an understanding of which was being prepared by theosophical spiritual science ('We learn that this is something that lays a huge
responsibility upon us, preparing as it does for the fully tangible
reappearance of Christ. The Christ will reappear because human
beings will raise themselves upward to him in etheric vision. If we
grasp this, then spiritual science appears to us as the preparation
of humankind for Christ's return [...]'[19]). In 1910 Rudolf Steiner
spoke of these things in many places in Europe, with great intensity and subtlety of presentation. We have no evidence to show
whether Neville Meakin attended any of these lectures in Berlin.
But two years later (spring 1912), the London jurist Harry Collison, who had joined 'Stella Matutina' after Edith Maryon, and
who had heard Steiner's Christological lectures in Rome in the
spring of 1910, organized lectures on the etheric reappearance of
Christ at his London studio. At the invitation of Collison these
were given by the Swedish theosophist Baron Carl Alphonse
Walleen, in close reference to accounts by Rudolf Steiner ('The
Turning Point of Evolution by Baron C.A. Walleen. Based on the
Unpublished Works of Dr Rudolf Steiner'), and were closely and
intently followed by Edith Maryon.

*

A few weeks after these lectures, at the age of 40, Edith
Maryon left England for studies in Italy, intending to follow
this up with a trip to Egyptian mystery sites. But she broke off
this journey in Milan, and returned to England.[20] According to
verbal communications and the accounts based on these by Rex
Raab, Edith Maryon travelled from Milan to Berlin and there
attended Rudolf Steiner's lecture of 14 May on the need for
a future depiction of Christ.[21] Documents in Maryon's estate

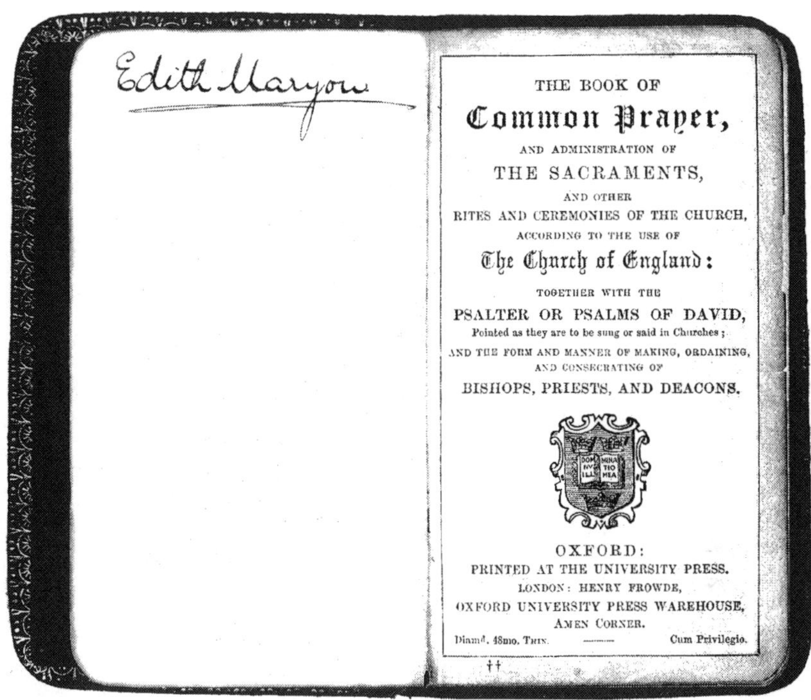

Ita Wegman Archive, Arlesheim

relating to her life awaken doubt about the historical authenticity of these reports, or her actual attendance at the lecture in Berlin referred to[22]—though not about the central importance of the content of the Berlin lecture for Edith Maryon's further life and work.

Rudolf Steiner's comments of 14 May followed on from a great, innovative presentation that he had given six days earlier in the ancient Dominican city of Cologne. There, on 8 May, a day held in celebration of Blavatsky who was revered in the theosophical movement, Rudolf Steiner had spoken, after some introductory comments, about the future of the Christ being on earth: by the end and goal of earth evolution, he said, Christ will have become its 'spirit' ('What will emerge once the earth has arrived at its goal, at its end? The Christ, who approached the earth from far distances and united with it, will be, at its goal, the real principle and reality, he will be the spirit of the earth'[23]). According to Rudolf Steiner, Christ had already become the 'soul of the earth' through the Mystery of Golgotha—since that time he was no longer an impulse working from the cosmos, but the spiritual impetus within the 'earth sphere'. But for his future, further enhanced and continuing efficacy on earth, the intensifying of 'spirit'—his full permeation of the earth— the Christ being required specific 'sheaths', needed 'a kind' of spiritual corporeality ('These are things that for the time being can only be hinted at. Through the Jordan baptism the Christ indeed descended into the sheaths of Jesus of Nazareth. He used these, lived within them, took the Last Supper with his disciples within these sheaths, passed through Gethsemane in them, in them was mocked and condemned, passed through the Mystery of Golgotha in them. Then he rose again and since then lives in union with the earth as its spiritual principle. He creates for himself something similar to what human beings possess in their bodily sheaths. Gradually, over the course of epochs, there forms around the original, purely spiritual Christ impulse that descended at the Jordan baptism, something resembling an astral body, etheric body and physical body. All these sheaths are created from powers that humanity must develop on earth'[24]). Then, continuing his lecture, Rudolf Steiner said of the development of these Christ 'sheaths' out of the soul-spiritual, moral powers of the human being and humanity:

> Those people who can find it in themselves to marvel at great perceptions and truths of the world of spirit, imbue themselves with this feeling of wonder, and over time this forms a power that signifies a power of attraction for the Christ impulse; it draws the Christ spirit toward them. The Christ impulse unites with the individual human soul in so far as the soul can wonder and marvel at the secrets of the world. Christ forms his astral body in earth evolution from all the feelings that have lived as wonder in individual souls.
>
> The second thing that human souls must develop, by means of which they draw the Christ impulse toward them, are all feelings of compassion. And whenever a feeling of

empathy or sharing in others' joy develops in the soul, this forms a power of attraction for the Christ impulse; the Christ connects with the human soul through such empathy and love. Compassion and love are the powers from which Christ forms his etheric body through to the end of earth evolution. [...]

A third element that enters the human soul, as from a higher world, is the conscience to which a person submits, to which he assigns a higher value than his own, individual moral instincts. The Christ unites with this in the most inward manner: from the impulses of conscience of individual human souls Christ forms his physical body.

When we know that the life body of Christ forms from human feelings of compassion and love, a biblical saying gains very real significance: 'What you have done to the least of my brothers, that you have done to me'—for Christ forms his life body through to the end of earth evolution from human compassion and love. Just as Christ develops his astral body from wonder and astonishment, just as he forms his physical body from conscience, so he creates his etheric body from feelings of compassion and love.[25]

Unexpectedly, after speaking these words, Rudolf Steiner then moved on to speak of their further intentional context, and, right at the end of his lecture in Cologne, added as an 'explanatory' addendum:

Why is it that we can say these things precisely now? Because a great problem for humanity is to be solved, that is, how to depict the figure of Christ in the most varied realms of life as he truly is. We will only behold the true nature of this figure if we consider much of what spiritual investigation can tell us; for this we should not look back to what occurred in Palestine, when, indeed, the Christ used the sheaths of Jesus. When, after long study and contemplation of the spiritual-scientific idea of Christ we at last attempt to depict the Christ, we will come to a figure in whose countenance is contained something that all art can, must and will wrestle to portray: in his countenance will be contained something of the victory of powers present only in the countenance, above all other powers of the human form. When people become able to create a living eye that shines out with nothing but compassion, a mouth that is not made for eating but only for speaking those words of wisdom that are the conscience upon the human tongue, and when a forehead can be created that is not beautifully high but beautiful in the clarity of form that curves forward to what we call the lotus flower between the eyes—when all this can at last be created then will be discovered why the prophet says: 'He is without form and beauty.' This is not beauty as we know it, but rather what will triumph over corruption: the form and figure of Christ in which all is compassion, all is love, all is the duty of conscience.

And so spiritual science passes over into human feeling as a seed, a kernel. All teachings that spiritual enquiry can offer do not remain as they are but transform themselves into intrinsic life within the human soul. And the fruits of spiritual science will gradually grow to be the actual circumstances and conditions of life, appearing as an outer embodiment of spiritual science itself, of this soul of future human evolution as it must become.[26]

In his lecture in Berlin on 14 May, Rudolf Steiner then returned to this approach to a future artistic depiction of Christ ('that all art can, must and will wrestle to portray'[27]). In Berlin Rudolf Steiner also spoke of the enhancement of our humanity by the powers of wonder, compassion and conscience, and of their decisively future-oriented quality in relation to the earth's evolution ('This is the meaning of earth evolution, that upon its foundation will be implanted into all evolution what would not exist without it: wonder, amazement, compassion and conscience'[28]), describing these powers and capacities as 'founding' or 'supportive' principles in the development of the sheaths of the Christ impulse. As in Cologne, he also ended the Berlin lecture by turning to art, to an artistic depiction of Christ, albeit now in more detail and differentiation, and largely in the language of sculptural form.

Here are his actual words in Berlin about the relationship between the sheath powers and the body of Christ:

> Indeed, even the outward, pictorial representation of Christ, how he should be pictured outwardly, is a question that still needs to be resolved. Many feelings will have to pass

Rudolf Steiner's notes for the lecture in Cologne on 8 May, 1912.
Rudolf Steiner Archive, Dornach

through human souls on earth if all the attempts that have been made in the course of past epochs are to be joined by one that will to an extent show what the Christ is as supersensible impulse that lives its way into earth evolution. Previous efforts to portray Christ do not even contain intimations of this. You see, something must emerge that expresses a developing outward appearance which incorporates impulses of wonder, of compassion and of conscience. What comes to expression here must be such that the Christ countenance becomes so alive that the principle rendering the human being earthly, our sensory and desire nature, is overcome through what the countenance spiritualizes. There must be the greatest strength in the countenance by virtue of the fact that everything conceivable as the highest development of conscience reveals itself in the singular form of chin and mouth: a mouth, when he stands before one, when the painter or sculptor has given form to him, that gives us the feeling that it is not made for eating but to express all the morality and conscience that has ever been cultivated within humanity, and that in addition the whole bone system [of the face], its dentition and lower jaw, is formed as mouth. This will come to expression in such a countenance. With this form of the lower face will be connected strength of a kind that radiates, dismembers and tears apart the whole of the rest of the human body so that this becomes another form, enabling certain other forces to be overcome: thus it will be impossible to give the Christ, endowed with such a mouth, any kind of bodily form such as the physical human being of today possesses. Then, on the other hand, one will also give him eyes from which all power of compassion will speak that it is possible for eyes to direct toward other creatures: not eyes to receive impressions but to pass with the whole soul into others' joys and sufferings. And he will have a forehead that defies any assumption that it thinks the sense impressions of the earth; a forehead, rather that will protrude to a degree over the eyes, arching over that part of the brain—not a 'thinker's forehead' that cogitates upon what already exists; but wonder, rather, will express itself through this forehead that protrudes above the eyes, and arches gently backward over the head, thereby expressing what we can call wonder at the mysteries of the world. This will need to be a head which cannot be found amongst physical humanity.

Edith Maryon, 1912

Such a portrayal of Christ would have to be really something like the ideal Christ figure. And the feeling that strives
for this ideal, that seeks to evolve toward it as humanity
progresses, in so far as humanity will reach for art in rep-
resenting the highest ideal through spiritual science, is this:
If you seek to portray the Christ you must not look upon
something that is already in existence, but you must allow to
work within you, must inwardly imbue yourself with everything that a spiritual contemplation of the world's spiritual
evolution can endow you with through the three important
impulses of wonder, compassion and conscience.[29]

*

On 16 October 1912, Edith Maryon wrote to Rudolf Steiner for
the first time and asked for a conversation with him in Germany:

> Dr R.W. Felkin (F.R.) told me I should write to you and ask
> you to grant me an interview. If I can arrange it, I hope to
> spend a few weeks in Cologne; and if you would write to
> tell me when you will be there, I will try to come there at the
> same time. I first have to find a position where I can live as
> an 'au pair' and give English tuition.
>
> I can only speak a very little German. Perhaps we could
> converse in French.[30]

When Edith Maryon's letter—written, with help, in German—
arrived at Motzstrasse, Berlin, Rudolf Steiner himself was in Italy
following eventful weeks during the summer and autumn. In
August, Steiner's third Mystery Play, *The Guardian of the Threshold*, had had its first performance in Munich, at the same time as
he was writing the meditation book *A Road to Self-Knowledge* (GA
16). During the subsequent course he gave in Basel in September on the Gospel of Mark, Steiner had taught a young woman
the first founding elements of eurythmy, as well as giving over
300 people individual personal advice. At the beginning of October he had visited the grounds of what would later become the
Goetheanum and then (after a short stay with Édouard Schuré
at the foot of Mont St Odile) had left for lectures and studies in

Italy. It was not until November that Rudolf Steiner was in Berlin again for a while—interrupted by further lecture tours—and there received Edith Maryon's second letter (in English), which once again asked him for a consultation:

> Would it be possible for you to see me and could you let me know when you will visit that town. I shall come to Germany specially to see you, and there will be a good many things to arrange beforehand, so that I shall be very grateful if you could let me know.[31]

When, once again, no answer reached Maryon from Rudolf Steiner, Harry Collison telegraphed Steiner's partner and colleague Marie von Sivers, and at the beginning of December exchanged a few letters with her to secure a date for Edith Maryon to speak with Rudolf Steiner in Berlin ('Would you be so kind as to ask the Doctor to make an appointment for her and would you be so good as to interpret?'[32]). Collison stressed the biographical urgency of this request ('[…] As she is in urgent need of advice and help, she can wait no longer and so is coming to Berlin at once'[33]) and asked her emphatically to receive the young sculptress, especially as she had never been to Berlin before ('It is the first time she has been in Berlin, she knows no one there and she does not understand German [but she is beginning to learn].'[34]).

Collison did not specifically explain why Maryon wished to consult Steiner, her 'urgent need for advice and help'. Part of the reason for Edith Maryon's overall situation may however have been the sudden death of Neville Meakin on 4 October 1912 in London, of which Harry Collison, at Felkin's request, had informed Steiner two days later.[35] Edith Maryon—like Robert Felkin—was a close friend of Meakin, and indeed had been ready to marry him in order to help him, as she was later to confide to Rudolf Steiner ('I would have done so at his request […] because I thought he might live longer if he had someone who took care of him.'[36]). Felkin himself was deeply affected by Meakin's death, but a few days after this had been compelled to leave England for Australia.[37] His advice to Maryon to turn to

Steiner may have been due to his concern about her. Maryon followed this advice twelve days after Meakin's death in a letter in
which—at Felkin's prompting—she also enclosed a photograph
of her depiction of Christ, *The Seeker of Divine Wisdom*.

*

Rudolf Steiner, circa 1912

After arrangements had been made between Harry Collison and Marie von Sivers, Edith Maryon finally reached Berlin on 9 December, very probably staying there until the end of December. During these weeks she may have attended three members' lectures and a public talk by Rudolf Steiner at the Architects House ('Science and Spiritual Research'). On 22 December, Christian Rosenkreutz was the focus of a lecture by Steiner to Berlin members of the Theosophical Society, Steiner regarding this lecture 'as a kind of Christ-medicine' for strengthening the heart—'as a strengthening of the powers of the soul, a strengthening we need if we wish to live safely with our soul within what life presents to us in the form of harmony and disharmony'.[38] Two days later, on Christmas Eve, the Christmas festival of the Berlin branch took place in the 'art room' at 17 Motzstrasse, attended by the Russian artists Andrei Belyi and Assja Turgenieff who had also been present at the lecture on Christian Rosenkreutz. They may have met Edith Maryon there for the first time. Not only was a Christmas play performed at this gathering,[39] but the founding of the Anthroposophical Society, which took place a week later in Cologne, was spiritually prepared through deep contemplation of the events of Christ's life ('The birth of earthlight out of the darkness of the Holy Night'). By way of introduction, Rudolf Steiner said the following among other things:

[We] may regard it as benevolent destiny that we can gather here precisely in this year and on this evening, and can impress this festival upon our hearts through a small contemplation because [...] this year we look forward to the birth of something which, if we understand it in the right way, must lie very close to our hearts: the birth of the Anthroposophical Society. If we have rightly experienced the great ideal that we seek to bring to expression through the Anthroposophical Society, and if we are minded to employ our powers in the right way on behalf of this great ideal of humanity, it will be evident that we must allow our thoughts to pass on from our present spiritual light, or faculties of light, to the dawn of the great light of humanity's evolution on earth, celebrated in this night of love and peace. In this night we do really have before us in spirit or soul what we can call the birth of the earth-light, of the light that is to be born out of the darkness of the Holy Night, which should shine into human souls and human hearts for everything these human souls and human hearts need to find the way to spiritual heights that the mission of earth asks us to attain.[40]

There is no documentary evidence to confirm whether the conversation between Edith Maryon and Rudolf Steiner that had been requested as a matter of urgency took place during these December days in Berlin, though it would seem highly likely given Harry Collison's initiative, as well as the fact that Rudolf Steiner gave numerous people consultations during this time.[41] It is very probable that Rudolf Steiner offered to continue his discussion with Edith Maryon a little while later in Cologne, where he was to give the lecture cycle 'The Bhagavad-Gita and the Epistles of Paul' and where the Anthroposophical Society was to be officially founded. Edith Maryon participated directly in this new Society, which had become necessary and possible through the Christological dispute with the Theosophical Society (Michael Bauer: 'Our battle primarily signifies a battle for our view of Christ'[42]) and she (like Assja Turgenieff and Andrei Belyi) travelled to Cologne at the end of December.

Nor are there any extant documentary details relating to the conversation which Edith Maryon had with Rudolf Steiner in Cologne on 31 December. It took place on the day of the fourth lecture of the course, at the end of which Steiner described the Christ being's engagement and relationship with Lucifer and Ahriman,[43] as further elaboration of his account in Berlin on 24 December with its accentuation of the Christ impulse and the adversarial powers opposing him.[44] The conversation, with translation by Marie von Sivers, called forth an intense and questioning echo in Edith Maryon's soul, as expressed in a further letter she wrote to Rudolf Steiner on New Year's Day 1913:

Baselerhof Hotel

1. 1. 13.

Dear Dr. Steiner,

I think you must be too busy to grant me another interview, but I do want to ask you two questions, so will write them.

You said yesterday I am far more developed occultly than I can bring through in this incarnation – does that mean in consequence of some fault I have committed or because there is some other kind of work for me to do?

Then for some years I have always felt there is something definite for me to do, & that some time I shall meet the Master who will tell me what it is & explain some of the things which have puzzled me

Letter from Edith Maryon to Rudolf Steiner, 1 January 1913.

was so much. For a long time I searched,
at last I thought perhaps it was Abdul Baha
who would be the right person, but when I
met him although I liked him so much I
knew he was not the person I was looking for.
Then I thought it possibly might be you, &
when I saw you in Berlin I knew at last I was
right about the Master, there remains only
the second face – is there really any definite
thing for me to do, or do I only imagine it?
If there is, may I know now what it is?
I think the time has come for me to know if it
is so, but I am quite sure you will know best,
& if I may have some of my muddles cleared
up or must still wait
       Believe me
          Yours sincerely
            S Edith C. Maryon.

Rudolf Steiner Archive, Dornach

I think you must be too busy to grant me another interview, but I do want to ask you two questions, so will write them.

You said yesterday I am far more developed occultly than I can bring through in this incarnation—does that mean in consequence of some fault I have committed or because there is some other kind of work for me to do?

Then for some years I have always felt there is something definite for me to do, and that sometime I shall meet the Master who will tell me what it is and explain some of the things which have puzzled me so much. For a long time I searched, at last I thought perhaps it was Abdul Baha who would be the right person, but when I met him although I liked him so much I knew he was not the person I was looking for. Then I thought it possibly might be you, and when I saw you in Berlin I knew at last I was right about the Master. There remains only the second point—is there really any definite thing for me to do, or do I only imagine it? If there is, may I know what it is? I think the time has come for me to know if it is so, but I am quite sure you will know best, and if I may have some of my muddle cleared up or must still wait.[45]

Thus in the conversation the previous day, Rudolf Steiner had told Edith Maryon that she would not be able to fully realize her high esoteric ('occult') stage of development in this life. Edith Maryon was now asking why this was so, as well as about her task, an intimation of which had clearly been living in her soul for a long time. Since 1902 only a few pupils had come to Steiner in this way—at an advanced stage of esoteric development, seeking their esoteric 'Master' and with the clear premonition of a work to be selflessly undertaken. Edith Maryon came to him with no personal wishes, concerns or needs: she came—as a trained and prepared sculptor—at the age of 40, and at a time when Rudolf Steiner had begun to speak of the need for a new, sculptural depiction of Christ. She came as a schooled occultist at the moment when the Anthroposophical Society was born out of the spirit of esoteric

Christianity, offering her selfless help close to the time of Rudolf Steiner's first move to Dornach.

*

Edith Maryon had to return to London in January 1913, very probably without having received an answer to her letter of New Year's Day. From there, at the end of February, she wrote to tell Steiner that she would attend his lecture course in The Hague from 20 March ('The Significance of Occult Development for the Human Sheaths and the Self'):

> Rather unexpected to myself I find it will be possible for me
> to attend your course of lectures at the Hague.

Edith Maryon excused herself for her still inadequate knowledge of German ('Forgive me that I still must write in English, I have almost no time for study, it must wait until my return to Germany, then I hope there may be more opportunity to learn') and indirectly requested a further conversation in The Hague, as well as admission to the cultic section of Rudolf Steiner's 'Esoteric School'.

In Holland Edith Maryon attended ten, wide-ranging course lectures that engaged in depth with esoteric schooling and the Grail, and, once more, with the human soul and the Christ being in the etheric, in relationship to Lucifer and Ahriman. On Good Friday Edith Maryon was able to attend an esoteric lesson with Rudolf Steiner for the first time, two days before a key lecture in The Hague about the astronomical constellation at Easter 1913. On the same day that she was admitted to the circle of esoteric pupils, Edith Maryon wrote as follows to Rudolf Steiner:

> I feel I must just write and thank you not only for your kind-
> ness in admitting me today to the F.M. but for all you so
> unselfishly and ungrudgingly give to us. I am indeed grate-
> ful to you for many things; I am no longer terrified by the
> future as I used to be. Some day I hope, through your teach-
> ing I may develop into a being who can be a little use to
> others, it is quite time I did so.[46]

At the end of her letter she asked Steiner if possible to give her some brief instruction about her meditative practice, which stood at the centre of her inner preoccupations—'Before I return to England perhaps you will be able to tell me if you consider I am carrying [out] all your instructions regarding my exercises—correctly?'[47]

*

On the day of her return to London, less than twenty-four hours after the course in The Hague had ended, Edith Maryon wrote once more to Rudolf Steiner:

> I think perhaps I ought to inform you that I have now quite definitely decided in my own mind, that when I leave England in May it will be altogether, and with your permission I hope to entirely cast in my lot with the Anthrop. Gesell. When I know more I hope it may be possible for me to do some work for it.[48]

Edith Maryon wrote this letter exactly twelve years before Rudolf Steiner's death on 30 March 1925 in Dornach; she wrote it with the spiritual decisiveness intrinsic to her, three months after the

I think perhaps I ought to
inform you that I have now quite definitely
decided in my own mind, that when I leave
England in May it will be altogether, & with
your permission I hope to entirely cast in
my lot with the Anthros. Gesell. when I
know more I hope it may be possible for
me do some work for it

Society was founded in Cologne—'I hope to entirely cast in my lot with the Anthrop. Gesell.' Edith Maryon had not only joined the new Society but now also united her whole life with it ('With decisive inner certainty she united herself with this [anthroposophic] movement.' Rudolf Steiner[49]). In this context she once again spoke of a task that awaited her: 'When I know more I hope it may be possible for me to do some work for it.'

In order to be able to better understand Rudolf Steiner's lectures and, indeed, anthroposophy altogether, and to prepare for the future, Edith Maryon very much wished to learn German ('it worries me dreadfully not to be able to understand German'). She wanted to learn it in Munich, where anthroposophic summer lectures and play performances were held—and then later go on to Berlin to work, as she likewise told Rudolf Steiner in her letter of 30 March:

> Then when I go to Berlin—as I unfortunately have no means of my own—I must look for some work to do, but I am not troubling myself unnecessarily about this, for I feel I have come to the right decision, and so when the proper time arrives the right work will arrive with it.[50]

Near the end of her letter, Edith Maryon stressed that the thought of coming to Germany made her very happy; and she ended with the German sentence 'Auf Wiedersehen in England' ['See you again in England'].[51]

*

Four weeks later, in fact, Rudolf Steiner was expected in London after an absence of eight years for two members' lectures to be held on 1 and 2 May. Baron Carl Alphonse Walleen translated these into English, thirteen months after his introductory presentations on Christology at Harry Collison's studio ('Our dear friends in this country, who have often visited us on the Continent have in the loveliest way forged an inner bond between our friends here and those abroad.' R. Steiner.[52]). The two London lectures of 1 and 2 May, which focused on esoteric development and Christology, were the first of Steiner's lectures that Edith Maryon was able to hear translated and thus absorb them word for word. To begin with they seemed to her to continue the conversation they had had in The Hague about relating to the dead,[53] but then went on to detail the workings of the anti-Christian adversarial forces, including especially Ahriman's influence on the human soul—whose effect Steiner outlined as, among other things, a 'fear of pure spirit'—before passing on to a positive surmounting of such effects through 'educating the soul in the virtue of moral courage, of inner, spiritual courage'.[54] Following on from this in his second lecture, Rudolf Steiner spoke in most striking and never previously heard fashion of the events of Golgotha and subsequent spiritual developments ('Of all mysteries, the Mystery of Golgotha is the hardest to comprehend, even for those advanced in occult knowledge; and of all truths to which humanity can form a relationship, it is the one that can most easily be misunderstood'[55]). On 2 May, Rudolf Steiner vividly characterized the Michael epoch that preceded the Christ event, as well as the new Michael Age that had begun again at the end of the nineteenth century, which would facilitate a newly dawning Christ consciousness ('Michael can give us a new spiritual light which we can regard as a transformation of that light that was given through him at the time of the Mystery of Golgotha, and the people of our era should place themselves within this light'[56]). The materialistic forms of thought of the nineteenth century, which human souls carried with them at death into the world of spirit, brought about, said Steiner, a 'repetition of the Mystery of Golgotha', a death-process martyrdom of consciousness amongst the third hierarchy. At the start of the dawning 'age of light', under Michaelic preconditions, this could now be followed, he said, by resurrection powers in the realm of human consciousness: 'This new dawning becomes humanity's clairvoyant vision in the 20th century.'[57] Michael, said Rudolf Steiner, is the inspiration for a science of the future—'in the next couple of centuries Michael will give the world something that is as important in a spiritual sense—indeed, more important since

more spiritual, immeasurably more important—than the materialistic science that has developed by successive stages since
the 16th century.'[58]

After his striking lectures in London, Rudolf Steiner went to
deliver lectures in Paris before coming to Cologne on 10 May,
where Edith Maryon—having now left England—had also
arrived. She attended both his lectures in Cologne, no tran-
scripts of which were made, and met him for a further discussion of esoteric questions. Shortly before travelling on to Munich
(and after his second Cologne lecture) she sent him her interim
address in Munich, and wrote:

> I have been writing down the thoughts which come imme-
> diately after my exercises as you say they are very import-
> ant. I never quite know however whether to bother you with
> results or not, or which to select. I have however seemed to

Edith Maryon: The Cross of Golgotha (undated)

receive a good deal of excellent advice from somewhere, and last night (among other things) I thought I heard, 'your probation is ended'. Since then I feel altogether different, and all my old life and views have faded away. I welcome a new one whatever it may bring.[59]

From 13 May onwards Edith Maryon lived at Türkenstrasse in Munich and studied German, very probably involving herself in the industrious and socially oriented Munich branch around Pauline Countess of Kalckreuth and Sophie Stinde. Edith Maryon made very rapid progress in her language practice ('With dedicated industry she overcame [...] this [language] barrier and thus in a relatively short time was able to immerse herself in everything that is given specifically in the German-speaking part of the anthroposophic movement.' R. Steiner.[60]). We can safely assume that Sophie Stinde drew Edith Maryon into the warm-hearted and artistically oriented life of this group in Munich, that she attended its weekly events and studied various books and lecture cycles by Steiner.[61] Though Maryon did not have sufficient funds to make the trip to Stuttgart to hear Steiner's lectures from 17-20 May, or to attend the esoteric lesson given there, in Munich she very probably soon heard of Steiner's announcement of the relocation of the St John's building project from Munich to Dornach near Basel, due both to Munich city council's obstruction of the plan over many years and a generous offer by Swiss anthroposophists. Sophie Stinde was on the executive committee of the St John's building association, and a driving force behind it. Nor will Maryon have missed the circular letter printed in Munich, 'To members of the Anthroposophical Society in relation to the St John's building', which reproduced the Stuttgart address of 18 May and the need, expressed there by Steiner, to initiate this building 'quickly' ('I intentionally emphasize the word "quickly", my dear friends.'[62]).

How greatly Edith Maryon engaged from the very outset with the greater destinies of the Anthroposophical Society and anthroposophic movement, despite her own uncertain future at

the time, is apparent from her letter of 3 June in which she drew
Steiner's attention to an article attacking anthroposophy in the
Church Times, a widely read British ecclesiastical journal, and
suggested counter-measures:

> Will you tell me if you think it should be answered?
>
> It seems to me that any reply should be given by an
> English writer, as only an Eng. person would be quite in
> touch with and understand the English church. And to be
> of any use to the reader of the 'Church Times' the answer
> requires to be written by as able a thinker as we can find.
>
> The most suitable name which has occurred to me is
> that of Mrs (Professor) Mackenzie. I think you met her at
> Dr Felkin's, she has been a member of his Order for 7 or
> 8 years; she is Professor of Education at Cardiff University
> (her husband is Prof. of Philosophy there). Both of them are
> members of the Anthrop. Society. She is a personal friend of
> mine so that I could ask her if she would write a reply, but
> of course I have no authority to speak on her behalf, nor do
> I know if you would approve, perhaps someone else may
> have a better suggestion to make.[63]

Edith Maryon asked Rudolf Steiner—who at the time of writing
was still in Helsingfors (Helsinki) and only returned to Berlin
in mid-June—for his appraisal of the situation and his wishes
('perhaps you would tell me what you wish'); and she was also
willing herself to do something to counter the article:

> Perhaps Prof. Mackenzie would be willing to collaborate
> with me—at least I could give her the facts, and she could
> incorporate them in an article. If she would undertake it, it
> would be well done, she is extremely clever.[64]

Years later—at the instigation of Edith Maryon—Millicent Mackenzie would become a key coordinator of Rudolf Steiner's pedagogical courses and aims in England. It is not known, however,
whether he replied to Maryon's suggestion of a counter-article

in the spring of 1913, though it does seem likely that he would
have done. At this time and in later years, Steiner received few
workable or thoughtful proposals—such as this one of Maryon's
—and increasingly suffered from an Anthroposophical Society
that showed little ability to actively protect its precious spiritual
resources.

*

At the time she wrote the letter above, Edith Maryon very probably knew that Rudolf Steiner was giving lectures in Scandinavia
(the courses had been announced in Mathilde Scholl's 'Anthroposophical Newsletter'). Thus she had sent her message to him
at Motzstrasse, Berlin, to await his return, and likewise her next
letter of 20 June, with its personal concern:

> Some time when you return, whenever convenient to you,
> please will you answer a question for me? Will you tell me
> what you consider it best for me to do after the Cycles? I can
> only afford to study and reflect until the 2nd week in Sept., by
> that date I must find some definite work to do, or be forced
> to return to England. There is a feeling that perhaps there
> may be something for me to do here, as I will not go back
> unless absolutely obliged. You will see that it is necessary
> for me to come to a conclusion about the kind of work I will
> do during the rest of my life, and I do want some advice, so
> forgive me if I ask you.
>
> If you will tell me what you think I will try to carry it out
> if in any way possible for me to do so.[65]

Edith Maryon had come to Munich to see the Mystery Play
performances scheduled for August, and perhaps even to help
with their realization, alongside her language studies. She also
wished to attend Rudolf Steiner's lecture course 'Secrets of the
Threshold' in the last week of August, with, by then, a better
knowledge of German. But any plans beyond this were as yet
very unclear. Although Maryon's words were also informed
by the economic uncertainty of her situation and by the fact
that she had hitherto been a practising artist in England, with

Türkenstrasse 27^{II}
München.

20. 6. 13.

Dear Dr Steiner,

          Some time when you
return, whenever convenient to you,
please will you answer a question for
me? Will you tell me what you
consider it best for me to do after
the Cyclus. I can only afford to
study & reflect until the 2nd week
in Sept. by that date I must
find some definite work to do, or
be forced to return to England.
There is a feeling that perhaps
there may be something for me to
do here, so I will not go back

unless absolutely obliged. You will see that it is necessary for me to come to a conclusion about the kind of work I will do during the rest of my life, & I _do_ want some advice, so forgive me if I ask you.

If you will tell me what you think I will try to carry it out if in any way possible for me to do so.

Your pupil

L. Edith C. Maryon.

Letter from Edith Maryon to Rudolf Steiner, 20 June 1913.
Rudolf Steiner Archive, Dornach

material independence, once again the question of her real task in life reverberated in them ('You will see that it is necessary for me to come to a conclusion about the kind of work I will do during the rest of my life'). It is unlikely that Maryon received a written answer to this question; but only nine days after she had written the letter, Rudolf Steiner arrived in Berlin for a two-and-a-half month period, during which, despite the many activities in progress, he had time and space for personal conversations.

Little is known about the subsequent months in Edith Maryon's life. She performed in the fourth—and last—Mystery Play, *The Soul's Awakening*, in the chorus of elementals, as one of the chorus of sylphs; but beyond that no evidence has survived of any help she may have given with the productions in an artistic or craft capacity. It seems that Edith Maryon's quiet and reticent manner meant that she was overlooked amidst the throng of busy activity in Munich, despite her lively, expressive and dynamic qualities and her service to a super-personal 'cause'. The dazzling reminiscences of these months describe other personalities and events. But Edith Maryon will have taken note, with great interest, of the announcement in Munich of Rudolf Steiner's October course on the 'Fifth Gospel'—and with inner sadness too, since a trip to Kristiania (Oslo) and attendance at the course were completely unaffordable for her. But at the end of all the festivities, on 28 August, in Munich's concert hall complex, Edith Maryon did attend the first eurythmy performance in the still young history of the Anthroposophical Society—and thus witnessed the birth of a new, 'plastic' art of the Logos in the twentieth century.

*

A further letter to Rudolf Steiner on 12 September shows us that Edith Maryon did at least remain for several weeks—if not months—in the Bavarian capital and in Sophie Stinde's circle, after the end of the summer events described above. Rudolf Steiner himself stayed for another two weeks in the city after his lecture course on the 'Secrets of the Threshold' had ended, among other things undertaking preparatory work there for the St John's building, with the aid of a wooden model of it. Edith Maryon sent him the letter below shortly after a personal conversation with him, and in continuation of it:

Dear, revered teacher

May I just tell you some of the results of my exercises? I meant to on Sunday but most foolishly did not, tho' I have been waiting two months to do so, and to ask some questions and now must wait until Berlin for an answer. I am afraid from something you said you thought I was not doing my exercises, but I simply love doing them, and try to put as much as possible into them, tho' I can never do enough. I believe I did not tell you my results because I think you can always see what you wish, and that perhaps my experiences are not important enough to relate.

I feel a warmth in the region of the heart which flows down through the arms and hands—is that 'kundalinifeuer' [kundalini-fire]? How can it be directed? There are all sorts of odd experiences with the LotosBlume [lotus flower] of the eyes. How can one direct the currents from it so that they come into connection with spiritual Wesenheiten [beings]? I often see on the mountains now what I imagine to be my 'höhere Selbst' [higher self]; and I thought through this I might be able to get further?

Then I feel as if something were forming itself before my face and chest, a kind of organ, I thought, for I feel, and in a sense see, all sorts of tubes, one going round my head and connecting my throat and ears—my throat seems to expand and something seems to well up in it.

There are all sorts of other things but I will not bother you with any more now.

In Verehrung und Dankbarkeit [with veneration and gratitude]

Your pupil Edith L. Maryon[66]

Schwanstrasse 10°
München.

12.9.13.

Verehrter lieber Lehrer,

May I just tell you some of the results of my exercises – I meant to on Sunday, but most foolishly did not, tho' I have been waiting two months to do so, & to ask some questions. I now must wait until Berlin for an answer. I am afraid from something you said you thought I was not doing my exercises, but I simply love doing them, & try to put as much as possible into them, tho' I can never do enough. I believe I did not tell you my results because I think you can always see what you wish, & that perhaps my experiences are not important enough to relate.

I feel a warmth in the region of the heart which flows down thro' the arms & hands – is that 'Kundalinifeuer'? How can it be directed? There are all sorts of odd experiences with the Lotus Blumen of the eyes how can one direct the currents from it so that they come into connection with spiritual Wesenheiten? I often see on the mountain now what I imagine to be my "höhere Selbst", & I thought thro' this I might be able to get further?

Then I feel as if something were forming itself before my face & chest, a kind of organ, I thought, for I feel, & in a sense see all sorts of tubes, one going round my head & connecting my throat & ears – my throat seems to expand & something seems to well up in it

There are all sorts of other things but I will not bother you with any more now.

In verehrung und Dankbarkeit
Your pupil,
L. Edith C. Maryon.

Letter from Edith Maryon to Rudolf Steiner, 12 September 1913. Rudolf Steiner Archive, Dornach

Maryon's letter to Rudolf Steiner adhered to the customs of the Esoteric School, which allowed for the reporting of the results of exercises and any problems to the teacher. Maryon's depth of spiritual experience was unusual however: 'Esoteric contemplation was the natural element in which this soul lived. Her inner life was characterized by seriousness in this inward endeavour. And she was close to many important experiences in the realm of spirit.' (Rudolf Steiner.[67])

*

Rudolf Steiner left Munich in mid-September 1913 for Dornach, to oversee technical building plans and to lay the foundation stone on 20 September. After this he travelled to Scandinavia to give lectures on the 'Fifth Gospel' and other themes, and in mid-October he returned to Berlin. No later than November, pursuing her original plan, Edith Maryon also arrived in Berlin and found lodgings in a building at the rear of 17 Motzstrasse, which had many floors and in which numerous anthroposophic colleagues, including Rudolf Steiner and Marie von Sivers, had also meanwhile been lodging. In Dornach, Switzerland, the joinery workshop was already built, and construction work was starting on the rest of the Goetheanum, while here in Berlin Edith Maryon not only attended Steiner's public lectures at the Architects House but—no later than 18 November—also heard presentations from the 'Fifth Gospel'. On 1 October in Kristiania (Oslo) in Norway, Rudolf Steiner had begun to relate 'facts of the Fifth Gospel',[68] that is, to present the actual details of the 'earthly life of the Christ'[69] through true spiritual investigation. In Kristiania Steiner spoke of the 'tangible events that occurred in Palestine',[70] in order to reveal to his listeners in ever greater clarity the nature of the Christ being 'through study of the life of Christ Jesus himself'.[71] According to Steiner, it was essential to gain a 'far more vivid picture of the workings of Christ Jesus',[72] indeed a 'far more conscious grasp of the figure of Christ Jesus':[73] 'In our time, it really is necessary,' he said, 'to renew our understanding of Christ Jesus, to gain a renewed perception of what actually occurred in Palestine, what occurred as the Mystery of

Golgotha.'[74] Without doubt, Steiner's presentations in Kristiania belonged in the context of his lectures in Cologne and Berlin in May 1912, which were likewise centred on the figure of Christ in his historical reality and in relation to his sheath-nature that would in future have to be formed from human powers. Understanding and keen experience of the content of the Fifth Gospel —the necessity for which Steiner repeatedly emphasized[75]—was quite clearly an intrinsic aspect of 'approaching the figure of Christ [...], the living, spiritually life-filled figure of Christ'.[76]

On 18 November, the day of the Berlin lecture on the Fifth Gospel, Edith Maryon had a conversation with Rudolf Steiner. It is not known if Steiner also asked Maryon—as he asked Assja Turgenieff, Andrei Belyi and Friedrich Rittelmeyer—what impression his accounts had made upon her.[77] In the first letter to Rudolf Steiner written unaided in German,[78] however, she wrote to him the following day:*

> My revered, dear teacher
>
>> I knew yesterday I ought to give you an answer about
>> your question, but there is a certain difficulty in speaking
>> of these things, and I too cowardly was—but this will not
>> happen again, and when later I have the opportunity to
>> speak with you again, then that too I want to say and ask
>> for your help.
>> In deep regard and gratitude
>> Your pupil
>> L. Edith C. Maryon[79]

*

In December 1913 Edith Maryon's financial means will still scarcely have enabled her to attend Rudolf Steiner's lectures in various German cities (such as Munich and Cologne), in which the 'Fifth Gospel' repeatedly and intensively figured. Steiner also regularly returned to Dornach for brief periods, and worked

____

*Translator's note: To give a flavour of Maryon's early efforts in German, some of her mistakes have been retained in the translation of the earlier letters. Later on, the errors became only very minor.

there on artistic models of the new building. But she must have attended the Christmas festival of the Berlin branch and have seen the performance of the Oberufer play there. On 24 December she wrote very briefly to her teacher (words that possibly accompanied a small Christmas gift):

> With much, much gratitude, not only to you alone, but also for you, for everything which has been given me through you.[80]

It is not known whether Edith Maryon was able to travel to Leipzig—not all that far from Berlin—at New Year 1913/14, as many Berlin anthroposophists did, to attend Rudolf Steiner's great course on 'Christ and the World of Spirit. The Quest for the Holy Grail'; but it seems possible. Certainly she will have attended the extraordinary lecture in Berlin at Epiphany, twelve days before the second General Meeting of the Anthroposophical Society: a presentation from the 'Fifth Gospel' which describes the journey of Jesus of Nazareth to the Jordan baptism and his encounter with luciferic and ahrimanic beings.

*

On the second day of the General Meeting, on 19 January 1914, Edith Maryon wrote another letter to Rudolf Steiner in which she told him that she had accepted an invitation from the Polish artist Thaddeus Rychter to collaborate on the building in Dornach. In fact this was two weeks after she had written to Rychter to say she would arrive on 28 January, and would be willing to undertake wood carvings, 'initially without payment'.[81] Now she wrote to Rudolf Steiner:

> I only want to say it has become possible me to stay in Germany until Easter. I think the time may have come when I might do something other than just sit here and study for myself; also I have a great wish if it were possible to do something for Theosophy and not only work for myself alone. I have thought much about finding a way but I do

Motzstrasse 17 II.

Mit viele, viele Dankbarkeit, nicht nur für Ihnen allein, aber auch für Sie, für alles das welche durch Sie mir gegeben ist.

L. Edith C. Maryon

♄. 24. 12. 13.

Letter from Edith Maryon to Rudolf Steiner on 24 December 1913.
Rudolf Steiner Archive, Dornach

not know what I can have accomplish or what kind of work I can find here in Berlin. Herr Richter has told me he needs 80 artists in Dornach, and that they do not yet have many, and so I thought I could perhaps work as sculptor, or help someone with something! I have here a few photographs of artworks already I made and which have already been exhibited in the last 12 years, if you like I can show you these photographs. It is a misfortune I have no photographs of the buildings have I already made. At Easter I must perhaps work in England for a few weeks, but then I will come back if I am lucky enough to sell something more my work in England, but naturally then I cannot yet know what will happen. [GA 263/I, p. 22]

Rudolf Steiner will have been fully in agreement with Maryon's Swiss plans. During the General Meeting in Berlin he showed models of the building that was taking shape in Dornach and on 23 January, at the meeting of the St John's building association, he spoke extensively about his conception for the site there, after Emil Grosheintz, a Swiss dentist and originally co-owner of the Dornach hill, had presented slides of it. Opposing—albeit with charm and humour—specific plans and wishes for the building expressed by some anthroposophists involved in its development, Rudolf Steiner clearly emphasized in Berlin that the whole site and its buildings was to be conceived as 'an ideal whole', in fact an 'ideal unity', and would manifest a new architectural style developed from spiritual science. ('For this reason I was, you may say, really disheartened when presented in the past few weeks with plans and proposals for houses that those settling there intended to build. Naturally these were made with the best of intentions, but all of them without exception displayed the abominations of an appalling style of architecture. Things really can be done differently if the good will for this is found [...] If settlers do not have the patience to wait for a time when it is possible to show how one thing or another could be *well* done, then nothing favourable will come of it.'[82]) More positively, and with regard to the social form of the architectural plans for Dornach, Rudolf Steiner then went on to say this:

> The architecture of the settlers' houses will show that the whole settlement is an ideal unity, will in fact outwardly express an inner harmony. What I'm saying now is partly my wish, partly my hypothesis, and partly also something that, well, I myself do not know what to call it: an expression of the inner harmony of those living there! It will be an impossibility, in terms of the Anthroposophical Society, for the least conflict or mutual intolerance, or even a negative word to pass between one member of the settlement and another; no one will even show irritation with someone else in their countenance. And it will be a lovely thing if this is also expressed in the external forms of buildings—as it were a personified peace enveloping everything. But even if it should actually happen that someone's small-mindedness causes them to sneer or make a cross face, the eyes in this face will turn to the shared, peaceful forms of these buildings and, because forms engender thoughts, a smile of peace and contentment will smooth out such distortions of the countenance.
>
> If we consider all this then we really do have the basis for an impulse for creating something unified and harmonious there.[83]

*

Edith Maryon's arrival in Dornach on 28 January 1914 coincided with that of Rudolf Steiner. Just a few days later she was occupied with the making of plaster models for the building—rather than wood carvings—which she had prior training and experience of.[84] Andrei Belyi who, with Assja Turgenieff, had arrived on the site of the future St John's building more or less at the same time as Edith Maryon and Rudolf Steiner, wrote in his reminiscences of these weeks of the 'Maryon workshop where plaster models were made';[85] and Assja Turgenieff, for her part, wrote the following:

> Behind [the joinery workshop] in a small studio, already
> almost full of Goetheanum models, Miss Maryon began
> to enlarge Rudolf Steiner's designs, and to prepare forms
> made of Dornach clay for cement casting. Always calm and
> cheerful, she was soon able to settle in to what were, initially,
> very basic surroundings. But it was noticeable that a certain
> distance divided her from her colleagues—as if she felt sus-
> tained by the awareness of a great task that she must fulfil.[86]

According to Belyi, Rudolf Steiner came to Maryon's 'workshop'
every day. Belyi described her as 'a tall, quiet and gentle girl,
who seemed made of nothing but skin and bones', and, for him,
was 'not of this world'.[87] Edith Maryon's niece also later wrote
this of her:

> She was so modest, reserved and unassuming in her whole
> being that I always asked myself, when I was a child, how
> such a gentle spirit could be a sculptor.[88]

Despite all her reticence and unassuming modesty, there lived
in Edith Maryon's 'gentle spirit' a clear awareness of the work
of futurity awaiting her energetic engagement in which required
the 'virtue of moral courage' (Steiner) and an absolute dedication
and commitment ('as if she felt sustained by the awareness of a
great task that she must fulfil').

*

When Edith Maryon arrived in Dornach at the end of January
1914, the shape of the small cupola of the double-cupola building
was already apparent in its wooden framework, and preparatory
work to erect the load-bearing wooden beams of the big cupola
was underway. In the following weeks of February and March,
the cupolas were then lined with wood while in the joinery workshop the pillars and the rough blocks for plinths and capitals were
being created. In mid-March carving work began on the capitals
below the future stage area, with many artists who had arrived
and willing helpers involved in this. Anthroposophic architects
collaborated with Rudolf Steiner in Dornach; first endeavours to

create the window-glass etchings began under the guidance of
Thaddeus Rychter, and plant dyes were created for the planned
cupola paintings. Many other associated activities and initiatives
were underway. Rudolf Steiner was still not giving any lectures
in Dornach but restricted himself to detailed elucidations of specific work on the emerging building.

Edith Maryon will have observed Rudolf Steiner's advocacy
of the developing building project with great attentiveness
through articles in local newspapers but will also have been
aware of the whole dispute, in rural Catholic regions of Switzerland, surrounding this strange, 'theosophical-buddhist'
temple. From the very outset, Edith Maryon had an alert and
keen awareness of the embattled aspect of Rudolf Steiner's
spiritual life's work, as can be seen in her letter from Munich
in June 1913. The spread of anthroposophy and of the esoteric
Christianity intrinsically bound up with it was received not
only with an expected psychological discomfort but also with
decisive resistance from the guardians of other orders—a conflict which would gradually intensify in coming years, reaching

St John's building, beginning of February 1914

levels of—at least partly intentionally incited—aggression and destructiveness. Edith Maryon showed a continual concern and anxiety about this and about the personal situation of Rudolf Steiner connected with it. But Steiner's text 'What is the aim of spiritual science, and how is it treated by its opponents?'[89] was one she could no longer study in Dornach since in mid-March, for financial reasons, she was compelled to leave the place where she had at last found her true work. She went to Munich, where she attended three further lectures by Steiner, learned of the death of the poet Christian Morgenstern and very probably took her farewell from Sophie Stinde, and then returned to England. As Maryon had told Steiner in January 1914, her funds were not sufficient, despite the most extreme frugality, to last her beyond Easter, and this necessitated her—at least temporary—return to England ('At Easter I must perhaps work in England for a few weeks, but then I will come back if I am lucky enough to sell something more my work in England, but naturally then I cannot yet know what will happen'). In Munich Edith Maryon had one further personal consultation with Rudolf Steiner, but did not dare to speak her mind fully ('On the last evening you asked me if I did not have much unspoken in my heart, and my answer "no" was not true, I thought only it was not a question to be asked.'[90]). She wrote this to him shortly after she arrived in London, in a letter that began with these word:

> Dear, revered teacher
> I feel that I must say something than perhaps a very long time can pass before it is possible for me to return to Dornach. There is not I can do and also I lack the German to clothe in words the much, much gratitude I must feel for my teacher, but it is a feeling so that it is always there and I want to say this once.[91]

At the end of this brief letter, Edith Maryon referred again to her work in Dornach, with a sense of cautious optimism for the future:

I hope that my karma will allow me to work a little more for the building until now.[92]

On the following day, Palm Sunday, she apologized in English in a postcard to Marie von Sivers for the fact that she had been unable to take her leave from them in Munich—'it is however so unpleasant to say Goodbye to people, that in preference I will say "Auf Wiedersehen". I hope that it may be at an early date in Dornach.'[93]

*

Edith Maryon did not feel well in London, despite the lectures given during these Easter weeks of 1914 by Baron Walleen at the home of Collison. According to Rudolf Steiner's subsequent words, Maryon had fallen ill on her journey back to England, following a physical breakdown she had suffered already in Dornach. On Easter Sunday her doctor, Dr Felkin, wrote about this to Steiner and asked for advice and help: 'May I ask you if you can give me any advice to help Miss Maryon? She is not at all well, and is very thin. I am very much afraid that, if she does not take great care, she could succumb to tuberculosis.'[94] Edith Maryon herself wrote to Steiner the same day, and then wrote again a week later to Berlin in the hope that he might have arrived there by then (as he had done, following a trip to Vienna and Prague). In this second message, dated 18 April, she wrote:

> Dr Felkin says that when I was so ill in Dornach, was I very close to the threshold of death, and this has now made my heart very weak etc. I already knew this more or less in Dornach, and in my letter [on Easter Sunday] I asked what I might do after 1 May once my work here is finished. Following a meditation and in the morning I feel perhaps is there still some work for me whether my physical body can be saved, but that is the thing, I have grown so much weaker than I was in Dornach all my surrounding here so difficult is; I feel like a plant without light and water. And so I ask you to send me a word, I need a little more strength to continue, or to pass through the portal of death. Without you

it is so hard but I want to do what my destiny is, if find it I can. Once I had a hope later to help a little, but this hope is now fading.[95]

It is not known how Rudolf Steiner may have come to Edith Maryon's aid in the difficult Easter weeks of April 1914. Many years later he hinted that she passed through a life-threatening illness at this time—'an illness that could be seen as one which, if it recurred, would have made it impossible for Edith Maryon to remain any longer upon the earth'.[96]

Edith Louisa Church Maryon stayed in England for several months and slowly regained her strength. She only returned to Dornach, to the St John's building site, during the summer, in June or July, shortly before the outbreak of the First World War, once again taking up her true work by the side of Rudolf Steiner.

*

II
'What she does, I have done'

Work on the 'Christ Group' and the First World War
(1914-1918)

> *My task in Dornach was to place within this building of the School of Spiritual Science the central Group that depicts the Representative of Humanity between the luciferic and the ahrimanic.*
>
> Rudolf Steiner, 9 June 1919[97]

It may have been in August of 1914, that, following discussions with Rudolf Steiner, Edith Maryon began her first study and model for the figure of Christ between Ahriman and Lucifer, made in wax and plastiline, and only 36 centimetres high. Rudolf Steiner's own model, developed from Maryon's preparatory study and giving this a different emphasis, followed immediately, whereupon Maryon continued work on the third study, which was twice as big. Thus this great work, first described by Steiner in May 1912 as a necessary and possible thing, took its first, well-nigh concealed beginnings in the autumn of 1914, a few weeks after the war had begun. Two-and-a-half years had passed since Steiner had first spoken of it—years during which he had undertaken further, profound investigations of the Christ mystery, and had given a wealth of Christologically oriented lectures to members of the Anthroposophical Society. He had, however, largely ceased his accounts from the 'Fifth Gospel' at the beginning of 1914, in the atmosphere of approaching war and given an audience not fully prepared to hear and receive what he said in this regard.[98] Now, six months after the death of his esoteric pupil and friend Christian Morgenstern, the Christ revelation in artistic form began to emerge in the quiet isolation of the Dornach joinery workshop and under the gathering clouds of war.

After the outbreak of the First World War, Rudolf Steiner was by no means permanently in Dornach; in the last week of August, he travelled to Berlin via Stuttgart, only returning to the St John's building site in mid-September for ten days, before he had to leave again. Subsequent months too were always interrupted by Steiner's absence. But despite all the tasks calling upon him in Dornach, and his intervening travels, his close collaboration with Edith Maryon began in the early autumn of that year—a collaboration that would gradually bring to realization what he had expressed in the Berlin lecture of 14 May 1912, in

Edith Maryon: the first model for the Group (autumn 1914)

work that Edith Maryon had been seeking for years. Her artistic work and support of Rudolf Steiner, for which she had deeply longed, was an experience of joy for her. From the very outset she perceived Steiner's inherent artistic capacity, his formative power arising both through and from spiritual science in the emerging realization of a work that she wished to support without ever relinquishing her own individuality in the process. In comments in 1924, a decade after their shared endeavour began, Rudolf Steiner spoke as follows about the special conditions of work required for the St John's building, later the Goetheanum, as illustrated by his *exemplary* collaboration with Edith Maryon:

> Today anthroposophy, my dear friends, is a cause that is
> not only subject to much attack in the world but is also hard

to accomplish, if taken seriously. If anthroposophy and the anthroposophic movement is taken seriously, really the individual can do nothing other than to take what he is able to integrate in one field or another and to offer it up, as it were, at the sacrificial altar of the life and activity of society. [...]

In a sense we cannot bear anything with us into the anthroposophic movement but must really first let go of what we already have if we wish to work actively in it. Those who do not believe this, do not yet have a far-reaching perception of the degree to which the anthroposophic movement, if it is to fulfil its mission, if it is to reach its goal, must be something that draws in a completely new way from the primary, originating sources of humanity's evolution. [...] It is perfectly natural, my dear friends, if someone introduces into it something from without, a particular art of one kind or another. But everything introduced in this way from outward training is inherently—and I beg you to take this in its profoundest sense—something I cannot really be in agreement with; always what is introduced in this way is not really anything I can assent to. Nevertheless, for the whole thing to thrive, it is necessary for the individual to bring their ability and skill with them. You will inevitably understand that each person must bring their abilities with them. The sculptor must bring their skills. The painter likewise, and so on and so forth. You will understand this, of course, for otherwise I would have had to execute the whole Goetheanum building on my own. Thus we had a very essential need for collaborators—for co-workers who bring with them the best of their ability; but at the same time who also sacrifice these best abilities because—to express the outward aspect of this—I can never be in agreement with what is introduced in this way. What I myself had to accomplish in the art of sculpture was naturally something substantially different from what Miss Maryon was able to bring. What therefore was involved here? It could not be a matter of working together in some way that produced some kind of result from the collaboration, but it could only be a matter of undertaking the work in a way I needed to have it, as it must be accomplished according to the aims of the Goetheanum that I had to represent. You see, my dear friends we must consider here the emergence of an entirely new interest: an interest in the work itself. This requires people who, without mingling anything else into the work, possess this interest in it, so that the work as such arises. Whether we are in agreement with each other or not, the work must come about, the work must be possible.[99]

Rudolf Steiner: The second model for the Group

As Rudolf Steiner expressed it, this 'interest' in the work lived in Edith Maryon, indeed a 'noble dedication' to the work of developing the mystery building and its central sculpture of Christ, but also willingness to fulfil many other tasks that necessarily arose in relation to the building. No later than the autumn of 1914—and throughout all the following years—Rudolf Steiner experienced Edith Maryon's absolute reliability in work selflessly accomplished ('It was not possible for anything I intended and that Miss Maryon was to execute not to be executed, for it not to be taken seriously in the fullest sense and brought to the point it needed to be brought to, in accordance with instructions.'[100]). This experience he had of her was one he recorded in a note after her death:

> If she said something, one could build upon it.
> If she undertook to do something, after a while it would be there.[101]

Edith Maryon's 'practical sense', her 'energy in tranquil work'[102] and the quiet, reticent, discreet strength of her engagement not only gradually made it possible for Rudolf Steiner to 'develop the sculptural work of the Goetheanum'[103] but was also an essential soul-spiritual factor in the emergence of the Christ Group: a work which, as we can suspect, would never have been possible at all without these moral qualities.

*

Only a few people were allowed access to the room where Rudolf Steiner worked with Edith Maryon on his models—and this was true, too, whenever Steiner was away from Dornach. But at Easter 1915, Maryon herself conducted Assja Turgenieff and her sister Natasha to the models so far created—the three first studies for the 'Christ Group', as well as the busts of Christ and Ahriman that Steiner had modelled:

> Miss Maryon showed us Dr. Steiner's latest studies for the
> planned sculptural group. Still very primitive, only roughly
> indicated, a Christ figure, his left hand raised to a falling,

winged Lucifer, his right extending downward to a twist-
ing and turning Ahriman with bat wings. The whole 40 cm
high. Everywhere one saw the little wooden ribs that hold
the plastiline together. Then also a head of Ahriman, modelled very simply but with a huge expressive power and
drama conveyed by the strength of surfaces so characteristic
of the artist. Then Miss Maryon showed us the life-size head
of Christ, which is more formed and developed. Inwardness, and a light that is at the same time warmth, warmth
of soul, is what we felt before this work. It was a gift that
lives on in us when we revisit it in memory. 'Herr Doktor is
not entirely satisfied with the demeanour of the head,' said
Miss Maryon, 'there is still a little pride in it, and Christ has
no pride at all—the position of the head is still to be inclined
downward a little more.'[104]

Rudolf Steiner: Study for the head of Christ, Easter 1915

Another guest who visited Edith Maryon and Rudolf Steiner in subsequent months was a Protestant priest, Friedrich Rittelmeyer. One year older than Maryon, Rittelmeyer had arrived independently, by his own religious and meditative path, at the question of what Christ truly looked like, and in the spring of 1915 had asked Rudolf Steiner about the possibility of experiencing Christ's corporeal form:

> In meditating on the words of Christ [in the John Gospel] I had a strong experience of the effect of these words upon my body. It was as if these words said, 'If we are to live in you, then we must first transform you.' The intimate spiritual corporeality that stands behind material corporeality like its spiritual architect, came to my awareness. I felt it undergoing changes. I was able to intensify my meditation on the words of Christ to the point where I experienced strong bodily sensations, and in fact vivid bodily pains. The subsequent echo of this was a powerful awareness of healing that gave me an intimation of what true health of the whole human being means. These experiences made me wonder if it was possible, by meditating on the words of Christ, to say anything about what Christ actually looked like. To do so one would have to observe, at certain boundaries of one's own corporeality, the ways in which Christ had to be other than oneself. The words of Christ told one with more or less clarity how the body in which they really lived must inevitably have appeared. [...]
>
> Without saying anything specifically about these observations, I asked Rudolf Steiner: 'Is it in fact possible, simply by meditating on the words of Christ, to come to a point where we can say something about what Christ actually looked like?'[105]

In his reply to Rittelmeyer, Rudolf Steiner described the countenance of Christ in the same terms as in his lecture in Berlin on 14 May 1912, but with more emphasis now on his own personal perception, saying for instance in relation to the mouth of Christ,

'When I first saw it, I had the impression that this mouth looks as if it has never eaten but rather has proclaimed divine truths eternally.'[106] Friedrich Rittelmeyer, who for the past few years had become increasingly absorbed by and dedicated to anthroposophic spiritual science (and to Rudolf Steiner himself), was astonished at this answer—and at the same time recognized its possible (and necessary) outcome:

> Astonished, I asked him: 'But if you know what Christ looked like, surely one should in some way make this picture of Christ accessible to humanity?' 'Yes indeed,' he replied, 'and that is why I have commissioned an artist in Dornach to create a Christ portrait according to my instructions.'[107]

Steiner then invited Rittelmeyer to come to Dornach and study the artistic work progressing in the studio there, which he then did in the last week of July and the first week of August 1915—at a time when Rudolf Steiner and Edith Maryon were already working on the sixth stage of their model, which was now two metres high and at this point bore both their signatures:[108]

> At midsummer 1915, while the thunder of cannons reached our ears from nearby Alsace, and spotlights strifed the landscape in the evenings, I sat before the bust of Christ in Dornach. [...]
>
> He [Rudolf Steiner] had indicated to the artist [Edith Maryon] that she should allow me to visit the studio at any time and sit quietly before the head of Christ. I took advantage of this permission, taking as much care as possible not to disturb the artist. And so, at that time, I experienced the Gospels as I sat before this head of Christ.[109]

*

Possibly partly at the instigation of Rittelmeyer's forthright question, but primarily because of the imperatives of the St John's building itself, from the spring of 1915 onwards Rudolf Steiner spoke in numerous members' lectures about the developing sculptural work—in over ten lectures that he gave between

May and October in Dornach, but also in Berlin, Prague, Linz in Austria, and Elberfeld near Wuppertal. Back in November 1914, in a striking account of the nature of man which he gave in Dornach, Steiner had spoken of the luciferic-ahrimanic contest for the human being, with a marked emphasis on physiology and anatomy ('Through spiritual observation of physiological and anatomical processes we must come to discern how Lucifer and Ahriman battle with one another'[110]). But with the Dornach lecture of 3 April 1915, which Rudolf Steiner gave in the presence of Edith Maryon, he initiated his actual, direct account of the 'Christ Group'.

In these remarks, continuing until October in relatively swift succession and with ever new emphasis, Rudolf Steiner pointed—at the first stage of the work's development—to how the sculptural Group would bring to expression 'what our souls should feel arising from our [anthroposophic] movement in the most intimate and also profoundest sense'.[111] The shaping and creating of the sculpture, he said, was bound up with a truly 'new configuring' of the Christ impulse in its inherent engagement with the adversarial powers.[112] Repeatedly he stressed the absolute contemporary relevance of the task formulated in this way, saying in Elberfeld on 13 June 1915:

> [...] This relationship of the Christ impulse to the Lucifer impulse and the Ahriman impulse is something that humanity will increasingly be able to understand in the near future. Lucifer powers and Ahriman powers hold sway throughout the world; and the human being, through his Christ consciousness, must become like a being sitting in a boat that inevitably rocks back and forth in the storms unleashed by Lucifer and Ahriman but must still find its passage through the ocean—whose living substance consists of Lucifer and Ahriman, but through which, nevertheless, the human being steers his Christ boat.[113]

As Steiner put it in his lecture on 18 May 1915 in Linz, Austria—almost exactly three years after his remarks in Berlin—one of the greatest spiritual challenges of the modern era is 'to find the balance between our relationship with Lucifer and our relationship with Ahriman'.[114] Only by clearly distinguishing between Lucifer and Ahriman as evil's dual figures, and thus perceiving the overall threefold nature of evolution's spiritual impulses, is it possible, according to Steiner, to gain an apt discernment of reality, also in a historical and political sense.[115] The human being, he says, lives in a real sense in the field of tension between the luciferic and ahrimanic—between powers and forces that have a cosmic justification, but which must find a balancing and transcending centre in the core of the human being:

> The human being must swerve toward the luciferic principle on the one hand, and toward the ahrimanic principle on the other, but be must also stand firm by developing what Paul spoke of when he said, 'Not I but Christ in me.'[116]

On 22 May 1915, in Dornach, Rudolf Steiner accentuated that true knowledge of Christ implied acknowledging the polar nature of the adversaries, and in fact was not possible without this ('Knowledge of Christ is only possible if the relationship of the Christ impulse with the luciferic and ahrimanic forces of the human soul has been clearly discerned'[117]). And seven-and-a-half months later he said in Bern:

> To understand how the Christ stands in the centre between Lucifer and Ahriman, and what he signifies in relation to them, is one of the chief tasks of the near future.[118]

In the modern era, said Steiner, it was necessary to perceive the forces at work and, in knowledge and perception to 'face' these active powers,[119] especially within that Central European orientation belonging intrinsically to the mission of the Dornach building:

> It is the task of Europe to establish a balance between East and West. In the East the pendulum swings in one direction,

Rudolf Steiner/Edith Maryon: The fifth study for the Group (May 1915)

in the West to the other. In Europe it is not simply our task to ape what happens either in East or West, but rather to stand independently upon our own ground and to fully acknowledge the justification of both the one and the other. Our Group expresses this. And thus what has been erected at a special place in our building is also geographically connected with our task. It stands in the East, but with its back turned to the East, and gazes toward the West; but it stands there in balance, bearing within it what it has experienced in long wanderings in the East, not allowing the purely ahrimanic culture the West can bring upon humanity to suffice it.[120]

In this sense, as Rudolf Steiner put it in lectures given subsequently, the sculptural Group in Dornach should be seen as the 'crowning'[121] of the new, Central European mystery site (the 'House of the Word') or as its 'central creation',[122] as a 'trinitarian Group'[123] expressing the 'secret of the trinity of the Lucifer, Ahriman and Christ principles'[124] while being at the same time nevertheless a real 'Christ Group'.[125] The Christ impulse, said Steiner, preserves and 'saves' the earth and humanity from being occupied and estranged in one-sided ways by luciferic-ahrimanic beings and forces; only a connection with Christ allows us to resurrect the image of the human being and to bear it onward through a process that is necessary in history and in the history of consciousness, without succumbing to the extremes of this determining process:

> For this reason the Human Archetype is positioned in pride of place in our Dornach building, in his original intrinsic nature and as he is to be recreated from within by Christ, surrounded by the luciferic and ahrimanic principles. This will constitute the meaning, precisely, of this central statue of our Dornach building. In regarding this central figure, one will be able to say, Yes, the good gods have intended this. Initially it was fractured, Lucifer and Ahriman appeared, but the Christ impulse emerges victorious, recreating from

within what was originally outwardly established, recreating it from within the human being and thus in his freedom.

The understanding of human evolution that needs to be cultivated is precisely what will be offered to humanity through our building and what it contains. The most essentially necessary thing for humanity in the near future is intended by this building, allowing to be perceived and heard from human evolution itself what is vital in the near future, and presented and discernibly embodied here.[126]

*

By contrast, on 10 June 1915 in Berlin Rudolf Steiner stated how the work begun on the sculptural Group was only truly in its early beginnings, emphasizing that the three beings upon which he had focused in various lectures would not only be depicted in the terms previously given—'what is to be added to them can perhaps be mentioned at a later occasion, since these things cannot be elaborated according to some prior, abstractly conceived notion but must draw upon intuitions of the world of spirit as these arise in the course of work'.[127] Indeed, the fourth model by Rudolf Steiner, in May 1915, had already brought about a doubling of the luciferic and ahrimanic beings—besides Ahriman in the cavern beneath and the falling Lucifer, a connection was now shown between the two, as yet unvanquished beings by the side of the Representative of Humanity.

In Berlin, too, Rudolf Steiner stressed in this context that the artistic elaboration of the 'figures' was accomplished solely on the basis of actual spiritual-scientific enquiry, saying:

> It is not a matter of merely symbolic representation but rather of every trait in the three beings being drawn in every minutest detail from spiritual-scientific vision.[128]

Above and beyond the many interesting details Rudolf Steiner mentioned in his early references to the Group in the spring, summer and autumn of 1915—for instance in regard to the sculptural configuration of Lucifer,[129] he repeatedly and decisively drew his listeners' attention to the figure of Christ itself, whose

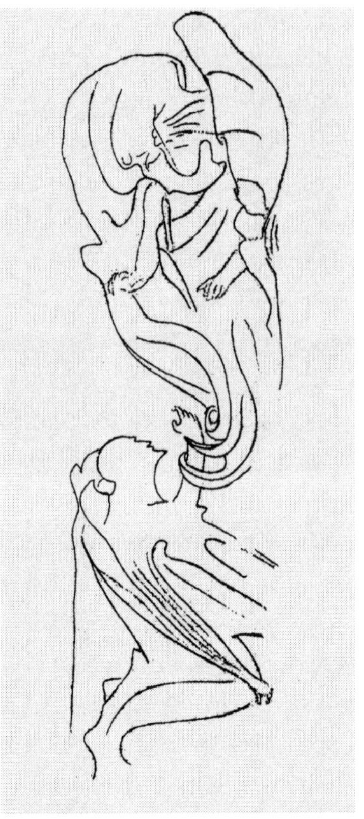

Drawing by Edith Maryon

artistic depiction in sculptural form he had described three years previously as a mission of the future. In his lectures in 1915, Rudolf Steiner spoke of the 'Representative of Humanity' or the 'Representative of the highest human nature that could develop on earth',[130] the 'Representative of the earthly human being in the greatest sense of the word'[131]—and on 22 May in Dornach he referred in specific terms to the 'Christ-permeated human being'[132] who holds the adversarial powers in balance, overcomes them and within himself—since the Jordan baptism—is the bearer of the cosmic Logos principle:

> It will be our particular task to shape this figure of Christ
> in such a way that one will be able to see on the one hand
> how the being in question inhabits a human earthly body,

but how at the same time this earthly body is spiritualized in every aspect and facial expression, in everything pertaining to it, by what drew into this earthly body from spiritual heights as Christ in the thirtieth year of life.[133]

Since 1 October, in his lectures from the 'Fifth Gospel', Steiner had presented the findings of his investigations into the life history of Jesus of Nazareth before and after the Jordan baptism, right into bodily aspects of his constitution and radiance. Now, with the help of Edith Maryon—and drawing on a capacity of seership that could look both back into the past *and* forward into the future, as he had clearly described back in 1912[134]—he set about depicting the being of Christ in his intimate engagement with the forces of temptation,[135] and in his victorious resurrection through the Mystery of Golgotha:

> This should therefore depict the significant events that occurred when the Christ being passed through the Mystery of Golgotha, in relation to the earthly relationship between Christ, Ahriman and Lucifer.[136]
>
> And so, between the principles of Ahriman and Lucifer, Christ appears here before us in his resurrection form as the Easter manifestation, the Easter manifestation placed before us: the resurrected Christ above whom luciferic powers hover, who is founded or grounded below on ahrimanic powers.[137]

But the sculptural depiction of the resurrected Christ is also intended at the same time to belong to futurity, to summon the future reappearance of the Christ being arising through evolutionary steps taken by the human being and humanity as a whole.[138]

*

During their visit to the studio at Easter, Edith Maryon had told Assja and Natasha Turgenieff that, once complete, Rudolf Steiner's head of Christ would have no sign of pride ('Herr Doktor is not entirely satisfied with the demeanour of the head.').

Likewise, in his first lectures on the Group which began at this time (April 1915), Steiner repeatedly emphasized that Christ's engagement with Lucifer and Ahriman in the sculpture would have nothing warlike about it. Thus on 10 June in Berlin, in relation to the depiction there of the overcoming of Lucifer, he said:

> The Christ is neither a figure who hates nor one who unjustly loves. He does not extend his hand to break the wings of Lucifer but is a being, rather, whose inner nature is such that he must extend his hand. He does not break the wings of Lucifer, but Lucifer, above, cannot endure what radiates from this hand, and breaks his own wings himself. [...] Lucifer feels within him something that means he himself breaks his wings. This is self-knowledge in Lucifer, self-experience. Similarly in Ahriman. [...] [Christ is] a being who through his very existence brings about what must occur within souls themselves.[139]

The left hand of Christ, pointing to Lucifer, points, as Steiner says in a later lecture, simply to 'the fracture, the breaking point in Lucifer' ('precisely where he breaks in two and plunges downward'[140]). But Lucifer, he goes on, is broken within and through himself and plunges downward because of this 'inward brokenness'.[141] Referring to the same context again, but this time with an artistic emphasis, and in line with the sculptural intention he would seek to execute ('Hopefully it will prove possible for us, through sculptural depiction, to avoid this false view [of the battle of Christ]'),[142] Rudolf Steiner also said in Linz on 18 May:

> What will have to be elaborated artistically with special vividness is how this Christ figure raises his left arm. You see, it is by this raising of Christ's left arm that the plunging being breaks his wings. But it must not seem as if the Christ breaks his wings; rather, the whole must be artistically shaped so that, as Christ raises his arm, it is apparent in the whole movement of the hand that he actually has infinite sympathy with this being. Yet the latter cannot endure what

streams upward through the arm and hand of Christ, which is visible too in the fact that something like engravures in the rock-face itself continue from the fingers of the upstretched hand. What this being [of Lucifer] experiences within himself when he comes into the proximity of the Christ being can be clothed roughly in the words, 'I cannot endure such purity radiating upward to me.'

This is what lives within this being, lives so essentially that its wings are broken and in consequence it plunges into the abyss.[143]

Four weeks later in Elberfeld, Steiner said that Lucifer breaks his wings 'through his state of soul as he comes close to Christ':[144] 'Because he cannot endure the power of Christ, the Christ impulse, he breaks his wings. This is not caused by Christ waging a battle against Lucifer but rather by something occurring within Lucifer himself—something Lucifer has to experience inwardly; not for a moment must we think it possible for Christ to feel hatred or antagonism toward Lucifer. Christ is the Christ, and fills cosmic existence with nothing but positivity; he does not do battle with any other power in the world!'[145]

No more than Lucifer can Ahriman endure the 'pure compassion with the world', the unsullied 'love' and spirituality of the hand of Christ,[146] and despairingly consumes himself: 'he fetters himself through what occurs in his soul'.[147] '[The figure of Ahriman] twists and contorts himself in consequence of something likewise lying in his own nature that pushes and throws him back upon his own being through the strength of the central figure.'[148] On 18 May 1915, for the first time, Rudolf Steiner described this specific mode of action of Christ as the 'Parzival element' of a forthcoming stage of culture ('The Christ [...] stands in the midst as the one who brings the Parzival element into the modern era: he brings the others to self-vanquishment not through his strength but through his very being and existence, so that these others must overcome themselves rather than him overcoming them.'[149]). Four weeks later, in Elberfeld,

Drawing by Edith Maryon

summarizing all this once more and heralding the Christ knowledge of the future, he said:

> The Christ being is so significant, and understanding of the Christ being so difficult that this [understanding] can only be attained over the course of time. Only in future will it be understood that Christ brings other beings either to condemn or redeem themselves simply through what he is. [...] The Christ [...] stands there non-personally, and the beings who come into his proximity judge themselves.[150]

*

In the spring, summer and autumn of 1915, Rudolf Steiner's remarks about the sculptural Group were kept to members of the Anthroposophical Society, but nevertheless they met with a complex inner situation in the first year of the war in Central Europe, which brought with it severe emotional crises and exceptional circumstances even in Dornach.[151] He asked the members not to stridently publicize his comments, especially about the figure of Christ in the Group, given the expected opposition from the Church,[152] but also because of artistic perspectives ('Art not only means something but is something.'[153])—and on 4 October 1915 he said in Dornach:

> Try not to irritate the outer world by speaking of a new religion. It would be a big mistake to speak of the Group as a 'Christ statue'. It is enough to say, Here stands the Representative of Humanity. Everyone can see for themselves what is meant by this. It is important for us always to find the right words; that is, we must consider how we place ourselves into the whole cultural world, trying to describe things with the right words. This is something that must continually be said. We should not say to others: Here at last we have presented the Christ in the right way. That is something we may know and keep for ourselves.[154]

In subsequent years, too, Rudolf Steiner would repeat this,[155] saying for instance in Dornach in 1919:

> If destiny wills it, and this building can eventually be completed, someone who sits in it will have directly before him as he gazes upon the being who gives earth evolution its meaning, something that will invite him to say: This is the Christ being. But this also requires an artistic sensibility. It should not be a merely intellectually spun thought—oh yes, that's Christ. Rather, it has to be felt. The whole is conceived artistically, and what comes to artistic expression in the forms is the most important thing. In a purely feeling way, with exclusion of intellect if you like—which ought only to guide us toward feeling—this should invite a person to look toward the East and say, 'That art thou' [...].[156]

Yet at the same time Rudolf Steiner made clear in a lecture in Bern at the beginning of 1916 that full understanding of the sculptural Group would only be possible on the foundation of modern spiritual science and its Christology:

> Naturally you can only understand an artwork if you live
> within the whole spiritual stream that gave rise to it. Thus
> only those embedded in this stream will understand our
> ideal figure with Ahriman and Lucifer. But this is common
> to the artworks of all ages—that they are only comprehen-
> sible for those within the cultural stream they belong to.
> They can only be true works of art within such a stream,
> possessing their particular spiritual or cultural orientation.
> Just as someone who understands the Sistine Madonna
> or, let us say, Raphael's Transfiguration of Christ, needs to
> know something originating with this spiritual stream out
> of which the painting emerged, so naturally someone who
> has observed something or other in our building must pos-
> sess in their soul, in their heart, something that belongs to
> our spiritual stream. But when we possess this in our soul,
> the artwork itself must speak to us—then no one will need
> to write something upon it as explanation, a name or such-
> like.[157]

*

In the spring of 1916, to accommodate the seventh and last study
model for the sculptural Group, planned to stand over nine-and-
a-half metres high, a plain, high studio was built on to the western side of Rudolf Steiner's and Edith Maryon's previous workshop, with big swing doors as passageway.

In Rudolf Steiner's absence—he was away in Germany for
more than six months from the second half of January, giving
lectures, writing, and involved in meetings—Edith Maryon with
a few helpers succeeded in constructing a suitable scaffolding
for the immense sculpture, attaching the necessary plaster base
for the rocks and—after production and endless stirring of tons
of plastiline—in transposing the two-metre-high, sixth stage of
the model to the form it now required, starting with the lower
and upper Ahriman figure and the falling Lucifer at the side.
Assja Turgenieff wrote:

Group of co-workers around Edith Maryon and
Assja and Natasha Turgenieff

On several occasions I had to stand in as model to help
Miss Maryon: lying upon a stairway with my head downward, my hand extended to the Lucifer hand clutching at
the rocks. This was the loveliest opportunity to observe the
development of the Group in a studio otherwise strictly out
of bounds.[158]

It was Assja Turgenieff who noted with wonder in her memoir
'the great strength and ability with which Miss Maryon sculpted
the various figures',[159] as she prepared the work meticulously
for Rudolf Steiner's arrival—with the harmony, artistic elegance
and well-proportioned qualities characteristic of her. But Turgenieff also described Rudolf Steiner's eventual arrival and the
process that began then of transformation, of the extraordinarily
dynamic reconfiguration and further elaboration of all that had
been prepared for him:

[...] Hardly had he returned and begun work again it
seemed as if a tempestuous storm had taken up in its dwell-
ing in the studio—everything, every surface and edge came

into motion, was taken up into the unfolding expression of a superhuman drama. The gaze could no longer rest upon the beautiful form itself, but must live with it, pass through it so that form itself vanished leaving only movement, expression, living being.[160]

Many years later Steiner would say in a detailed recollection of his collaboration with Edith Maryon:

> The artistic impulses given through the Goetheanum can only come into effect if those who go to work upon it with real ability are not hindered by any artistic wilfulness. I had to let impulses issuing from anthroposophy stream into the work. In the process it is often difficult to overcome contradictions that arise from the clash between customary forms of art and new intentions. With Maryon I could collaborate in sculptural form without this clash having any significance. For her, the freely felt necessity for the work to be created stood above and beyond all possible artistic opinion. And sustained by this feeling, Maryon allowed all that she was accustomed to in art stream into the new impulses in quiet yet energetic fashion.[161]

*

From 25 July 1916 onwards, Rudolf Steiner was in Switzerland for six months uninterruptedly, working—apart from a few public lectures in Swiss cities—almost entirely at the Goetheanum and on his sculptural Group. In the early autumn, Andrei Belyi and his brother-in-law Alexander Pozzo—Natasha Turgenieff's husband—had to leave Dornach to be Russian army conscripts, like many before them.

Things became increasingly quiet at the building site, which had seen such lively activity in the spring of 1914; nevertheless, the construction and artistic work continued to a limited degree, in a socially tense, even sometimes militant atmosphere caused partly by attacks on Rudolf Steiner and Marie Steiner-von Sivers by Édouard Schuré, as well as by emotional breakdowns and the psychopathology of some individuals in Dornach.[162] In the early autumn of 1916, Rudolf Steiner announced the withdrawal of Marie Steiner-von Sivers—at his request and for her personal protection—from her position on the Vorstand or executive committee of the Anthroposophical Society, saying in this context in relation to himself:

> I cannot withdraw myself [from honorary presidency of the Society]. I have to retain these duties and obligations undertaken since the building was begun, so as not to disappoint those who have made sacrifices in this respect, to ensure we stay connected with the building. This is why I said recently that nothing will induce me to voluntarily relinquish what connects me with the building. Do not imagine that I speak these words without reflection and without considering the

Rudolf Steiner, 1916

seriousness of the situation. But it must be said very clearly for once. I will continue as adviser and I will see whether a sufficient number of people come to recognize what kind of mendacity it is to speak of power lusts or suchlike, words that are devastating for everything that lies within our movement. And if such lies are expressed as they now have been, our movement cannot continue.[163]

In an incident during the following autumn or winter months in Dornach, about which no further details are known, Rudolf Steiner nearly fell from the scaffold while working on the Christ statue and could have been killed, but was saved by the quick action and presence of mind of Edith Maryon ('My accident in the studio'[164]):

> It happened at the time, due to a gap in the scaffolding, that I nearly fell and would quite certainly have fallen upon a pillar with a sharp point if Edith Maryon had not stopped

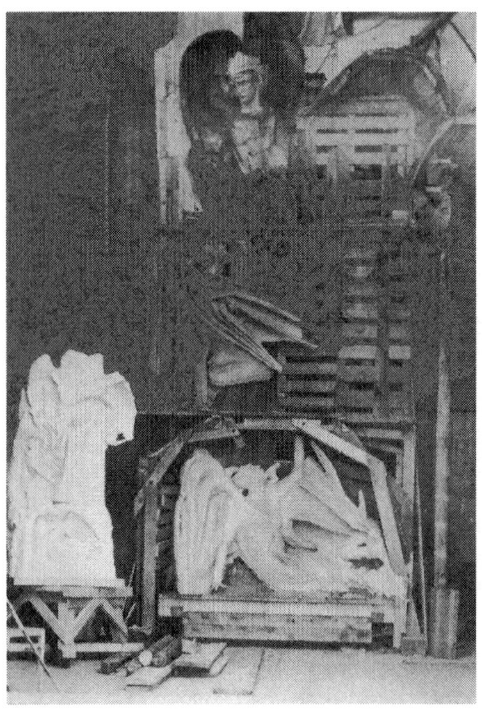

me from falling. And so it must be said [...], if the Anthroposophical Society considers that my work since then has had a value for it, that in a sense it must be grateful for the fact I was saved in this way.[165]

Many years later—in addresses and a memorandum—Rudolf Steiner referred to this rescue by Edith Maryon in no uncertain terms as a 'karmic symptom'[166] and a 'karmic context'[167]—and said that as a direct consequence of the incident he was now 'karmically connected' with Edith Maryon.[168] According to Assja Turgenieff, Rudolf Steiner also said in this context, 'What she [Edith Maryon] does, I have done'—in this way describing a fundamentally altered mode of their relationship and collaboration, which Turgenieff explained decades later in the following words:

> He has [now] taken on responsibility for everything that Edith Maryon did. Before this time, if Maryon made a correction or revision that someone did not understand or was not in agreement with, it was still possible for them to go to Rudolf Steiner to see what he thought about it. Afterwards this was no longer possible, since he had made this statement. And so if henceforth she made an alteration, this was the final word![169]

Only during the Christmas Foundation Meeting and the refounding of the General Anthroposophical Society seven years after his near-accident and following further, momentous years of crisis in the Anthroposophical Society, did Rudolf Steiner say that in future *he* would lead the various sections of the School *through* their leaders (based on an esoterically initiated working and research community). To Ita Wegman, the secretary (i.e. responsible correspondent[170]) of the esoteric Vorstand, he said in a mantric verse: 'So take my hand of soul / Extended to you by / My I, your own. / And act as I desire. / The work that is done will be / As if my very self / had held the pen.'[171] The active presence of mind shown by Edith Maryon at the end of 1916, which bore the signature of her whole collaboration, friendship with, and pupilship of Rudolf Steiner, clearly saved Steiner's life and spiritual work in the middle of the First World War with its destructive, Christ impulse-opposing forces. At the same time, with the initiate Rudolf Steiner, she configured the form of an effective social dynamic that would become the substance of a future School of Spiritual Science with its view of the work of the Sections.

*

Rudolf Steiner remained in Dornach until the beginning of February 1917, very largely completing the big model for the sculptural Group. Most uncharacteristically he repeatedly postponed his departure for lectures and work in Berlin, planned for the end of 1916, and on 6 February, in his first Berlin lecture, explained this by saying:

> Allow me firstly to express my great pleasure at being once again in your midst. I would have come sooner if there had not been an urgent necessity for me to continue work on the Group, which we have often discussed here, and which is to stand at the Dornach building's eastern end, depicting the Representative of Humanity in reciprocal interplay with the ahrimanic and luciferic powers. I needed to bring this work to a point where it can now be developed further without me. In our era one has to have forethought for the future, in a sense, and it seemed to me very necessary, given events that may transpire, to advance the Group as far as has now been possible.[172]

In this opening lecture of his Berlin cycle, Rudolf Steiner again spoke of the spiritual conflicts of the day, and the forthcoming appearance of the Christ being in the etheric ('And as true as it is [...] that, at the time of the Mystery of Golgotha, the Christ walked in physical form amongst human beings at a particular place on the earth, so it is likewise true that in the twentieth century the etheric Christ will walk amongst humankind world-wide. And if the earth's salvation is not to be undermined, humanity must not pass this occurrence by unnoticed but must practise the right attentiveness for it so that a sufficient number of people are prepared truly to behold the Christ who is to come and who must be perceived.'[173]). As in former years—since no later than 1908[174]—Rudolf Steiner characterized anthroposophic spiritual science as real preparation for this occurrence, for perceiving and experiencing it, and for its true fulfilment. At the same time, toward the end of this same Berlin lecture of 6 February 1917, Steiner expressly stated that these events were connected with the actual influx of active Christ impulses into the progress of social, scientific and cultural life, but that there was no certain assurance that this potential Christ-permeation of greatly endangered civilization would actually be realized. As Steiner put it, the Christ being *could* increasingly come to the aid of human beings and humanity, *could* stand beside them when they consulted him, and offer those prepared for this, good counsel in weighty decisions demanded by forthcoming times:

> [...] The time must come, and cannot be far off, when the immortal aspect of the human soul asks Christ, in relation to what it seeks to establish, 'Should this happen or should it not?'; when the human soul sees beside it the Christ as its loving companion in each circumstance of life, gaining not only solace, not only strength from the Christ being but also instruction and advice about what should happen. The kingdom of Christ Jesus is not of this world, but it must work in this world, and human souls must become the instruments of the kingdom that is not of this world. From this standpoint we must observe how little the question is posed that must be asked of Christ in relation to individual deeds and events. But humanity must learn to consult and question Christ. [...]
>
> Why do we study spiritual science? It is as if we need to learn the vocabulary of the language through which we approach Christ. And to those who endeavour to learn to think about the world as spiritual science endeavours, to those who endeavour to exert their head to a degree that enables them to gaze into cosmic secrets as spiritual science

seeks to do, to them will the figure of Christ Jesus draw near from the dark and obscure ground of cosmic secrets and be the vigorous strength in which they will live, standing by his brotherly side as he guides them so that they can be strong in heart and soul and be equal to the tasks of humanity's future evolution. Let us therefore not seek to acquire spiritual science as mere teaching, but let us try to acquire it as a language, and wait until we find in this language the questions that we may ask of Christ. He will answer, yes indeed he *will* answer! And a wealth of soul powers, soul strengthenings, soul impulses will accrue to those who hear the counsels, the advice of Christ emerging from the grey depths of spirit that underlie the evolution of humanity in this era, advice which Christ seeks to give to those who seek it in the very immediate future.[175]

*

Until the end of September 1917 (thus for a total of seven months) Rudolf Steiner remained in Berlin and Germany, working to cultivate spiritual science and Christology. At the request of Otto Count Lerchenfeld he wrote memoranda for a new, peaceful social order in Central Europe along social threefolding lines (and thus in accord with the Christ impulse seeking realization), wrote the book *Riddles of the Soul* (with his first outline of the tripartite human organism and its functions) and gave numerous lectures on the theme of contemporary events. For her part, in May, Edith Maryon in Dornach began to execute the 'Christ Group' in (elm) wood, preparing with her helpers the separate figures, work upon whose final surfaces (last 2.5 centimetres) was to be reserved for Rudolf Steiner:

Enormous, layered wood blocks stood there before us, and now we had to measure them and quake in our shoes. 'Up to the last two centimetres' hung over us like a sword of Damocles—the permitted limit to which we might bring the preparatory work. And to the point of despair we walked back and forth with a long, moveable measuring needle, fixed to a board—from the workplace to the model—to find each point, and behind us—also very understandably—Miss Maryon trembled for her two centimetres. She herself was working on the central figure. [Assja Turgenieff][176]

This stage of the work had been preceded by transportation of the glued ('layered') elm-wood slabs in large cuboids into the

Photographs by Edith Maryon. Ita Wegman Archive, Arlesheim

high studio—an important and complex labour that had been carried out from May 1914 with the help of gantries and hitches, as recorded in photographs taken by Edith Maryon and her colleagues.

Rudolf Steiner left Berlin, finally, on 28 September, the day before Michaelmas, a week after he had sent his essay on 'The Chymical Wedding of Christian Rosenkreutz' to Alexander von Bernus, and returned to Dornach. Immediately the next day, in the joinery workshop, he embarked on a major, wide-ranging lecture course on the battle of Michael with the 'spirits of darkness' and its reflection in contemporary events, a few weeks before the Russian Revolution and the gradual build-up of Soviet power in the East.

Six months previously, in April 1917, America had entered the war as decisive, future-determining Western power, heralding subsequent West-East confrontations. In the autumn of 1917 Rudolf Steiner did not give any 'political' lectures in the narrower sense, but his presentations in Dornach focused again, and more deeply, on the spiritual battle for the European centre, and also for the threatened centre in each human being ('It is Europe's task to establish balance between the East and West. For us in Europe it is not our role merely to mimic the East or mimic the West; rather it is our task to stand independently upon our own ground and to fully acknowledge the justification of both the one and the other. This comes to expression in our Group.'[177]).

In a room directly adjoining the lecture room (in which, on 29 October, Rudolf Steiner also gave a major art-history lecture with slides on the development of the view of Christ in art[178]), his work on the wooden statue of Christ began soon after, again—as Assja Turgenieff recorded—involving radical reshaping of what was already there:

> The sculpture stood there resplendent, like a figure of
> Apollo, with beautifully rounded muscles in the soft-as-silk
> outlines of the wood when Rudolf Steiner returned from a

Photographs by Edith Maryon. Ita Wegman Archive, Arlesheim

long trip away. 'This English Lord is not my Christ,' he said, laughing; 'My Christ is not so muscular, he has no fat on him.' And energetically he drove his chisel into the lovely form. No trace of annoyance, nor any sense of hurt at all could be discerned in Miss Maryon.[179]

According to Assja Turgenieff, Edith Maryon's sole wish was to be Rudolf Steiner's 'helping hand' in executing the necessary work, and she herself had a keen sense of the barriers posed by her classical training—'Our powers were very inadequate, and Miss Maryon perhaps felt this most keenly, feeling herself hindered by a too rigid academic training' (Turgenieff[180]). Despite Turgenieff's striking account ('And energetically he drove his chisel into the lovely form'), Rudolf Steiner certainly did not destroy Edith Maryon's substantial preparatory achievement but further sharpened and intensified it, deeply grateful for the work that had been done for him and yet taking overall responsibility for it ('it could only be a matter of undertaking the work in a way I needed to have it, as it must be accomplished according to the aims of the Goetheanum').

*

In the period described by her, Assja Turgenieff herself belonged to the small group of wood-carvers working on the figures of the 'Group', and she soon began to work on the figure of the upper Ahriman:

> 'He is a fine man,' said Dr Steiner encouragingly as I worked. 'It is a lovely thing when the ugly is made ugly. Then it is true. In art ever more heed will have to be paid to ugliness.' He also said: 'Ahriman is a mighty Lord, he affects and acts upon his surroundings, he informs them with himself. Behind him, in the cave, one must incise his negative profile as shadow, and, in the rocks strewn around, one must draw forth hints of his emerging facial features. Nature too is everywhere seeking to form a face. That is its goal. When I walk around outside I continually see faces that are trying to emerge…'[181]

In her reminiscences Assja Turgenieff also noted her impressions of Steiner's own work on the wooden sculpture—his 'hand shaping forms out of inner experience alone':

> On one occasion I was at work in Dr Steiner's studio. The whole body of the central figure was already emerging from

The Christ figure. Photograph by Assja Turgenieff. Ita Wegman Archive, Arlesheim

the sheath of its preparatory stage. 'I sought to bring soul into it everywhere,' he said. 'In stone, the ancients sculpted out of impulses of wisdom. In Christian sculpture one has to engrave warmth into the living material of the wood.'[182]

Assja Turgenieff noted down these remarks in 1928, in a first manuscript about the work on the Group; there (though not in a later version in the 60s) she added to these last-quoted words a comment by Rudolf Steiner directly related to it ('In this way the dead can also see him [the Christ]') and wrote about them standing together before the sculpture:

> For a long time we stood there, and, as if feeling a ques-
> tion from him I dared to say, 'It is beautiful, Herr Doktor.'
> So great was the modesty of the one who had accomplished
> such a great work that he was pleased at my remark.[183]

*

At Christmas 1917,[184] Rudolf Steiner first showed the completed large-scale study model in plastiline to the eurythmy group around Marie Steiner-von Sivers and Tatyana Kisseleff, having begun working in the previous weeks on painting of the small cupola, the future intended location for the sculpture. Once again Assja Turgenieff recorded the atmosphere and the various details of this presentation in the high studio:

> Stirred, as if still pervaded by the warm pulse of his cre-
> ative strength, in deep seriousness and yet selfless humility,
> he stood there in his self-evident humanity. It was as if he
> wished to discern in us the effect of his creation.[185] My gaze
> was gripped by the cramped fingers of the hands of Ahri-
> man, extending towards Lucifer. 'Yes, there is a great trag-
> edy in these hands,' he said, picking up on my thoughts. 'I
> had to soften much about these figures, for otherwise people
> could not have endured it.'[186]
>
> I gazed at the arm movement of Ahriman, simultane-
> ously grasping and pulling towards him. 'Yes, a great
> pain, a great longing lies in this movement,' said Doctor

Steiner. [...] 'Everything convulses in Ahriman, since he wants to make everything cramped, contorted, hardened, gristly, bony. If you can get a sense of this, you discover [the nature of] his organism. That is why he is also smaller than a normal person, in the same way that Lucifer is bigger. Imagine an organism consisting only of blood-heat, air and lungs—that is Lucifer. He seeks to disperse, spread wide, the blood rises to his head, inverts itself in the lung-wings which are also ears. He listens to the cosmic music, intercepts and absorbs the sound ether with his wings. And precisely in the middle, if you bring together all the forms and configurations of the one and the other, you find the figure of the Representative of Humanity. Also in the whole treatment of surfaces. Each individual is free to regard him as the Christ, he does not urge himself upon us. He does not judge, he is simply there. One should not feel anything aggressive in his gesture: it also expresses itself in everything, in the forms of the body, in the asymmetry of his countenance, and also in the way he is sculpted. The new element here is to pass from form to movement. He strides forward calmly, the others cannot endure his proximity and judge themselves. In Christ's *proximity* Lucifer breaks his own wings and Ahriman entangles himself in the earth's veins of gold, but this is not done by Christ's hand. At the side you have them both as they are intrinsically, untouched yet by the power of Christ. There is great tragedy in the relationship of these two to each other.'[187]

The intensity of the effect of this model upon those who viewed it can be compared with that of a natural phenomenon. Only in the central figure striding upon the waves did one find tranquillity again. One could also come to a more vivid experience of time at such moments: an answer was here found to humanity's quest through the centuries, from primitive Romanesque reliefs of the Last Judgement through to Michelangelo's work.[188]

The big model, 1917

It was very probably during this showing in the high studio in Dornach that the Dutch artist Mieta Waller, a close friend of Marie Steiner-von Sivers, addressed the unbalanced over-all shape of the sculptural Group ('"Herr Doktor, the Group is tipping to the right, it is not in balance" was the first reaction of Mieta Waller. She had the invaluable gift of saying what she thought, whether it was tactful or not'). Steiner immediately took up this observation and comment (' "You are right", he replied after pondering for a moment, "to balance it I will need to add something on the left"'). In the following weeks this led him to create the additional 'Rock Being' at the top left of the artwork—as a figure who 'observes' the earthly events of Golgotha. 'He comes from the cosmos and gazes into earthly events.'[189]

In the context of the same visit,[190] or a little while later,[191] Marie Steiner-von Sivers asked Rudolf Steiner for a 'literary' supplement to the work (' "Herr Doktor, you must tell us a fairytale about the Group," said Frau Doktor [...]'[192]), thus stimulating Steiner's account of a 'new' or 'different' Osiris-Isis myth which he began, on 7 January 1918 in the joinery workshop, with the words:

> It was at the time of scientific profundity, in the middle of the land of Philistinism. There, on a lonely hill of the spirit, was erected a building that people in the land of Philistinism thought very strange. [...] If one wished to use the language of Goethe, one could say that the building embodied an 'open secret', for entry to it was denied to no one: the building was open to all, and anyone who wished could take the opportunity to see it. But the great majority of people saw nothing at all. The very great majority saw neither what had been built nor what the building showed. The great majority of people stood—to speak again with Goethe—before an open secret, an entirely open secret which divulged nothing to them.
>
> The centre of the building was conceived as the location for a statue. This statue represented a group of beings—the Representative of Humanity, then also luciferic and ahri-

manic beings. The people regarded this statue but, in the age of scientific profundity within the land of Philistinism, they did not know that this statue is fundamentally only a veil for another, invisible statue. They did not perceive the invisible statue, for that was the new Isis, the Isis of a new era.[193]

*

Only two weeks after this 'Isis tale', Rudolf Steiner had to relinquish his work in Dornach again for eight months, for lecture tours, meetings, writing and research in Germany. As three years before, he also spoke to members of the Anthroposophical Society in various German cities about the sculptural Group, illustrating his comments with slides of the developing artwork. Quite clearly, Steiner wished to enable those who belonged to the Anthroposophical Society to follow the details of processes unfolding in Dornach and the central Christ Group in particular. At the same time he unveiled deeper aspects of the artwork, and the knowledge of the human being underlying it. On 15 February 1918 in Munich, for instance, he said:

> An attempt has been made to create a sculpture in wood, a Group, which, let me say, represents an archetypal human being, but does so in such a way that what is otherwise only potential or predisposition, but is suppressed by a higher life, is depicted so that the whole form initially becomes gesture, and the gesture is then in turn brought to stillness. In sculpture the attempt has been made to awaken gesture suppressed in the ordinary human figure—not the gesture one makes to express the soul, but the gesture that is only deadened and suppressed in the soul through the life of the soul—and then to bring it to stillness again. Thus we have tried to first bring into gestural motion the calm surface of the human organism and then return it once more to stillness. By doing this we came very naturally to the sense that what is also predisposition but is self-evidently held back by higher life, the asymmetry that exists in every person—for no one is configured the same on their left side as on their right—could be accentuated more strongly. And now

therefore we accentuated this, in a sense dissolving what is made to cohere in higher life; and then one has to reconnect it again, with humour, at a higher level; then one has to again reconcile [it with] what appears outwardly naturalistic. It becomes necessary to artistically reconcile this violation of naturalism committed by accentuating asymmetry, by also having let various things pass into gesture and then having brought them to stillness again. This inner violation was one we had to redress again by showing, on the other hand, what is overcome when the human head passes through metamorphosis into a dark, oppressive figure that is now again overcome by the Representative of Humanity: the figure is at his feet and is such that we can feel it as a limb, a part of what represents the human being. The other figure we had to fashion embodies a sense of what happens when, apart from the head, the rest of the human form becomes so mighty as it is already in life, though restrained, held back by higher life—when what otherwise remains atrophied starts to proliferate: think of the shoulder blades, for instance, what begins in them, what already lies unconsciously in the human form and is a certain luciferic element in it, one that seeks to emerge from the human being. When everything that exists as predisposition or potential in the human form assumes form by sprouting forth from drives and desires, whereas otherwise it is overlaid by higher life— by the life of the mind, or rational life that configures itself, realizes itself in the human head, then it is possible to unlock from nature the spell of its open secret, to draw this forth by presenting parts, aspects, that nature otherwise deadens or kills in order to fashion a whole from them, to present these parts separately so that viewers of the work must accomplish in their sensibility what nature has otherwise performed before them. Nature has done all this. It really has attuned the human being, composed him from diverse separate parts into a harmonious whole. By dissolving what lies enchanted, spellbound, in nature, we dissolve nature into her supersensible forces. […] We become able to redeem something supersensible that is already present in sensory existence, that lies spellbound there, to release it from the sense realm, whereas otherwise it lies there under a spell of enchantment. Thus we become able, really, to be supernaturally naturalistic.[194]

If you look at a human being—you need only consider the skeleton—even a very superficial appraisal will show you that the skeleton is composed of two very strongly differentiated parts […]: the head or cranial part of the skeleton which in a sense is only appended above, and the rest. Those who have a feeling for form will discern—not through some kind of anatomical study but through a feeling perception of the skeleton of head and body—that the one is a metamorphosis of the other; that one can conceive of the cranial bones, in terms of their form, such that wherever there is some kind of bump or protuberance this can also grow and develop, and on the other hand that wherever such excrescence exists, this can recede. Through mere transformation of this kind— through changes of morphology—we can indeed derive the skeleton of the head from the rest of the skeleton and, to a certain degree, the rest of the skeleton from the head. And so we can say that the whole human being lies spellbound in the head. Even if we look at a skeleton without a head, if we wish to get further than sensory observation we will seek in a sensory-supersensible fashion to add the head to this skeleton; will seek to allow a vision of the head to emerge from the skeleton of the body. It is impossible however for the skeleton of a human trunk to appear in nature without the skeleton of the head. If you want to do more than observe nature in an abstract way but instead to bear the essence of nature herself within your own feeling and sensibility, thus feeling the natural object to be as it inevitably must, then it is self-evident that a vision of the skeleton of the head will arise for you out of the skeleton of the body. For those who understand such things it is true to say that if we have only the head and now complement this in vision by allowing the whole human being to emerge from it, this human being will be different from what emerges when we do it the other way round. The two will be similar and yet different. And so we can say that in outward nature a whole is fashioned in the human being that consists in the distinction of the head from the rest of the organism; but each separate part seeks to be a whole human being. In a higher whole the life is killed, deadened, that lies spellbound as whole human being in every separate part. If we exclude the thought that rises in us when we encounter the human being, then we find it necessary to recreate within us what we deprive him of when we analyse him. And in this way, like nature herself, and in imitation of her, we become creative builders. We create this infinitely intensive, significant process of harmonization of what must first be killed off in the limbs to appear again at a higher level. And naturally it becomes different when we recreate it in the spirit. [...]

In Dornach, in our building there, in a sculptural Group that is to be executed in wood—it is important that it should be made in wood, it can't be done in stone—we attempted [...] firstly to reunite at a higher level in a central figure something that is also united in the human being, but by nature herself, where the membered parts are suppressed or destroyed by a higher principle. Every person is asymmetrical. But we can feel what it is that desires something quite different in the left side from the right, and then we have two people before us, as it were, a left-hand and a right-hand person. What is specialized to our left-hand or right-hand being is united in nature to form a higher unity by killing off what the limbs would otherwise be in their separate idiosyncrasy. Encountering the will of nature, artistic apprehension perceives what I will call the full shape or form of the left-hand person and the right-hand person rising before it. Each basically seeks something different, and the artist—though this can remain very unconscious—can re-experi-

ence the process that nature accomplishes at another level
when it stifles the idiosyncrasy of our left-hand and right-
hand nature and balances them in our whole being. If we
actually succeed in artistically fashioning a figure whose
form indicates that the human being is asymmetrical in

Edith Maryon: Lucifer study. Ita Wegman Archive, Arlesheim

nature, then something else must be added. Perception in this sensory-supersensible realm requires us to add what then becomes necessary as other or further limbs. For this reason we had to create different figures. It was necessary for us to balance the diverging and reuniting of the left-hand and right-hand being by indicating the two other antitheses. What lives in us as a vision if we enlarge the human trunk into the whole human being? Then we would have living in the outer form what rises from the trunk into the head as drives and instincts, which we could call the luciferic. We will seek to fashion this luciferic principle in a different way from that undertaken by nature: for instance, we will reconfigure the shoulder-blades into wings; and then we will in turn try to combine these wings that nature constricts with the shape of the ears and the head.

Something other than an ordinary human being as created by nature will emerge from these sensory-supersensible human limbs, but it will depict a certain aspect of the human being that ought not to be depicted on its own. It would be ghastly if someone sought to present such a thing as a single figure on its own, but together with the human being, and placed into the right composition, we can imitate nature's own power of composition. On the other hand, what seeks in the human head to become a whole human being, becomes ossified and rigidified when we elaborate it into a whole human figure. This is what we must continually overcome in ourselves, what in fact we do overcome when, besides the impulses we bear within us from our head, we also have those active forces issuing from the rest of the organism that keep this rigidifying element fresh. What is head in us we must overcome through what derives from the blood of the heart organism. Here the sensory-supersensible view of the human being makes it possible to recreate in separate figures what nature herself secretly composes in the single human form.[195]

*

At the end of May 1918, Edith Maryon sent Rudolf Steiner in Berlin new photographs of the developing sculpture, which he used in his lecture there on 3 July. This lecture was devoted to the whole building, ending with a detailed account of the sculptural Group ('It aims to depict what must necessarily become part of human spiritual perception today and in the future'[196]) and the distinctive collaborative work being done by Edith Maryon. Six years after the seminal lecture of 14 May 1912, Steiner now said that Maryon had 'very wonderfully' found her way into the necessary 'reconfiguring of a worldview into an artwork'.[197] In his presentations on art in Berlin, Steiner not only pointed specifically to the distinctive fashioning of surfaces in the Group in the polarity between Ahriman and Lucifer,[198] but, elaborating on a primarily gestural and expressive rendition of the two beings, he said:

> The figures were not easy to create [...] because this required us to fashion something spiritual—for the main figure something partly spiritual and for Lucifer and Ahriman purely spiritual—and it is the hardest thing of all to create a spiritual form in sculpture. But we attempted to achieve what was necessary especially for our aims: to dissolve form, albeit necessarily remaining artistic form, entirely into gesture, entirely into facial expression. The human being is actually very limited in his capacity to use gesture and facial expression, whereas Lucifer and Ahriman are entirely gesture and entirely facial expressiveness. Spirit figures do not have finished and circumscribed forms. If you wish to sculpt a spirit it is the same as trying to sculpt lightning. The figure assumed by a spirit at one moment changes the next moment. That is something to which we must attend. If we sought to fix a spirit form as it is at a single moment, in the same way as one sculpts a resting figure, we would get only a rigidified gesture. Thus instead we have to convey gesture, nothing but gesture. In the figures of Lucifer and Ahriman, therefore, nothing but gesture has been fashioned, and to

a degree we had to attempt this for the central figure also, who is of course a physical figure, that of Christ Jesus.[199]

In Berlin Rudolf Steiner spoke extensively about the specific depiction of Lucifer and Ahriman, about Lucifer's beauty and Ahriman's ugliness, openly and directly relating the curious tale of the 'Rock Being' ('The Group was ready, and once the scaffolding had been taken down something curious became apparent: that, as Miss Waller felt, the centre of gravity of the Group—I mean of course only in aesthetic terms—lay too far to the right, and something needed to be added to balance this. Karma dictated it. Now it was not a matter of simply adding a lump of rock but of pursuing the sculptural idea further'[200]). Then he went on to explain the marked asymmetry of his sculpture:

> You will observe one thing particularly with this being, though only hinted at: you will see that the moment we are dealing with spirit figures, asymmetry comes into play, and must immediately strike you. In the physical realm this only comes to expression to a very limited degree: our left eye is different from our right and so on; our ears and nose likewise. The moment we enter the realm of spirit the etheric body acts in a radically asymmetrical way. The left side of the etheric body is quite different from the right, and this becomes immediately apparent when one tries to create spirit figures. If you walk around this being, you will see something different from every angle. But you will see that asymmetry is necessary to it because it is the expression of the gesture, implicit in which is a kind of humour, with which this being gazes down from the cliff to the Group below.[201]

On 3 July 1918 in Berlin, for the first time, Rudolf Steiner also stated the absolute necessity of making the Group in wood, because of the work's intrinsically Christological foundations,[202] and emphasized, remarkably, that the underlying context of this requirement was only partially apparent to him:

The Rock Being

A wooden Group. This thought arose for me, one I believe
I have grasped in thought, but whose deeper, underlying
occult reasons are not yet clear to me. I am sure that esoteric investigation will in future reveal them. But it seems
absolutely right that all motifs of antiquity are best depicted
in stone or metal while all Christian motifs—and ours is
pre-eminently a Christian motif—are better executed in
wood. All I can say is this: I always felt it would be necessary to rethink Michelangelo's pieta in Rome, the sculpture
in St Peter's, as a work done in wood. I believe that only
then would it depict what it should; and in the same way I
have had to change into wood in my thoughts other Christian sculptures that are executed in stone. I am quite certain
that something underlies this, though I myself have not yet
discovered the reasons. And thus our Group must be conceived and executed in wood.[203]

*

After his return in the second week of August, at the beginning
of his first lecture in Dornach (17 August 1918), Rudolf Steiner

thanked his co-workers for their 'dedicated' work over the past eight months ('You will I am sure believe me when I say that it gives me the deepest satisfaction to take up work again in your midst upon and around this building of ours. It is indeed true to say that anyone who approaches the whole aura of this building will become aware, not only after profound reflection but even on cursory reflection, that it relates in some way to the most significant and gravest tasks of humanity's future. And after a longer, enforced absence it is quite natural of course that one experiences the profoundest satisfaction to find oneself again at the site where this building stands as a symbol of our cause. And I would like to add that every time I return after a longer absence, I feel the deepest satisfaction to see how work on this building has continued, in beautiful and significant ways, through the dedicated work of those labouring here. Especially during these recent months of my latest absence, where work has been done under such difficult circumstances, some of the artistic work has been accomplished in an incomparable way, has progressed in a spirit that must pervade this whole endeavour'[204]). He then went on to speak, among other things, of his lectures on the Group to members of the Anthroposophical Society in Germany, stressing the effect of this on their souls just a few months before the end of the First World War, with all its catastrophic destructiveness:

> One could see [...] how powerful impulses, in fact, could enter the souls of those who, because of the circumstances of recent years, have never been able to set eyes on what is happening here. A new understanding of the human being is already emerging from the way in which our Group conceives, depicts and reveals the ahrimanic-luciferic along with the Christian. When what is given through these things approaches people's souls, their souls are deeply moved.[205]

Until Easter 1919, Rudolf Steiner remained at the 'Goetheanum'—as the original St John's building was renamed from the end of 1918, at Steiner's suggestion. In lectures in the autumn and winter of 1918/19, Steiner also for the first time spoke of

Rudolf Steiner, 1918

the sculptural Group within an anthroposophic and cosmolog-
ical context, explaining further design motifs in the Group and
the building.[206] For the rest, Rudolf Steiner worked on the Christ
figure and undertook major lecture courses on contemporary
history at a period of decisive change in Central Europe that
would affect the whole twentieth century. On 15 October 1918
he inscribed the following verse in Edith Maryon's copy of the
new edition of his *Philosophy of Freedom* (which he had revised
in Berlin in the spring of that year and thus made available in
expanded form for the post-war era):[207]

> In the free human being
> The universe concentrates itself
> Therefore concentrate yourself with free intent
> And you will find the world within you.

Bear yourself into the world
And through you the spirit of the world
Will come into being![208]

Seven weeks later, he noted in her copy of the book *Goethes Weltanschauung* ('Goethe's World View'):

You wish to think 'God':
Thus speaks Goethe's soul;
With this will, you plunge yourself
Into contradiction and doubt.
You should think in a 'godly' way;
And 'God' works within you:
This was the solution Goethe intimated
To the riddle of God
And in the same way spiritual science
Must be the solution of thinking.[209]

Thus ended the war-years, far from the Front and yet in the very thick of spiritual battles. In his lecture in Ulm on 30 April 1918, six months before the war ended, Rudolf Steiner had said of anthroposophy, the social impulses seeking to become active, and the nature of the Goetheanum as a School of Spiritual Science:

Humanity is now living in the midst of a terrible catastrophe. If it does not resolve to really integrate the new spirituality intended here, these catastrophes will keep recurring again and again, perhaps at very short intervals. This catastrophe and all its consequences can never be healed with the means humanity knew previously, before this catastrophe erupted. Anyone who still thinks it can be, is at odds with humanity's evolution on earth. This period of catastrophe will last—even if it can seemingly be bypassed for a few years—until humanity comes to interpret it in the only right way, that is, as a sign that human beings are turning to the spirit that must pervade purely physical life. This may seem a bitter truth to many, since it is an uncomfortable one, yet it is a truth.[210]

Im freien Menschenwesen
Faßt das Weltall sich zusammen
Drum fasse Dich mit freiem Sinne
Und du findest die Welt in dir
Trage Dich in die Welt
Und durch Dich wird der Geist
       der Welt!
E. Maryon, am 15. Oct. 1918
       zur Erinnerung
       R. St.

Inscription for Edith Maryon in the second edition of
The Philosophy of Freedom. *Ita Wegman Archive, Arlesheim*

DIE
PHILOSOPHIE DER FREIHEIT

GRUNDZÜGE

EINER

MODERNEN WELTANSCHAUUNG

VON

RUDOLF STEINER.

SEELISCHE BEOBACHTUNGS-RESULTATE NACH
NATURWISSENSCHAFTLICHER METHODE.

2.—6. TAUSEND.

WESENTLICH ERGÄNZT UND ERWEITERT.

1918
PHILOSOPHISCH-ANTHROPOSOPHISCHER VERLAG
(BERLIN W., MOTZSTRASSE 17).

Title page of the new edition of The Philosophy of Freedom,
1918. Ita Wegman Archive, Arlesheim

III

'With the essential being / of another soul'

Inner Accompaniment and Continuing Work
(1919-1922)

In the studio everything is slowly progressing;
it longs greatly for correction and collaboration,
and hopes that the time for this will soon come?
Edith Maryon, 21 May 1919[211]

I write these lines from the orphaned sculpture
studio, that longs for its director [...]
Rudolf Steiner, 9 August 1920[212]

Rudolf Steiner, 6 January 1919

Edith Maryon, who was keenly attentive to political and historical events, and possessed a highly developed social conscience, had followed Rudolf Steiner's accounts and emphases at the end of 1918 with keen interest.[213] In mid-November 1918, following a lecture in Dornach in the series on 'Evolutionary and Historical Foundations for Developing Social Discernment', Stuttgart factory-owners Carl Unger and Emil Molt first discussed with Steiner possibilities for a comprehensive initiative to realize social threefolding. At the beginning of February 1919, at their request, Steiner then wrote his 'Appeal to the German People and the Civilized World' a few days before he started to write *Towards Social Renewal*—a book which Edith Maryon immediately began to translate into English ('[…] If she said something, one could build upon it. If she undertook to do something that needed her practical sense, after a while it would be there even if what needed to be done was very far removed from her actual professional work.' R. Steiner[214]). Just nine days after Steiner's departure from Dornach on 20 April 1919 for extensive public lectures to support the new threefold movement in Wuerttemberg, Edith Maryon wrote to him in Stuttgart to say she had already sent her translated texts of the preliminary remarks and the first chapter of the book, as well as her translation of the 'Appeal', to England for checking and proofing. Along with this news, Maryon sent a few words about circumstances in Dornach since his departure: 'The weather […] is dreadful, snow, rain and cold, in the studio the temperature is only 2 degrees. Frau Stein read out to me a letter from her husband, from Stuttgart, it was very interesting to hear something about the work there; here we are falling asleep again somewhat!'[215] Rudolf Steiner's reply of 10 May initiated their real epistolary correspondence, which would become a key aspect of the remaining five years of Edith Maryon's life:

My dear Miss E. Maryon

> Many warm thanks for the letter. I am in the midst of such excessive work here that, if this is to be done carefully, I can only look through and send back the page you enclosed in a few days' time. To give at least one lecture every day, with discussion at the end, taxes the old organism greatly, and I would be happy if between times I could exert parts of the body, in our artistic work in Dornach, other than just the larynx, as I do here. But all this has to be. And since the day before yesterday it appears that people understand me better than previously. But this can always change again. Naturally I think a lot about the work in Dornach, and will be pleased when circumstances once again allow me to collaborate on it. The work here will take some time still.
>
> Warmest greetings for today
> Rudolf Steiner[216]

Why no such correspondence between them had developed during Steiner's long absences in the two previous years (since the accident in the studio at the end of 1916), or why it has not been preserved if it did occur, is not known. But in the period after Easter 1919, in the midst of Rudolf Steiner's threefolding work during the social upheavals of that time—an initiative that enormously sapped his strength and made the following years an uninterrupted test of endurance and engagement—an ever-growing correspondence began between them that testified to a high degree of trust and a deep sense of connection.

In the letter of 10 May Rudolf Steiner spoke with a directness unusual for him about his own situation and compromised forces, but also of his glad anticipation of their forthcoming artistic work and collaboration in the studio. Eleven days later, at the end of a long message that was concerned, among other

Stuttgart, 10. Mai 1919

Mein liebes Fräulein E. Maryon!

Vielen herzlichen Dank für den Brief. Ich bin hier in solcher Überarbeit darinnen, dass ich das mitgeschickte Blatt, wenn es sorgfältig geschehen soll, erst in einigen Tagen durchsehen und zurücksenden kann. Jeden Tag wenigstens Einen Vortrag mit daran sich schliessender Discussion zu halten, mutet dem alten Organismus viel zu, und ich wäre froh, wenn ich dazwischen an unserer künstlerischen Arbeit in Dornach auch noch andere Körperglieder anstrengen könnte als hier nur den Kehlkopf. Doch das alles muss eben sein. Und seit vorgestern scheint es, als ob man mich besser verstehen würde als vorher. Aber das kann immer anders werden. Ich denke natürlich viel an die Arbeit in Dornach und werde befriedigt sein, wenn die Verhältnisse mir wieder gestatten werden, mit zu arbeiten. Die Arbeit hier wird noch einige Zeit dauern.

Für heute herzlichste Grüsse

Rudolf Steiner

Stuttgart, Landhausstraße 70 (bei Kinkel).

Letter from Rudolf Steiner to Edith Maryon, 10 May 1919.
Rudolf Steiner Archive, Dornach

things, with threefolding activities in Switzerland and translation of *Towards Social Renewal*, Edith Maryon wrote:

> Everything is slowly progressing in the studio, it longs
> greatly for correction and collaboration and hopes the time
> for this will soon come? I would be very pleased to hear lec-
> tures are necessary only every other day and not daily.[217]

As Maryon put it on 21 May, the 'studio…longs' for Rudolf
Steiner and the continuation of the work there; and she herself
expresses concern about the situation of her teacher in Stuttgart.
The aptness of Maryon's concerns is confirmed by Steiner's subsequent accounts in a letter that arrived in Dornach two weeks
later:

> I have long wanted to reply but I am burdened by a great
> deal of work—and work that really requires long and care-
> ful thought. Naturally everything would be easier if one did
> not, on top of it all, have to continually encounter misun-
> derstandings. Everything one says immediately becomes
> something different when it is repeated. One sees how peo-
> ple fight one from all sides, by giving mistaken reports. Peo-
> ple seek to push everything into a fixed, partisan form, and
> when it is something that has nothing to do with anything
> fixed and partisan, they turn it into something altogether
> different. It isn't only our opponents who do this but also
> those who support the cause I represent and wish it well.
> And so all real work is very difficult.
>
> I am very pleased to hear that the sculpture work in
> Dornach is progressing, and I will be very glad indeed
> when I can work there artistically again, far from all the
> present commotion. But the needs of the time must be
> met. It is wrong to withdraw from any duty or obliga-
> tion. I hear that my book on the social question has now
> appeared in Switzerland; I hope that people will be able
> to see from this what I really intend, and that what has
> arisen only from the gossiping of opponents and also

beginners can calm down again a little perhaps. But I am content to know that there are also, after all, people who do understand me correctly. [...][218]

'But the needs of the time must be met. It is wrong to withdraw from any duty or obligation.' Like Maryon, Steiner here also expresses a 'longing' for his return to the artistic work ('far from all the present commotion'), and, wrestling his way through the difficult circumstances of misunderstandings and disparagement,[219] feels himself to be absolutely understood by Edith Maryon ('But I am content to know that there are also, after all, people who do understand me correctly'). Only a few days later he read her answer:

> Your letter is very welcome to me, although I am sorry to hear all the obstacles and misunderstandings one must battle with that the so difficult work [so that the difficult work] can progress. I can only recommend everyone thoroughly studying the book [*Towards Social Renewal*], then one has no need to introduce all sorts of things that have nothing to do with it.[220]

She goes on to say that she will have completed her translation in the next few days and will then embark on its critical revision. On 8 June she writes further about the situation at the studio in Dornach:

> Is there some hope that the work in Stuttgart will be far enough along at the end of this month, that you can take

Euer Brief ist mir sehr willkommen, obwohl der Inhalt tut mir leid zu hören unter wieviel Hindernisse und Missverständnisse man kämpfen muss so dass die schwere Arbeit vorwärts kommen kann. Ich kann nur jedermann empfehlen das Buch gründlich zu studieren, man hat es dann nicht nötig alles mögliche hinein zu bringen was gar nicht mit der Sache zu tun hat. Ich werde mit der Uebersetzung zu ende kommen

up the work here again? Everything is slowly advancing, on the South side of the Goetheanum the scaffolding has been taken down between the columns and the windows so that the cupolas and columns stand free, the capitals can be seen; it is really wonderfully beautiful and gives a sense of the impression it will make when wholly liberated from the forest of scaffold poles.

I would like to have the cast made of the head (plastiline) of the 2nd Ahriman in the big studio so that when one works on the wooden head in the small studio the model can stand alongside it. But of course this will spoil the original. May I do this or would you prefer us to wait a while?[221]

Rudolf Steiner did not return at the end of June 1919 as Edith Maryon wished—further threefolding lectures and discussions followed almost daily until August. At the end of June Steiner wrote to her again from Stuttgart, in explanation:

The work here must continue for some time still. But I think it will not be too long now. I greatly long for the work in the sculpture studio in Dornach. And no doubt I can get back there after a while, and return here again for the founding of a school planned for Stuttgart. But as yet I cannot say anything certain about my forthcoming schedule. The circumstances of the times do not allow any such certainty. It is very difficult to find understanding for what is, precisely, the most vital thing in these contemporary conditions. It is difficult for people today to understand what is needed based on spiritual foundations. Under the sway of materialistic habits of thought they have distanced themselves from an understanding of how the spirit also works within matter. They believe that material things can only be improved by material measures. And thus they do not recognize that any attempt merely to do this must inevitably lead to further confusion. My book is incomprehensible to many simply because it contains things that are different from what they have been accustomed to thinking. It is hard enough for people to change other habits, but it is hardest of all with habits of thought. And yet nothing healing and wholesome will develop in our era unless by changing thoughts, by relearning. I think much about our work in the sculpture studio in Dornach, and I would be glad to be doing it. But the work that duty requires has to be done, and I can only be there in thoughts.[222]

In the first week of July, Edith Maryon sent Rudolf Steiner a new photograph of the head of Christ ('the best one so far'), described the progress of work on the sculptural Group, that is, the preparations for Steiner's awaited return ('In the studio the last blocks are arriving this week, everything will then be ready, the work longs now only for the chief sculptor, especially to work on the Christ figure'[223]). She also reported on the lack of accommodation

Sofie Bauer and Edith Maryon in Dornach

and its increasing expense in Dornach, and expressed her intention to do something about this ('I have been speaking a great
deal to Herr Bay about the possibility of building small houses
and leasing rooms at around 30-35 francs'[224]). Edith Maryon pro-
ceeded with great independence and inner assurance, but then
waited for Steiner's casting vote before trying to implement her
plan with the help of Paul Bay and wealthy members ('But I will
wait to see what you think once you come'). At the end of this
letter she wrote:

> There is also *much* work to do here, Stuttgart has already
> received a *very* great deal.[225]

Nevertheless, Edith Maryon had to remain patient with 'Stuttgart' and Rudolf Steiner's delayed return ('But the needs of the
time must be met')—a patience she found in her awareness of the
intrinsic connection between the Dornach sculpture and Rudolf
Steiner's social commitment in the service of a future culture of
selflessness[226] ('Only the very fewest have sufficiently esteemed
Christ's entry into time.'—Michael Bauer[227]). Only three weeks
later, at the end of July, did she receive another letter from Steiner
with a broader survey of the situation, in which he outlined his
activities in Stuttgart again and hinted again at the difficulties
involved:

> My work here has not grown any less. For example, in the
> last few days I gave a lecture here on Sunday, in Heilbronn
> on Monday, on Tuesday in Ulm, on Wednesday here again;
> on Thursday I spoke for a eurythmy performance here,
> today I had many meetings and so on. Between times much
> to discuss and write. How glad I would be to get down to
> our artistic work again. The interim plan is to go to Dor-
> nach in the first half of August. But at present everything is
> uncertain. However, I am definitely hoping to do this. But
> then I would have to be back in Stuttgart in the second half
> of August where I must give a course for the teachers of a
> school that is to be founded on my principles. But if all goes

as I now think, I would be back for a short while to work in the sculpture studio.

The outlook and ideas meet with little understanding. Certainly there are a few who show understanding. But there is much misunderstanding and progress is far too slow for the circumstances of the time.[228]

Gratefully, Steiner wrote about Maryon's work on translating his book ('But it will be very important for this translation to appear in the world') and added at the end of his letter:

Recently I have also given anthroposophic lectures along-side those of a different character [exclusively devoted to the social question]. One might even say that there is more receptivity for these than for the others. In the intervals free from work I think a great deal about the sculpture work in our studio. It will be satisfying for me to be there again. Let us see if this will happen in the first half of August.[229]

*

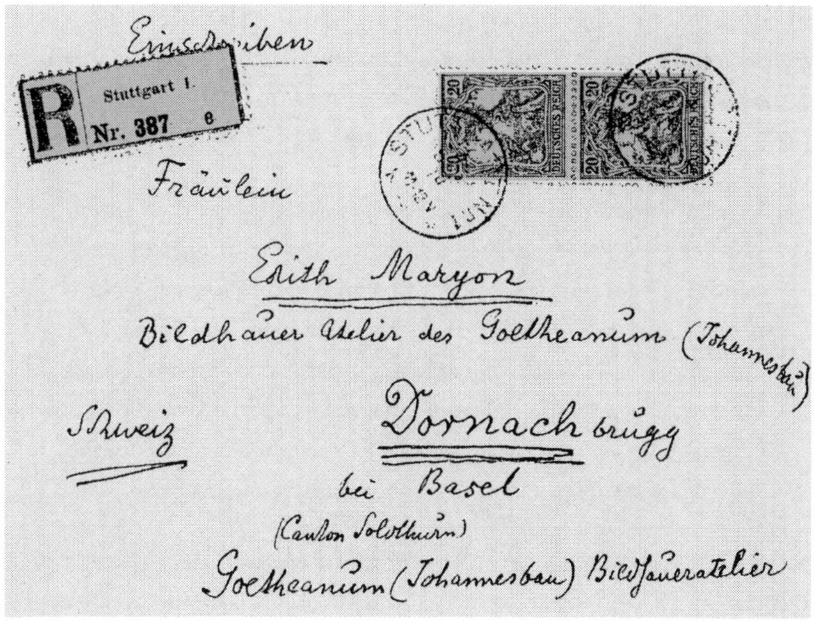

In fact—after almost five months of the endeavours in Wuert-temberg—Rudolf Steiner did not return to Dornach until 8 August 1919, for just ten days during which he gave six lectures on pedagogy and concerned himself with countless details of the building, before returning to Stuttgart to prepare for the opening of the Walfdorf School. Edith Maryon was greatly affected by the dynamic of events, the ever-increasing demands on Rudolf Steiner and his compromised state. But though she stood once more in an empty studio after Steiner's quick depar-ture ('The studio seems empty and silent now. [...] This week I will begin again to carve the Ahr. head and the hand of Lucifer, and will keep myself in equilibrium by doing so'[230]), she also felt deeply and inwardly involved in the success of the new, inde-pendent school, and thus in the beginning of an exemplary 'free life of culture' along social threefolding lines:

> I hope that the opening festival at the school will be very
> beautiful, I will be present in thought.[231]

As in all succeeding years, Rudolf Steiner enabled Edith Maryon, unlike anyone else living at a distance from him, to be 'present in thought' in what was happening, sending her detailed, daily accounts and in this way keeping her informed of his work in tangible ways. On 4 September, for instance, three days before the school opened, he wrote to her about his curriculum lectures:

> There is much work to be done here setting up the school.
> Each morning we start at 9 a.m. with a lecture on general ped-
> agogy, followed, after a 15-minute break, by a second lecture
> on the specifics of methodology and practice. After these two
> lectures it is 11.30. In the afternoon the seminar runs from 3
> to 6 and then there are usually meetings of some kind. So you
> could say the lectures run all day. Between times I think of the
> work in Dornach, especially of our sculptural Group.[232]

After the school opened, Rudolf Steiner went to Berlin and Dres-den to work and give lectures, stopping in Stuttgart again for five days on his way back to Dornach, where he arrived on 30 September.

*

The opening of the Stuttgart Waldorf School along with subsequent endeavours by Stuttgart entrepreneurs around Emil Molt to create business associations in line with social threefolding ideas—something that would turn out to be extraordinarily complex—absorbed much of Rudolf Steiner's strength and energy. Despite her deep commitment to social issues, Edith Maryon observed these developments with the greatest concern. While good progress was made on the sculptural Group in the late autumn and winter of 1919, Steiner's lecture tours and, especially, the rapidly increasing number of financial and business meetings, brought much turbulence with them. There were also difficulties within the anthroposophic movement—Edith Maryon's translation of *Towards Social Renewal* was sidelined by English members in favour of a freer version that was published at the beginning of 1920. Given the expertise and professionalism of this alternative version, Maryon respected this decision absolutely, but was concerned that it deviated from Steiner's wordings.[233]

Rudolf Steiner, however, continued working tirelessly, as it seemed, supporting the developing business activities despite his personal scepticism, speaking in numerous Swiss cities about the future of society and, in October and November 1919, holding his great Michael lectures in the joinery workshop in Dornach. These picked up again on motifs that had first sounded in London in May 1913, encompassing the social threefolding debates of the present and incorporating the Christ sculpture between the two adversarial forces:

> [...] This is to come to expression in the [...] sculptural Group, whose central figure is the figure of Christ, which we have attempted to fashion such that one can picture that this is really how the Christ walked the earth in the human being Jesus of Nazareth at the beginning of our era in Palestine. Conventional images of the bearded Christ are actually only

creations of the 5th and 6th centuries and are not in any way—
if I can use this expression—true likenesses. That is what has
been attempted: to create a faithful portrait of Christ who
is at the same time intended to be the representative of the
seeking human being who strives for equilibrium.[234]

Walking through the Goetheanum from West to East becomes,
as Steiner puts it, an increasing process of human self-knowledge that culminates in the Christ Group ('Know thyself in the
striving for balance'[235])—thus a process of self-knowledge and
transformation leading to Christ in the Logos house of the Word,
which was most inwardly connected with the true centre of the
human being.[236] 'The spirit of Christ holds sway throughout our
school', said Rudolf Steiner in Stuttgart, in repeated variations[237]
or rather intimations of the form of the new pedagogy, drawn
from spiritual science and strengthening the core of the human
being.[238] Five days before Christmas he said in another Stuttgart
lecture on social issues:

> [...] As central figure in this building we are working on
> a wooden sculptural Group nine-and-a-half metres high,
> which aims to depict the enigma of the human being in our
> era, but in an artistic form.[239]

But from Dornach, Edith Maryon—to whom Steiner had sent
brief Christmas greetings 'to our sculpture sanctuary'—wrote:

> Our studio looks very empty and abandoned, as if no one
> had been working there for a month now.[240]

*

1920 brought with it not only further work by Rudolf Steiner
and Edith Maryon on the sculptural Group but also on the
living quarters for co-workers conceived by Maryon in 1919,
and realized architecturally by Steiner (with Paul Bay). On 25
April, in a general meeting of the Goetheanum Association,
and following painful preliminary experiences in Dornach,
Steiner said: 'This matter will now be my own, most personal

concern.'[241] Six weeks prior to the general meeting, Edith Maryon, in Steiner's absence, had already shown models of the dwellings and of the sculptural Group to official visitors to the building, writing to him in Stuttgart to tell him about this ('Yesterday we had visitors from [to] Dornach, the presiding judge and seven or eight elevated creatures. They were friendly and had some understanding of the thing, afterwards they bought various books. A few of them even carved on the large Lucifer, something they found very amusing. They liked the models of the dwellings, I told them it was an attempt to meet the need for housing, and the intention was to execute them very simply, no luxury, but their architecture somewhat adapted to the building. They were very interested. We all tried to make a good impression. The presiding judge seemed to me particularly benevolent, if it was genuine').[242] Maryon and

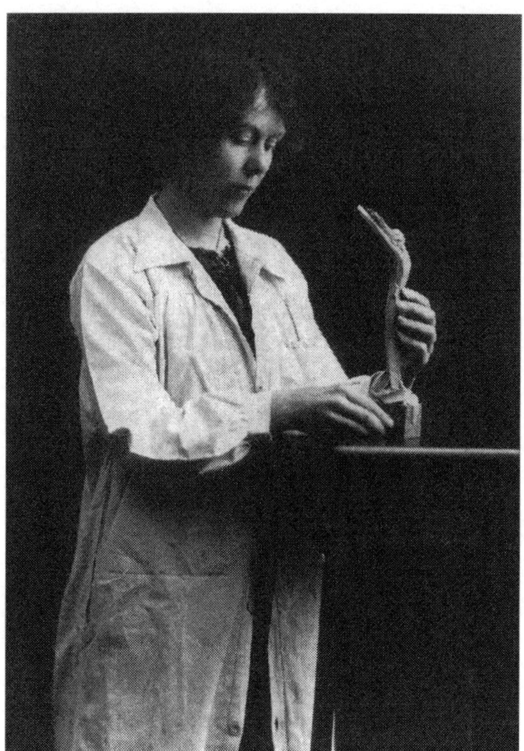

Edith Maryon, 1919/20

Steiner also collaborated on a house for the Dutch astronomer and mathematician Elisabeth Vreede (with whom Maryon had lived for some time after her return from England in the summer of 1914[243])—in line with the overall social conception of the Goetheanum and its 'ideal unity', as explained by Steiner in January 1914 in Berlin.

As ever, Rudolf Steiner was often in Stuttgart: at the school, taking part in negotiations by the 'Kommender Tag' joint-stock company, giving science lecture courses, and involved in academic initiatives that arose in relation to the Waldorf School and its teachers. In the periods of Steiner's absence, Edith Maryon wrote many letters describing the impoverished life in Dornach without him, one whose partial monotony and tedium—despite singular efforts—stood in marked contrast to the energy of developments in Stuttgart ('It is somewhat boring here and people wish it were possible to be present at the course in Stuttgart and to see the city again instead of going on working here sensibly!' 'I seek to grow wise in the loneliness here [...]'[244]). But more than anything else, Edith Maryon showed care and concern for Rudolf Steiner, who was finding only limited support for three-folding activities in Stuttgart, and whose colleagues there left something to be desired, as Steiner clearly expressed it to her. Thus in a letter of 23 June 1920, three months after the founding of the 'Kommender Tag' joint-stock company in Stuttgart, and shortly before Steiner's return to Dornach after several weeks in Stuttgart, he wrote:

> Of here I can scarcely say anything other than that I will, despite everything, be leaving much undone work behind. What we lack are focused people with expertise, whom one can hardly find at all. Work of such dimensions as we have started here weighs heavily upon the soul. And such a burden leaves little room for consideration of whether one is more tired or not. Certain things simply *need* to be done. I long greatly to work in our studio again. Well, it will soon happen. For today, my very warmest greetings.[245]

Four weeks later Steiner wrote again to Maryon, whose 'practical sense' and 'energetic tranquillity' he often painfully missed amongst the leading figures in Stuttgart:

> Business expertise that we now need is, sadly, largely lacking. The few people we have are over-burdened, and others cannot be found anywhere.[246]

Edith Maryon's concerns, or indeed anxieties, related also to the public attacks on Steiner to which he was increasingly exposed in Stuttgart and Dornach—in newspapers, journals and universities, from pulpits and nationalist groups.[247] The post-war Weimar Republic was an unstable set-up, showing early signs of unsolved problems and of a tendency to resort to violence. Maryon, with her highly developed sensitivity and alert historical insight perceived this long before the majority of those active in the Anthroposophical Society ('I hope the lectures yesterday and today were well attended and that things are running calmly? I am still anxious about the events in Germany'[248]). For his part, at intervals often of only a few days, Rudolf Steiner wrote letters to Maryon, messages which he—invariably under pressure of time—sometimes composed in the Stuttgart Waldorf School itself, and in which he often sought to reassure her ('Warmest greetings for today, and be assured that there is no need for anxiety. I will no doubt not be back on Monday, but soon afterwards'[249]). Yet neither did he dissemble the real dangers that existed. Even the emerging Christ sculpture in Dornach itself became the subject of a grossly distorting pamphlet put out by opponents.[250]

*

After a six-year absence from England, including the whole period of the First World War, Edith Maryon visited her family again in the summer of 1920. Immediately on arriving in Britain, she wrote a postcard to Steiner in Dornach:

> My very dear teacher
>
> I'm writing these few lines at a very uncomfortable post-office counter! I arrived safely, and not too tired. Please open

the little window in our studio at night-time, otherwise the
air is too bad. I will write a letter tomorrow or the next day.
For now just Aufwiedersehen. I'm already longing for Dornach, and find London ghastly!

With warmest greetings
Edith Maryon[251]

Rudolf Steiner had himself often spoken in his letters from Stuttgart—or other places where he was working—of 'our sculpture
studio'. On the day Maryon wrote her postcard in London, 8
August 1920, he also took up his pen in Dornach:

> I'm writing these lines from the orphaned sculpture studio
> that longs for its director, but does not want to cause her any
> trouble by cutting short her stay.[252]

But despite Steiner urging her to stay longer in England,
Maryon was not at ease with her old and now strange-seem-
ing homeland. She felt she belonged in Dornach, and to her

The Goetheanum, 1919

work with Rudolf Steiner, the spiritual-esoteric centre of her life ('I long greatly for Dornach, and no longer like London. I hope all is going well in the studio, and that the Christ is not yet finished, I would like to see for myself how he grows'[253]). But Rudolf Steiner's support for a long stay in England was because of her need for complete recovery, and on 13 August he wrote to her again:

> All is well at the studio. I was only away for a day and a half and made sure that no disorder occurred—though this was the cause of some agitation for Miss Geck. But now, though the studio longs for its director, I want to ask you not to hurry if it would be desirable to lengthen your stay there by a few days. It is a cause of anxiety to think that the long, tiring journey was undertaken for such a short stay. So please, if necessary, take a few more days. In such matters one should be sensible.[254]

We do not know exactly when in August 1920 Edith Maryon returned to the Goetheanum and her sculpture studio from England. But Steiner's lecture in Dornach on 27 August, in which he elaborated again, strikingly, on the aspect of differentiated equillbrium in the Group, in terms of body, soul and spirit,[255] will certainly have taken place in her presence. The 'opening' of the Goetheanum, with extensive 'School courses', was planned for four weeks later, even though Steiner spoke out against using the term 'opening' and the intention of such an event at this time was not one that came from him.[256]

*

> When the building had reached a stage of completion that allowed courses and performances to be held there, we were full of a burning wish to see the Group in the surroundings created for it. Aspects concerning its appearance from a distance still needed work. But Miss Maryon met our wish with the words, 'There is still time, there is no need to hurry...' [Assja Turgenieff][257]

But in a memoir she wrote in 1928, Assja Turgenieff wrote the following about the same situation:

> Certainly the building could not be completed without the Group, could not be inaugurated, but from Herr Dr we knew that we, that the time, was not ripe for inaugurating the building.[258]

And in a later essay, in a slightly modified and clarified version:

> During our work on the Group we heard from Edith Maryon that Dr Steiner [...] did not yet wish to erect it [in the building]: the time, and the members, were not fit for this; one must wait...were his words as she repeated them.[259]

Despite his pleasure at the energetic initiative of the young Swiss jurist Roman Boos, who had organized the School courses, Rudolf Steiner left those closest to him in no doubt that he did not think the time had yet come for a festive inauguration and true 'opening' of the Goetheanum. Assja Turgenieff's memoirs also testify to the fact that in the autumn of 1920 Steiner did not wish the 'Christ Group'—despite the work on this being now far advanced—to be placed within the building as its true 'crowning' and culmination. At the end of September and beginning of October 1920, therefore, the lectures from the speaker's lectern and the festive eurythmy performances, took place in front of the empty space at the eastern end of the small cupola surrounded by ash pillars. It was Edith Maryon who, when asked by her co-workers about this, passed on the decisive words of Rudolf Steiner that 'the time, and the members, were not fit for this; one must wait...'.

The opening event at the Goetheanum, in particular the academic lectures given there, showed that Steiner was right in his diagnosis of the situation: they scarcely belonged to the form-language of the building; they did not raise themselves to its heights and were, ultimately, alien and inappropriate to it, despite being inspired by goodwill. The Christ-permeation of thinking, and thus the spiritualization of knowledge and science by Michael forces of the heart, of which Rudolf Steiner had spoken six months earlier—in his Whitsun lectures in the Dornach joinery workshop on the philosophy of Thomas Aquinas—was something as yet very imperfectly accomplished by Steiner's co-workers and pupils; and to some extent this was not yet even recognized as a profound problem and task. Rudolf Steiner did not seek a merely 'additive' extension of conventional academic or scientific ideas through anthroposophic insights but a complete transformation of thinking through the active and dynamic Christ impulse. Only a week after the three School weeks ended, he described in evening lectures in Dornach the extraordinarily difficult contemporary situation, in which real Christian impulses of the future were not being taken up ('The Christ will not come, in a spiritual sense, if people are not prepared for this'[260]). In this context, Steiner spoke for the first time of an 'inner opposition' to his own intentions and the core of his work amongst anthroposophists, arising in particular from a self-willed arrogance in the realm of business and economics, in 'the field of practical life'.

The Goetheanum, 1919

Only a few days later he wrote in Edith Maryon's copy of his essays 'On Realizing the Threefold Social Organism':

> The only wholesome thing is when
> In the mirror of the human soul
> The whole community is reflected;
> And in the community lives
> Each single soul's strength.
> That is the motto of social ethics.[261]

Steiner had written the various essays in this collection the previous summer and winter—immediately following his mostly failed social threefolding endeavours in Stuttgart—as leading article in the Stuttgart journal *Dreigliederung des sozialen Organismus* ['The Threefold Social Organism']. In these essays, as he wrote in the Introduction to the edition published in book form, he did not wish 'to express the thoughts of one individual, but the unconscious will of European humanity'.[262] And now he gave them to Edith Maryon, endowed with an important 'motto'. When writing these articles, some of them composed in Stuttgart, Rudolf Steiner may often have been thinking of Maryon—of the sculpture studio in Dornach and her love of work which she placed wholly at the service of social endeavours. As Steiner wrote in one of his essays, the individual's impetus for work should not succumb to the egoistic quest for profit, but requires the same 'love for the human social order [...] that, say, the artist has for the creation of his works'.[263] As a unique artist, Edith Maryon worked beside Rudolf Steiner 'to transform esoteric impulses into the shaping of a social organism which would come to sculptural expression in the Goetheanum building'.[264] She worked on the central Christ Group but also on housing development and various other fields whose necessity for the social community she selflessly perceived.[265] In the late autumn of 1920, the difficulty of Rudolf Steiner's situation was matched by the encouragement and faithfulness of Edith Maryon, who had committed herself fully to Steiner's destiny, and that of the anthroposophic movement and its society:

> The only wholesome thing is when
> In the mirror of the human soul
> The whole community is reflected;
> And in the community lives
> Each single soul's strength.

*

Despite his wide-ranging Christmas lectures in Dornach on the Isis myth and the Sophia motif, which were not without notes of warning ('Humankind is preparing itself for a next great world war. Culture will continue to be demolished'[266]) and his ongoing sculptural work during the Christmas period,[267] he also spent many days and weeks in Stuttgart during the winter months of 1920/21, consolidating the enterprises that had been started and giving social guidance to the people involved in them ('If only people could work together in good, human ways; but that is what is most lacking. There is so much to do [...]'[268]).

A day after Epiphany, on 7 January 1921, Steiner again sent Maryon the items of his very busy schedule (including public lectures on economic and social questions, branch lectures on spiritual science and karma knowledge, supervisory board meetings and industry conferences as well as an ongoing course on astronomy and science), and wrote:

> I hope that I will accomplish this without any flagging of
> mood this time. Otherwise everything is the same except
> that the attacks here too are growing ever uglier.[269]

At this point, for the first time since her major crisis seven years before, Edith Maryon was ill and weakened. But she sent reassuring words to Rudolf Steiner:

> My health is really better. I have found a means to eat with-
> out taking medicine. It mostly consists of infant meal, beaten
> eggs, milk etc (with no further vomiting). I must proceed
> very slowly and continue this method for a while. Yester-
> day I was inoculated, and Frau Dr Wegman is coming again

Ich hoffe, dass ich so ofne alle Stimmermüdung die Sache diesmal durchbringe. Sonst ist alles das gleiche außer dass die Angriffe auch hier immer hässlicher werden.

tomorrow. I am still a little short of breath. My heart pounds a little when I have to exert myself.

But I keep wondering if proper care you are taking? I hope things are going well in Stuttgart—I think a lot about it and hope there are no night-time sessions. Naturally I have not heard about the lectures that have begun.

Herr Vreede visited me and brought me fresh eggs, Miss von Blomestein brought me a flower and said that her house would now soon be finished, that many people have visited it and thought it very beautiful. I was very pleased indeed that people are happy with what we are trying to do.

Miss Kucerova looks after me faithfully.

I think a lot about how the [threefolding] work is going in Silesia etc.[270]

A few weeks later, on 9 February 1921, her 49th birthday, she received from Rudolf Steiner the following seminal verse:

Knowledge speaks to the human soul:
Reflect upon destiny
Behold it with acceptance;
In the beholding of destiny,
In feeling acceptance, you will
Achieve your freedom,
In freedom forge bonds
With the essential being
Of another soul.[271]

Es spricht Erkenntnis zur Menschenseele:
Bedenke das Schicksal
Erschaue es duldend;
Du wirst im Schicksalschauen
Du wirst im Duldendfühlen:
Erringen deine Freiheit
In Freiheit deine Bande
Mit andrer Seele
Wesenheit.
9. Februar 1921.

Ita Wegman Archive, Arlesheim

On Edith Maryon's birthday, which concluded seven seven-year periods of her life, Rudolf Steiner was in Dornach where, in the last few days, in members' lectures, he had engaged intensively with the fierce opposition to anthroposophy, and again urged members to show alertness and initiative. But only three days later, Steiner began yet another six-day training course for speakers on threefold issues in Stuttgart, in which, in lectures and question-and-answer sessions, he comprehensively elaborated on the inner and outer preconditions for their future work,[272] before travelling to Holland for public and members' lectures.

On 16 February, two days before his departure for Amsterdam, Edith Maryon, wrote to him in Stuttgart:

My dear, respected teacher

Now I am back at work, having stayed at home for three days to get rid of my cold at last, and now it is a good deal better, and I have sorted out my diet somewhat better.

I hope you didn't catch a cold?

I think about the work in Germany a great deal, and send my best wishes for many good things to be achieved—and success in Holland too. But I am jealous of those who travelled there yesterday! I would so much have liked to travel with them.

Today the electrical work has been finished (this change coming somewhat late in the day) and half of the scaffolding has been taken down. There is a great deal of dirt but already one can see Luc. and the being clearly from the ground.

I've been told it is terribly cold in Holland, no hot water in the rooms, only 2 blankets on the bed, unheated rooms and corridors, lecture hall etc., so that one has to be very careful not to catch cold.

I hope you took the eucalyptus with you?

With best greetings
Edith Maryon[273]

Rudolf Steiner also wrote the day before his departure, briefly summarizing his efforts in Stuttgart ('All went well, except for the fact that there is so much work to do that not everything could be done') and ended with solicitous words about Maryon's health:

And now a last meeting still awaits me, so I can only add that I hope you continue to get much better.[274]

*

While Steiner's wide-ranging work continued in the second half of February and beginning of March in Holland (where, on his 60th birthday, a plan for founding a 'World School Association' was drafted in The Hague), Maryon in Dornach oversaw occupation of the three now completed 'little houses', including her own move, with her few belongings, into very modest rooms there—with a view of the Goetheanum and the sculpture studio.

Once again she received from Steiner an extensive report on his work, which the latter had written in Amsterdam a day after his birthday ('I am in the midst of lectures here'), testifying to

The Goetheanum, the high studio and the three eurythmy buildings

a moderate optimism ('Much has gone very well here; other things could have gone better') and a recurring problem ('But we lack people with a real sense of practicality').

Rudolf Steiner also acknowledged that Edith Maryon's concerns about his voice had not been wholly unfounded ('I have been very careful, and yet it is arduous to have to speak so much'[275]).

Back in Dornach for only a week, Rudolf Steiner had to leave again for Stuttgart in mid-March to participate in the 'Anthroposophic Schooling Courses' there, contributing eight lectures of his own to an audience of more than 800 and attending numerous discussions and assemblies with over 500 seminar participants. Here in Stuttgart, where a large anthroposophic clinic with related research and medicines production facilities was to open three months later, Steiner was once again exposed to public attention, experiencing numerous journalistic attacks upon his person.[276] Edith Maryon observed these developments with anxiety and increasing alarm at the lack of protection and

the wholly inadequate defence given to Rudolf Steiner both by
the educated classes and anthroposophists:

> I think a great deal about this and hope that people in the
> right places will understand how terribly cruel and base
> are these attacks upon you, and how they militate against
> all truth. They are abominable, one really has to ask one-
> self where the people with true insight are in Germany, and
> whether broad-minded and clear-sighted people are entirely
> lacking.[277]

Rudolf Steiner's letter on 21 March 1921 described both the possibilities and limits apparent at the big gathering in Stuttgart:

> Overall, the participating students have been receptive so
> far. But one always has the sense that in so short a time one
> can give people so little, and that it is very difficult for them
> to form their own views—which is after all the critical thing.
> The difficulties we face are enormous. In the face of them it
> remains true to say that we can do little, indeed too little. It
> would be a big task to show people what the nature of the
> opposition is, and this cannot be achieved without almost
> unending work. My voice has held out well so far. In pauses
> in the work I live repeatedly in thoughts of our sculpture
> studio. This has to be, for it gives strength. And I will be
> happy when I can be there again.[278]

*

The year 1921 continued very much in this vein. Little time
remained to Steiner during his stays in Dornach to dedicate

himself to the sculptural work he loved. He had scarcely arrived back in Switzerland when he was compelled to deal with big problems—including financial problems—at the Goetheanum too.[279] Nevertheless, he took every opportunity to collaborate further with Edith Maryon on the Christ Group, working especially on the statue of Christ itself, even in the very midst of the members' lectures which he had begun in Dornach:

> A short while before lectures, one saw Dr Steiner coming through the door of the sculpture studio, accompanied by Miss Maryon, whose regal, slim figure immediately conveyed her Englishness: her red hair and delicate, transparent skin tone, the blue eyes that looked into the world with such alert awareness, and the strongly formed chin. A grace and charm lay upon her tall figure.[280]

Often after Rudolf Steiner had departed again, Maryon spoke of the 'orphaned studio' as a living being ('The studio seems very empty to me, it assumes a different character once you

The eurythmy buildings and the Goetheanum

have gone'[281]). She repeatedly described to him the tentative efforts to continue with anthroposophic lectures and studies in his absence ('Yesterday Miss Vreede gave a lecture on the development and history of mathematics—very interesting. Afterwards Wachsmuth, Storrer, Pfeiffer and Herr Stadlin asked questions. Wachsmuth spoke about [Chladni] tone forms, Pfeiffer wanted to know the extent to which the Egyptians based their astronomy on mathematics. He doesn't speak badly, but too monotonously. There were quite a few of the members present despite a heavy downpour, but perhaps only three or four outsiders unfortunately'[282]). Thus she described a situation in which, despite Steiner's avoidance of any emphasis on his personality, people were drawing entirely on the grandeur of his spiritual investigations, his mode of working and charisma so that, when he was away, things shrank to an almost pitiful stature despite the imposing forms of the Goetheanum itself. But Maryon also wrote to him about daily anxieties connected with the new dwellings, whose administrator she had more or less become ('Frau Kisseleff was the only one who paid her rent immediately. Each person tried to persuade us how little electrical light they were using—so we will no doubt face our first difficulties when the time comes to calculate electricity bills and distribute the costs'[283]). Or she told him about her preparations for his planned trips to England the following year.

In the summer of 1921, after an intensive international 'Summer Art Course' at the Goetheanum which she had helped prepare, at which Baron Walleen translated Rudolf Steiner's lectures, she went to Ticino for a short recuperation. Here her thoughts, however, continued to be filled with Rudolf Steiner, his situation and all his endeavours:

> I hope that no plans have been made [for activities] too close
> to the theological course and the Christmas course, and that
> you give your voice a holiday from 7 September onwards???
> It will surely be necessary. How is the voice at present? And

are you too tired? Or are you trying really to rest a little every day?

Farewell. Warmest greetings

Edith Maryon[284]

She wrote another letter to him at the end of August/beginning of September from Lugano:

> Dear, respected teacher
>
> I am pleased to hear that the hand-wound has healed and I send all good wishes for the voice. It is good that the many lecture demands, which always increase infinitely, will not prevent you resuming the work in Dornach. One *must*, after all take time between these demands to breathe again, especially after such strenuous work as in the last three weeks; otherwise the voice will really be completely wrecked.[285]

The day after the 'Summer Art Course' had ended, Rudolf Steiner had left again for Stuttgart to attend the congress on 'Cultural Prospects of the Anthroposophic Movement', where he gave seven more lectures and involved himself in numerous other tasks (including for the Anthroposophical Society, the threefold social order movement and the Waldorf School). Despite Maryon's well-meaning advice, Rudolf Steiner made the hoped-for contributions to all these ventures almost without ceasing, complaining only, as so often before, of the lack of collaborators ('One needs more co-workers for the cause. Every hour shows this'[286]). Finally, on 12 September, even before she herself had returned to Dornach, Maryon wrote to him:

> What date will you arrive back in Dornach? We need you very much in the studio from Monday onwards before the theological course starts since then you will be in such demand that everything else must take a back seat. I will prepare for Monday in the hope you come.[287]

This letter was forwarded to Steiner, who was already in Berlin—among other things to give a public lecture at the Philharmonia Hall. Before he had received it he wrote to her from 17 Motzstrasse on 13 September, in a more leisurely tone:

My dear Edith Maryon

Have just arrived in Berlin, and send my warmest greetings. I was unable to write sooner, unfortunately, since the last days in Stuttgart were very full and busy. It is all very well saying one shouldn't do this, but it simply isn't possible, for then one is neglecting an absolute obligation. Outwardly, actually, I am very well; hand and voice are cured. But inwardly there are many worries, and they grow ever greater. The congress really went extraordinarily well—beyond all expectations. But now everything else comes toward me, and for this we need capable people—those who have discretion and who would really feel that general concerns and matters are their own. But such people cannot be found at all in the business world. Instead people are intent on disagreeing with one another. Only the fewest help one get further, and these few are, indeed, too few.

From all sides I am invited to give lectures, but I have to refuse all such requests here. I will leave here on Sunday evening, travelling to Stuttgart firstly. Then as swiftly as possible from there to Dornach. I very much want to work in the sculpture studio again, understandably. The theological course is due to begin on the 26th. I send warmest greetings ahead of my arrival. I hope all is going well. Thanks for the letters.
Rudolf Steiner[288]

*

Rudolf Steiner eventually returned to Dornach on 22 September with the general manager of the Waldorf-Astoria Company, Emil Molt. The members' lectures there began the following evening, and were concerned, among other things, with the nature of evil; then, on 26 September, the two-week 'Theologians Course' began, which would lead a year later to the founding of The Christian

Community. Regular lectures for the workers at the Goetheanum also started in the middle of October.

Rudolf Steiner was able to stay no more than two months in Dornach in the late autumn of 1921, and continue work on the Christ sculpture, along with much else that was in hand there. In the middle of this period—on 27 October—he was with Edith Maryon to inaugurate and lay the foundation stone for Haus Vreede which they had both designed, and which was situated on Arlesheim's 'Zur Hoehe' street ('Path to the Heights'):

> In this house may soul live
> May it be pervaded by spirit
> That seeks firm will
> In its *foundations*
> And so acquires
> Devout intent
> In all this building's rooms;
> So that from *above*
> The spirit's blessing can join
> With the grace of God
> In all who live *within* it.[289]

*

Rudolf Steiner's last major trip of 1921 took him from Berlin to Norway at the end of November. In her letter of farewell, Edith Maryon wrote to him at Motzstrasse on 16 November, three days before another, expectantly awaited Philharmonia Hall lecture:

> I dreamed of Goethe continually last night, I do not know why, waking up around 4 in the morning and pondering on it. Today it is very empty in the studio and one has enough time to think; it seems as if I have been only developing my 'Martha' qualities for a long time, at the cost of more 'Mary' qualities, and that I would need very much a spiritual deepening in many directions. During your absence I will try to work better in this guideline [sic] and to meditate. So great a lack and inadequacies also in respect of you come ever more to my awareness.

I hope […] for much success on Saturday and will be thinking about it a lot until I know that all has gone well in Berlin. I also very much hope that the trip to Norway goes without [you] catching a cold, but it is easy to wish this without much hope of it being so.[290]

Two days later she wrote again:

I am thinking a lot of Berlin and soon the journey to Kristiania [Oslo], and wish it were granted me to be there too.

Letter from Edith Maryon to Rudolf Steiner on 16 November 1921.
Rudolf Steiner Archive, Dornach

I very much hope you will not catch a cold in the great cold-
ness. I will be glad when Berlin is over, I hope it won't be
necessary to give lectures in Munich??[291]

During these weeks—alongside her artistic work—Edith Maryon
was very much involved in the last preparations for a course for
English pedagogues at the turn of the year. But at the same time
she was also organizing many other things, including a studio
stove for Rudolf Steiner's artistic labours in the winter. She was
very preoccupied with the intensifying mood of extremism in
Germany and the increasing sway of nationalism, the seeds
of developments that would also pose an existential threat to
Rudolf Steiner.[292] But during the three days he was in Berlin he
wrote two letters to her, and reflected on their collaboration at
the Goetheanum ('I hope that all goes well in our studio. I will
be glad to be back there again'[293]). At the same time, his essay on
the nature of the opposition to anthroposophy appeared in the
weekly Dornach journal. Meanwhile, the stove ordered by Edith
Maryon arrived at the studio, its pipe passing through the whole
space up to the roof ('it heats very well, but looks like a giant
creature, otherwise it is not unpleasant once you have recovered
from the first shock of it'[294]). Edith Maryon wrote of this and various other things ('There is still a great deal to do in the houses, I
have now become secretary, house-painter, seamstress and other
things, and will not [be] dissatisfied if I have got everything in
order by the end of next week'[295]) to Rudolf Steiner in Kristiania:

> Dear, respected teacher
>
> I heard that there was a deep snow-storm on 21-22, and I very
> much hope you arrived safely in Kristiania without catching
> cold? I also hope the Norwegians did not arrange you to give a
> lecture in the station waiting room on your arrival—no doubt
> they would have made use of the time if they had heard too
> soon that you were going to arrive one day earlier![296]

In Norway (besides internal lectures at the Vidar branch), Rudolf
Steiner gave many major, public lectures—at the Nobel Institute

(at the invitation of a 'Pedagogical Association') on 'Education and Teaching Methods founded on Anthroposophy' and, to almost 2000 students and university teachers, on 'The Reality of Higher Worlds and Paths to Develop Knowledge of These Worlds'. He lectured in the old university lecture hall on the foundations of anthroposophy, at the 'Theological Association' on 'Jesus or Christ', at the 'Economics Association' on 'The Key Question of Economic Life' and, in his last evening lecture, on 'The Need for Cultural Renewal'.

Though she herself was an artist preoccupied with her inner life and with its esoteric foundations, Edith Maryon wholeheartedly welcomed Rudolf Steiner's social, cultural and scientifically-oriented activities. Entirely in keeping with this, she also prepared the necessary bridge for his work in England that would begin in 1922 with great energy, starting with the pedagogical course at the turn of the year. Edith Maryon herself took part in this ground-breaking course, initiated in collaboration with Professor Millicent Mackenzie, in the 'White Hall' at the Goetheanum. Consisting of 16 lectures and question-and-answer sessions on 'The Healthy Development of the Human Being',

South aspect of the Goetheanum, with the 'White Hall'

the course was also attended by teachers from Scandinavia, Holland, Germany and Switzerland.

During the course, Rudolf Steiner wrote in her copy of 'The Fundamental Social Requirement of our Time' the following lines:

> To replace spirit that is thought with actively working spirit means, in these times, to feel the fundamental social requirement.[297]

Rudolf Steiner's course for teachers, extending through the Holy Nights until 7 January 1922, was a great success, comprehensively highlighting the underlying ideas of Waldorf pedagogy and many of its consequences, right into physiological and medical aspects. At the same time, in frank answers to questions during the course, Rudolf Steiner gave clear expression to his real concerns for the future of the educational system, despite the successes and achievements of the Stuttgart Waldorf School, describing a totalitarian tendency that was in the process of making 'the state into a great machine' and the human being to a 'cog within it'.[298] The Stuttgart Waldorf School, which had been founded in the autumn of 1919 at a time when 'the economy and the state had collapsed' and 'cultural life was in a state of complete bankruptcy',[299] sought only to be, and could only be, according to Steiner, the exemplary model for a large-scale, far-reaching school movement founded on a 'free cultural life', the latter, however, being nowhere in sight yet in the past two-and-a-half years:

> [...] When the Waldorf School was founded, I said: It is a fine thing that such a model now exists, but this does not solve the problem. It would only be solved, or at least a beginning would only be made in solving it, if at least a dozen Waldorf schools were to be founded within three months. This did not happen. And therefore what has so far happened in this domain cannot be regarded as a success; all we have is a few 'model schools' as they are called in German. We have a model as basis. But this model does not yet stand there at all in the way one would wish it to.[300]

Continuing these comments after enlarging on the situation in Central Europe, and in Germany specifically, Rudolf Steiner spoke of a possible pedagogical initiative in England and of the current state of the anthroposophic movement and the Society:

And so if something like the Waldorf School were to arise in England, for instance—and it would of course have to be done differently to take account of the particular context of the country and the nation—this would very probably be a huge step forwards. When I saw that there was no Waldorf school movement as such because the [Stuttgart] Waldorf School remained the only one, I tried to get the idea of a 'World School Association' off the ground since, after all, one achievement can be noted: you see, in recent years, in Central Europe at least, we have witnessed a very great expansion of the anthroposophic movement. Today the anthroposophic movement is a real factor in the Central European world. As a spiritual movement it is a factor. [But] we have no organization for guiding or directing this movement in any way. The Anthroposophical Society—it has to be said, since it is good to recognize this—is not in a position to carry the anthroposophic movement since the Society is so pervaded by sectarian tendencies and so cannot sustain the anthroposophic movement as it now is, as it has developed. But I wanted to appeal one last time to the powers that might or could have existed in the Anthroposophical Society, believing that a final effort and exertion might after all emerge from these powers in order to cultivate something like the 'World School Association'. This did not happen. The 'World School Association' is dead and buried. You see, such things cannot just be talked about but must be taken in hand practically, and for this a number of people must be involved. And so the 'World School Association' as such is defunct.

The Waldorf School in Stuttgart emerged from the German revolution, not as a revolutionary school but out of a revolutionary mood. But if there are people somewhere like England

> with an overview of the world situation, and if something like the Waldorf School were to be founded there with full understanding, then we would make some progress.

*

Only a few days after the pedagogical course ended and its participants had dispersed, Rudolf Steiner travelled to Stuttgart again for school meetings, financial meetings and a public lecture in the Recital Hall entitled 'Natural Death and Spiritual Life'. At this time, in a snowy Dornach, Edith Maryon was carving the 'garment of Christ' ('If rightly depicted, it should be nothing but streaming love', R. Steiner[301]) and anxiously reflecting on Rudolf Steiner's imminent lecture tour through major German cities ('The Being of Anthroposophy') which was being organized by a professional agency and was due to begin in Munich on 16 January. One day before this first lecture in Munich she wrote to him:

> Tomorrow evening the lecture in Munich is to take place, I will be so pleased to receive news that everything has gone well, that the lecture has passed without mishap and that you have left the city. Until I receive news I am compelled to keep thinking about it.[302]

Almost by return of post, on 16 or 17 January, Edith Maryon received news that the lecture had gone without incident, and that Steiner was now travelling on to subsequent lectures in Stuttgart, Frankfurt, Mannheim, Cologne, Elberfeld, Hanover and Berlin. Initially she felt reassured but not relaxed:

> I am very grateful that everything went well in Munich. I am also worried about Frankfurt but I very much hope that

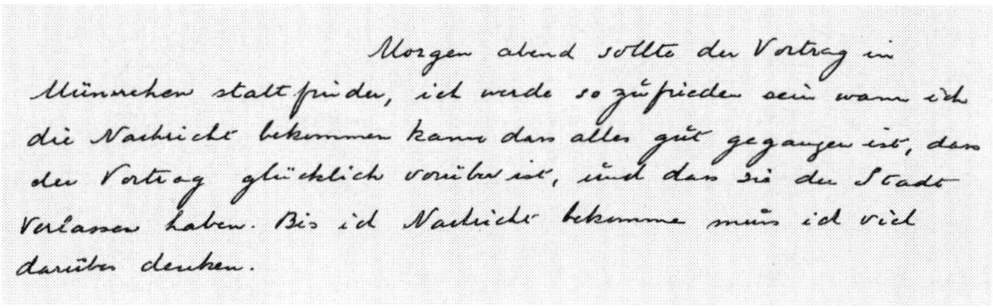
Morgen abend sollte der Vortrag in
Münnchen statt finden, ich werde so züfrieden sein wann ich
die Nachricht bekommen kann dass alles güt gegangen ist, dass
der Vortrag glücklich vorüber ist, ünd dass sie der Stadt
verlassen haben. Bis ich Nachricht bekomme muss ich viel
darüber denken.

nothing untoward can happen there. I hope to hear that all
has gone well and that you neither caught a cold nor that
your voice has suffered from over-exertion? And that you
are not overtired?[303]

Edith Maryon's concerns were—as always—well-founded in
reality. But Rudolf Steiner repeatedly sent her cautiously positive reports of his various lectures, along with expressions of
his desire to be back in the studio in Dornach ('Now all I have
left to say is that I think particularly of our studio; please do not
overtax yourself; I will be pleased when I can work in the studio once again.'[304] 'I am often in the studio in my thoughts, and
greatly long to actually be there again. I will have some details
of this trip to relate. So far the lectures were very well received
by the public. Of course one cannot do much with a lecture,
only offer stimulus. Really one is always at the beginning of the
work'[305]).

Maryon herself kept her bearings in the loneliness of Dornach,
and was continually at work ('Here it is empty and boring but
there's enough to do'[306]), both with her studies and inner work:

> I carve as much as I can, but carefully, sort things out in the
> houses and here, and darn all my old clothes. I also read the
> religious lectures, which are extremely interesting, and wish
> that February had already arrived.[307]

When there were short intervals between Steiner's separate
accounts of the lecture tour, her worries were again exacer-
bated ('I have had no news since Mannheim and hope very
much that all is well with your health? It is exhausting to
travel so much, to give a lecture every day and other things,
without rest. I wish I knew how everything is going; but I
am sure you have no time at all for yourself'[308]). Edith Maryon's own health was unstable as ever ('All is going relatively
well here, but boring. Suddenly I cannot carve much, I could
do *much* more but I start aching and then have to stop since
it would be more stupid to do myself an injury, otherwise I

would risk it'[309]). Nevertheless she was determined to accompany Steiner on the trip to London and Stratford which she had helped prepare:

> I am well, I'm just thinking how I should fabricate money—out of nothing, to buy a ticket to England etc. I'd best like to sell an old artwork and in this way defray my costs, but that is not so easy.[310]

During his major lecture tour in Germany, Maryon was already corresponding with Steiner about the details of his planned pedagogical course in Oxford in August, once again witnessing his great and uncomplicated modesty ('As far as the title of the lecture is concerned, "Spiritual Values in Education" seems best to me. But any title will do fine. Especially also "Education as a World Problem". As to the translator, the people there should decide. Scarcely anyone will translate better than Kaufmann. The location for the summer [course] should be decided as best meets the needs there. I have no particular wishes about it'[311]).

Steiner finally returned to Dornach safe and sound two days after her fiftieth birthday, and on 9 February 1922 gave her a notebook for future journal entries, on whose first page he had already written a further verse for her:

> Seek the will in thinking
> and you will find
> your self:
> for your own being's
> workings become apparent;
> seek in willing
> thoughts
> and you will find
> the world;
> for the thoughts of the cosmos
> actively reveal themselves to you.[312]

*

Suche im Denken
den Willen
Und du findest
dich selbst :
denn des eignen Wesens
Weben gehet dir auf ;
Suche im Wollen
die Gedanken
Und du findest
die Welt :
denn die Weltengedanken
Kraftend enthüllen sich dir.

9. Februar 1922

Rudolf Steiner

Ita Wegman Archive, Arlesheim

In the lectures he gave in Dornach immediately after his return, Rudolf Steiner spoke of the schooling of thinking and the will.[313] In the meantime, the joint-stock companies founded by anthroposophists and co-funded—sometimes unwillingly—by Steiner, had fallen into major financial crises. He was increasingly preoccupied by dealing with this. He was only able to work for two weeks in his beloved studio, snatching hours here and there for this, before he had to travel back to Germany—for a School course in Berlin and further crisis negotiations in Stuttgart ('I hope you are not overtired? The last few weeks were really awful. If only you could have a *really* long holiday in Berlin!'[314]). For her part, Edith Maryon was engaged in intensive carving work on the Group at the beginning of March 1922; she also organized the transport of further wooden blocks for finishing in Rudolf Steiner's studio, and was preparing for his return there:

> There is much work and also a lot of dirt; I will be very pleased when everything is in its place and you are back here at work. I am arranging things so that there will be as much space gained as possible for your statue, I am looking forward to it very much.[315]

Six days later, on 8 March, she wrote an additional account of progress in the studio and at the Goetheanum to Steiner in Berlin:

> Today the fourth Luc. block has been brought over, and by tomorrow evening I hope to have sorted the studio out again somewhat. It would have been impossible for you to work here while this was going on. Your corner with the table and everything has been cleared away altogether, and a sort of track has been built upon which the blocks can be conveyed. And where Ahriman stood, now a forest of beams and poles is standing. The studio furniture and the models are all piled up in the corners. It is very awkward but necessary. Between four and ten workers as well (I try to improve the air a little with eau-de-cologne!). And from time to time all the doors are open. But by the end of the

week everything will be fine again. I should think by next
Tuesday or Wednesday at the latest.[316]

Steiner stayed just three weeks in Switzerland at the end of
March/beginning of April, and then, via The Hague, departed
for England and London in the company of Maryon.

*

In his three London lectures, after an introduction to the method-
ology of supersensible cognition, Steiner focused on an esoteric
understanding of Christianity, speaking, in relation to the Pauline fomula 'Not I but Christ in me', of the experience of Christ
in modern initiation and the change that occurred in human
existence and human consciousness through the Mystery of Golgotha. He described the cosmic spirituality of early Christianity
('But today the time has come when humanity must definitely
recall this spiritual comprehension of Christianity in the early
Christian centuries'[317]) and the reincarnation background of the
Anglo-Catholic theologian John Henry Newman, who was connected in subtle ways with the 'deeper mysteries of Christianity'.
However, at the end of his third lecture in London, Steiner also
gave a striking account of the current influence of adversarial
ahrimanic powers already gaining a hold on human beings in
their pre-incarnatory phase of life ('Ahriman achieves his great
success by shortening the second half of the period of human
existence between death and a new birth. [...] By so doing he
grasps hold of the human brain and its thinking power with great
haste and energy. In a sense he hooks himself into the brain'),
and not least distorting the influence and work of Newman. In
this context Rudolf Steiner said of the current situation of anthroposophic spiritual science—and indirectly of himself:

> What [...] seeks to unfold through anthroposophy has very
> strong enemies inspired by ahrimanic powers. These pow-
> ers are growing ever stronger. That is what I wish to say
> to you today, so that you are not surprised if what seeks
> to emerge in the world as the anthroposophic movement
> will have to do battle more and more with terribly hostile

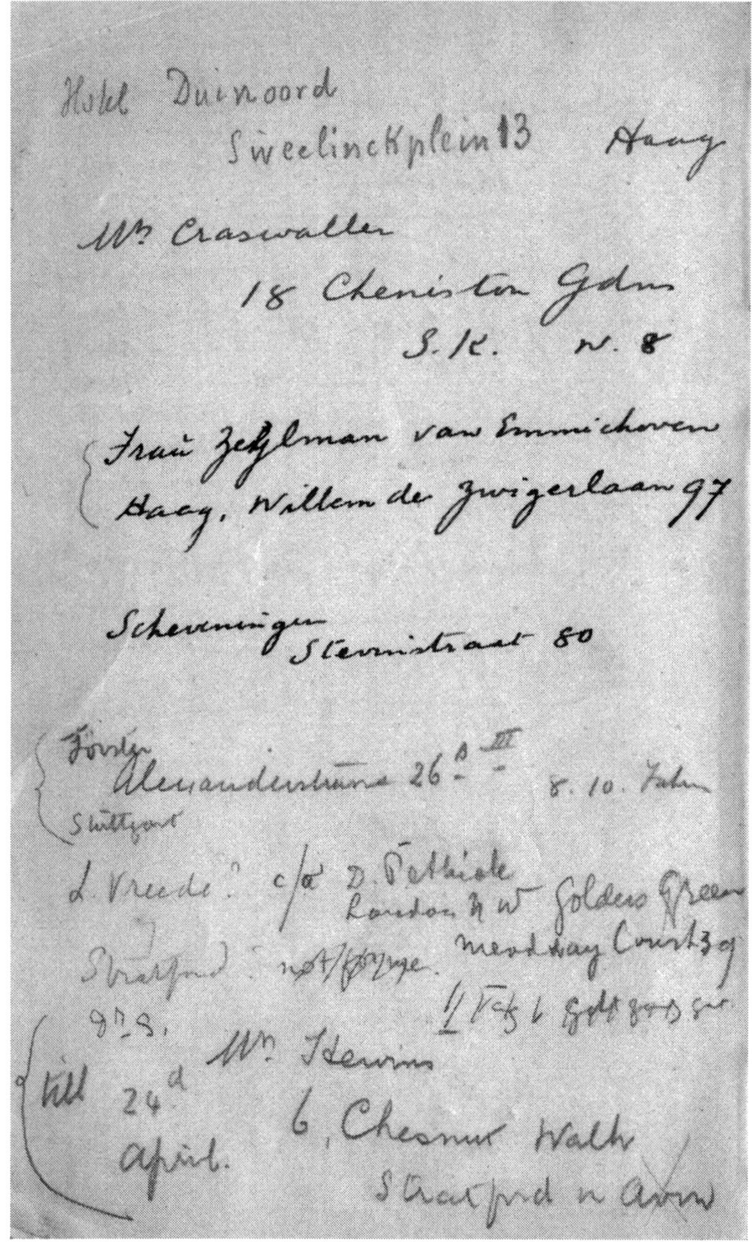

Notebook entry by Edith Maryon, April 1922

Dornach ab   1. 18
Basel   ab.   2.55? oder. 3.25.
Stuttgart an P.M 8.40
  „   ab. P.M. 9. 40.
Haag an   12.58 / nach Zeit.
  „   ab. P.M. 10.23   9.15
Hork an.   11. 17
  „   ab   11. 45
Harwich an
Harwich ab. A.M. 7. 50
L'pool St. an A.M. 9. 30

Municipium 10 Uhr Donnerstag.
24. April 7 Uhr.
74 Grosvenor St.
Paddington
9.0. A.M Wed.
10.20.   „   „

Ita Wegman Archive, Arlesheim

Edith Maryon: Ahriman study. Ita Wegman Archive, Arlesheim

forces. In consequence, we must in a sense recognize what these anthroposophic endeavours seek to achieve, remaining alert to the terrible calumnies or other forms of attack by enemies that do not wish to see this movement develop. But however strong such adversaries may be, they must be matched by each human being's own positive strength and energy.[318]

In Stratford-upon-Avon Rudolf Steiner also gave three impressive lectures. But the three Christological lectures in London that framed his trip to England and were accompanied by an esoteric lesson on Easter Sunday ('After the two first lectures I also gave another in a smaller circle of people who had been part of the anthroposophic movement for many years'[319]) were intrinsic to Edith Maryon's core experience in her native land. Eight years previously she had left England for good to become Rudolf Steiner's esoteric pupil and to collaborate in his work, especially on the 'Christ Group' in Dornach, seeking his proximity with 'wakeful eye also [...] for the terrible calumnies or other forms of attack by enemies that do not wish to see this movement develop'. This path had been strewn with pain and hindrances but so far all adversarial powers had been unable to stop the progress of Rudolf Steiner's spiritual science and her committed collaboration (her, as Steiner put it, 'energetic tranquillity'). 'But however strong such adversaries may be, they must be matched by each human being's own positive strength and energy.'

*

Only two weeks after Steiner returned to Stuttgart and Dornach, his second, professionally organized lecture tour through Germany was due to begin—a trip which this time would be aggressively disrupted by militant nationalists and was an extraordinarily dangerous undertaking. On 9 May Edith Maryon wrote to him from Dornach:

> Now I hope you will take great care in Berlin; but much more so in Munich.[320]

Rudolf Steiner received these lines from Maryon at Motzstrassse, Berlin, following a lecture in Leipzig to students and academics on 11 May ('Agnosticism in Science, and Anthroposophy') and immediately before embarking on the lecture tour on 12 May, a trip that would take him via Berlin and Breslau to Munich before returning to Leipzig via Mannheim, Elberfeld, Cologne, Bremen, Hamburg and Berlin. After the first lecture of the cycle in Berlin, before his onward journey, Rudolf Steiner responded to Edith Maryon:

> My dear Edith Maryon
>
> Many thanks for your kind letter. So far there was a great deal to be done everywhere. I have given two lectures—in Leipzig the lecture to students, which went well apart from a few, fairly low-level objections, and then the one in Berlin, which went very well.
>
> Please be assured that I will take care as far as possible. I'll send word about Munich as swiftly as I can. But please do not be anxious. I would gladly be in the studio, and will be pleased to be back there again. Only these brief lines for today, and warmest greetings from
> Rudolf Steiner[321]

The same day, 11 May 1922, Edith Maryon wrote in advance from Dornach, 'I hope the lectures on 12, 13, 14 May went well? And please take very great care in Munich—not going out alone etc.'[322] In the following days her great anxiety about the event in Munich did not fade.[323] She sent her letters to the hotel addresses which Rudolf Steiner had given her, as he always did before he set off. In her letter to the hotel in Cologne which she wrote in the studio on the afternoon of 15 May, a few hours before his lecture in Munich, she again emphatically reiterated:

> I am thinking especially today of the lecture and send all my good wishes for all going well.[324]

In Munich, back at the end of 1921, Hans Büchenbacher, an academic philosopher active in the social threefolding movement, had heard of a forthcoming plan by German nationalists to assassinate Rudolf Steiner and—in vain—had warned the Stuttgart executive committee of the Anthroposophical Society.[325] On the morning of 15 May, Büchenbacher personally collected Steiner from Munich railway station, informed him of the threats that had been repeated in publications ('Hopefully German men will be found to prevent this gentleman even setting foot in Munich.'[326]), and accompanied him during the day and through the evening, as well as organizing security in the lecture hall. Rudolf Steiner survived unwounded the attack that did indeed come at the end of the lecture, escaping into the green room and, at Büchenbacher's advice, spending the night in a different hotel room. He left Munich next morning one hour earlier than he had planned, at 6 a.m. on 16 May ('[…] His departure by passenger train went without incident. When the 7 a.m. train was due to leave, beside anthroposophic friends the attackers also appeared.' Büchenbacher[327]). Arriving in Mannheim, Rudolf Steiner asked Andreas von Grunelius to

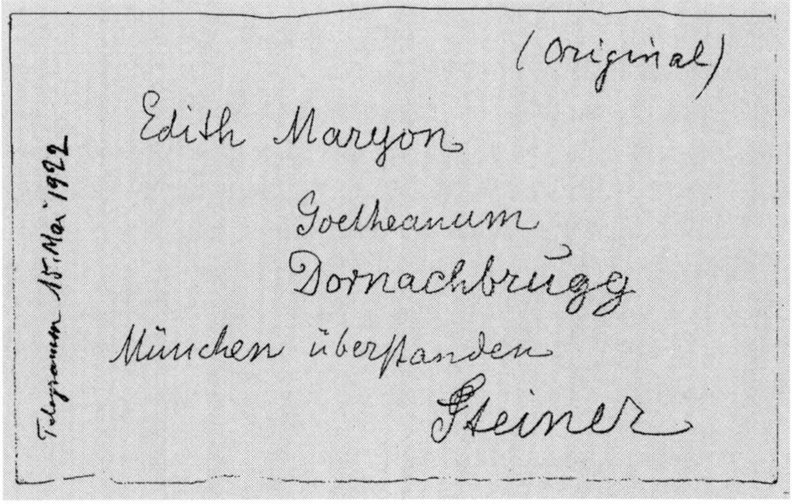

Telegram from Rudolf Steiner to Edith Maryon. Mannheim 16 May 1922.

wire Edith Maryon the telegram message 'Survived Munich. Steiner', which she received in Dornach the following day: Maryon replied immediately:

> Dear, respected teacher
>
> Ehrsam brought me the telegram this morning—many thanks! But I couldn't tell from it whether the lecture went well, without incident—for I was fearful! At least you have arrived in Mannheim, hopefully without burned fingers in either a soul or a physical sense. I am admonishing myself to await further news patiently, but I am in fact impatient! [328]

Having learned more details of the incident in Munich during the course of that day, she wrote to her teacher once again the same evening, 16 May:

> I have just got back from Basel and have heard about the commotion in Munich—it is just as I feared, I could not understand why it was so dark, and thought that noise and incidents had also occurred. I am very happy that you have left but I am now troubled about how the other lectures will go since these people might also travel there. Please take great care, perhaps especially in Leipzig. I hope other gentlemen travel with you and that you do not go out walking alone. Please be very cautious. I hope to get news soon of how the rest of the lectures go, goodbye for now.
>
> With warmest greetings
> Edith Maryon [329]

Edith Maryon received the next message three days later, a letter from Rudolf Steiner in Bremen about how the 'rest of the lectures' were going:

> It went very well in Mannheim and Cologne; in Elberfeld there were disturbances but everything was kept at bay. I will tell you another time about Munich. It was not particularly edifying. Please do not be anxious any more. I am well.

> It is just that the trip allows me almost no free time since the
> journeys are usually long and the trains depart early in the
> morning. I hope things are also going well there; I long to be
> back in the studio and I send my warmest greetings.
> Rudolf Steiner[330]

Exhausted and altered, Rudolf Steiner finally returned to Dornach for six days on 24 May ('[…] it seemed as if his figure had grown more slender, his gaze still more serious and quiet'[331]) before he had to leave again for the East-West Congress in Vienna. Once again Edith Maryon remained behind in troubled mind. Again letters went back and forth.[332]

The escalating attacks and disturbances in Germany, and the widespread failure of the Anthroposophical Society—in its lack of protection for his person and his work, its inadequate realization of his lectures, and in the continual demands it made on his attention[333]—prevented Steiner from pursuing the path of public activity upon which he had embarked. The second lecture tour in May 1922 was, despite full houses, the last such activity undertaken by Steiner, even though he would continue to teach anthroposophy without interruption until the end of September 1924. For the sake of the future of anthroposophy, and of the sculptural Group in Dornach, but also for the sake of Steiner himself to whom she was lovingly and attentively devoted, Edith Maryon will have been relieved that public lectures on a scale of these two tours had come to an end. But the battles surrounding Steiner and anthroposophy would continue unabated, something apparent to Maryon not only from the London lectures she had heard at Easter about the workings of Ahriman but also a certainty that arose for her on her path of esoteric pupilship ('…so that you are not surprised if what seeks to emerge in the world as the anthroposophic movement will have to do battle more and more with terribly hostile forces').

*

After Rudolf Steiner had returned from Vienna and Stuttgart, for the first time in a long time he was once more able to spend nearly seven weeks at the Goetheanum, and also work intensively in the studio. This period immediately preceded the second trip to England that year, which would take Steiner and Maryon to a pedagogical lecture course, again initiated by Millicent Mackenzie ('Spiritual Values in Education') and which, like the previous course, was accompanied by eurythmy performances. In recent months, at her own initiative, Edith Maryon had been working on a pictorial representation of eurythmy gestures, made in plywood and painted. Rudolf Steiner also had a refashioning hand in this process and so, in August, the figures went with them to England and were presented there for the first time by Steiner.

The events in Oxford were a great success and met with a sympathetic and considered reception, at least by comparison to the atmosphere in Germany. From Oxford, on 19 August, Edith Maryon wrote the briefest of reports to her friend, the painter Sofie Bauer:[334]

> All is going excellently. Lectures well attended, warm reception from audience—high-quality audience, many teachers and personalities from public life.[335]

Vowel sound I—sketch by Edith Maryon, plywood figure by Rudolf Steiner

Edith Maryon (left) in Oxford, August 1922

Later Rudolf Steiner would say of Edith Maryon and her
English activities:

> To her selfless efforts must be attributed the fact that the
> course for teachers was arranged here a while ago around
> Christmas time, and was attended by English teachers. It
> is due to her selfless efforts that Mrs Mackenzie became so
> strongly and energetically committed to the movement in
> English-speaking lands, especially in the field of education.
> And finally, it is also due to her selfless efforts that the Oxford
> course and the visit to Shakespeare's birthplace of Stratford
> took place, and that various other things were made possi-
> ble involving contact and communication between the head-
> quarters of anthroposophy and English-speaking regions.[336]

*

Once again, Rudolf Steiner ended his stay in Oxford and London at the end of August with Christological presentations centred on the 'teachings of the resurrected Christ' and the three Rosicrucian sayings *Ex deo nascimur—in Christo morimur—per spiritum sanctum reviviscimus*. And again in London he concluded by speaking of the resistance to modern spiritual science and stressed:

> This 'per spiritum sanctum reviviscimus' is what the modern initiate must strive for above all. If you consider this and compare it with the outlook emerging today from science, you will see that there must be huge opposition, perhaps of a nature whose extent you can as yet have no idea of, expressing itself in actions whose primary tendency will be to render initiation science completely impossible. And when I speak in this kind of smaller circle, what I would gladly inscribe in hearts and souls is this: to convey what arises from initiation science in a way that awakens strength so that there may really be some people who find their place in the right way between what seeks to enter the world from worlds of spirit and what, arising from the world, seeks to render impossible this influx of spirituality into life on earth.[337]

Only three days after Rudolf Steiner's return to Dornach on 3 September, the third theology course began in the Goetheanum's White Hall and, entirely in keeping with the words Steiner had spoken in his lecture in London at Eastertide, would lead to the founding of The Christian Community as the fulfilment of anthroposophy's desire to be a 're-enlivening of Christianity' and of the 'religious sensibility':

> It is because the human being does not seek only an enlivening of the old religious outlook but because, by this means, he acquires a new religious sensibility through knowledge, that one can say that anthroposophy in no way seeks to be anything sectarian. No more than any other science does it seek

Rudolf Steiner: bust of Christ

to be so. Anthroposophy does not desire to form sects but wishes to serve the religions that already exist, to re-enliven Christianity accordingly. Thus it wishes not only to preserve an old religious sensibility, not only advance and perpetuate an old religious life, not only enliven it but rather help to resurrect religious life since this has suffered so greatly from modern existence, from modern civilization. For this reason anthroposophy desires to be a messenger of love, not only a re-enlivener of the old religious sensibility but an awakener to new life of humanity's inner religious sensibility.[338]

*

The founding of The Christian Community and the idealism and active commitment of the young people involved was a joyous matter for Rudolf Steiner —who fetched from his studio for the celebration of the first Act of Consecration a copy of Vincenzo

Foppa's Milan painting of the Resurrected Christ ('I myself must count among the festive moments of my life what I experienced with these theologians in the small hall of the South wing [...] in September 1922. Here it was possible to pursue with a number of nobly inspired people the path that leads spirit knowledge into the religious life'[339]).

But many other developments—or rather stagnations—in the Anthroposophical Society weighed heavily on Rudolf Steiner's soul during the late autumn of 1922. On 11 October, during his 'Pedagogical Youth Course' given to young anthroposophists who had problems with the Society, and in the midst of many crises in Stuttgart, Steiner wrote to Edith Maryon:

My dear Edith Maryon

This time the quantity of work in Stuttgart cannot be reduced. The young people who have gathered here to work within anthroposophy want all sorts of things, and the old matters still need attention too. Especially at present the school needs a great deal. The affair with the various young rascals was handled by the teachers in an incredibly stupid way. I don't want to write anything more about it since really the situation is too ludicrous and will do the school an immense amount of harm. Then also the gentlemen in Stuttgart are losing all connection with the anthroposophic movement. They sit on their chairs playing at being a governing committee and the people wish to have nothing to do with them. Here's one example: I should have been in Stuttgart on Monday already but, since I couldn't be, I phoned Uehli asking him to give a lecture to the young people on Monday evening. They said they didn't wish to hear a lecture by him. And so there is no connection at all between all the people and the leadership in Stuttgart. One has to do everything oneself. And so there is always more and more work to do but no increase in the number of colleagues to help do it. And for this reason also it is impossible to do anything to defend ourselves against opponents, for one never even gets round to dealing with such things. And the fact that I have been absent from the school so long has also bitterly avenged itself. The teachers have lost contact with the pupils in the higher classes. [...]It might be said that these people do not have the skills! Well, yes. But that's not what is lacking. What is lacking is enthusiasm, an active joy in work. They want the daily round, routine; they want to be a heavy mass rather than a kindling element. Basically they are sluggish. [...]

I'm writing this letter quickly at 6.30 in the morning so that I can finally send a few lines to our studio, where I would so gladly be once more.

For now I send my warmest greetings there.

Rudolf Steiner

I will leave here on the 15th or 16th.[340]

Edith Maryon was deeply troubled by this message from Steiner and by what was going on in Stuttgart. Along with a draft programme for the next trip to England, which was to start in only three weeks' time, she wrote to him on 14 October:

> Your letter made me very sad, it is really terrible that the people have so little understanding and enthusiasm, and without these qualities, despite the strenuous work and a workload that has long been excessive, one does not make sufficiently rapid and sure progress. One cannot be everywhere at once, after all, but has to have trusted and energetic colleagues.[341]

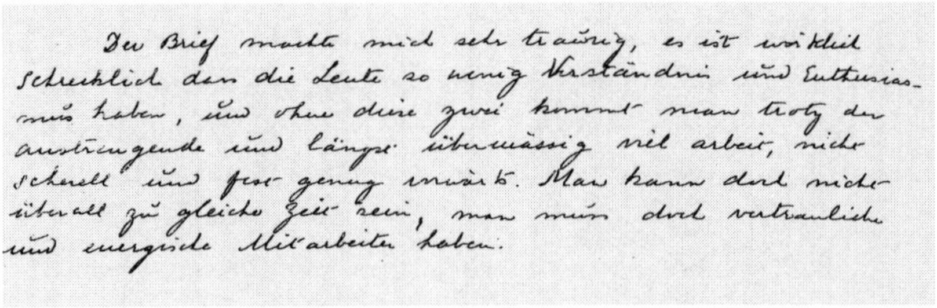

There were not many fields in which Rudolf Steiner had 'trusted and energetic colleagues' like Edith Maryon. A day later, on 15 October, in the charged mood of a meeting with the college of teachers of the Waldorf School, he spoke of a 'slumbering' Anthroposophical Society.[342] Similar phrases would repeatedly surface in Stuttgart over the next two months in a marked sharpening of Rudolf Steiner's tone, which sometimes testified to real despair about the extent of opportunities missed and work left undone.

*

After three striking lectures on the spiritual formation of the human organism, given in Dornach in the second half of October—aspects of which Steiner elaborated in relation to compositional and representational elements of the sculptural Group[343]—and a further period of lecturing in Holland, Rudolf Steiner reached London again in the second week of November for a three-week working stay. Edith Maryon had again followed Steiner to The Hague with a series of eurythmy figures which she had made at the last minute especially for the trip to London. She wrote humorously to Sofie Bauer about the sea crossing to England but then fell ill in London and struggled to shake it off ('now I am slowly improving') and among other things suffered from the English weather ('The weather is horrible, days of fog, it is like swallowing thick, black lead!').[344] Nothing more is known about Maryon's condition during this time in London, but Rudolf Steiner's mighty lecture of 16 November about the 'terrible battle' for the human being waged by Ahriman and Lucifer[345] will have moved her deeply.

Four weeks later, in Dornach, Rudolf Steiner gave her this verse:

> When the human being reinvented the world
> As endlessly fragmented in atoms,
> His power of knowledge
> United with the death of nature;
> Now he should strive in spirit
> To find what overcomes fragmentation
> And he will guide his knowing
> Toward the growth of the world.[346]

*

When she received these lines on the second day of Christmas 1922, this followed further difficult weeks for her and Rudolf Steiner—weeks which Steiner experienced as ones of 'inner opposition' and inactivity in Stuttgart and elsewhere. In The Hague and London, Steiner had once again emphasized that the financial situation, not least, would prevent him from completing the Goetheanum and thus from creating a site dedicated to the future of science, art and religion, and oriented toward the 'growth of the world' like no other in the world at this time ('We started building the Goetheanum with enthusiasm, an enthusiasm which has dissipated now precisely amongst those who developed it as the project began. And they have now left me alone with the anxiety about how it should continue'[347]). What Steiner had said to Maryon repeatedly about the lack of suitable, innovative and practical people—or their lack of persistence, selflessness and commitment—became ever more apparent in its consequences. At the same time Rudolf Steiner and anthroposophy were the subject of journalistic attacks of undiminished acerbity, a situation that could not be described as anything other than dramatic, albeit entirely unheeded by many anthroposophists.

On the last day of 1922, five days after Edith Maryon had received the verse above, and after the evening event in Dornach had ended, Assja Turgenieff—who was now living in the same house as Edith Maryon —noticed changes in the neighbouring Goetheanum:

> I knew something awful had happened and I rushed out of
> the room. In the hall stood Edith Maryon, as if paralyzed
> by agitation: she was trying to get the Minimax fire extin-
> guisher out of its stand. I wrenched it out and ran with it to
> the building.[348]

According to the reminiscences of Ita Wegman it was Edith Maryon who informed Rudolf Steiner about the Goetheanum fire by telephone soon after 10 p.m., after she had come running from her flat.[349] Steiner spent much of the night in Maryon's company, close to the burning building, in a small hut, and in walks around the site of so many years' work, the intended centre for a great, spiritual initiative of the future to overcome materialistic powers of destruction and death:

> Standing close to the joinery workshop I could see two shadows coming up the footpath slowly in the dark. Bent, and with a heavy step, Dr Steiner, followed by Edith Maryon, went into the joinery workshop [Assja Turgenieff].[350]

Threats from nationalist, clerical and occult-theosophical groups, which Steiner had referred to years before,[351] became a final reality with the almost wholesale destruction in Dornach on New Year's Night 1922/23. '…You will see that there must be huge opposition, perhaps of a nature whose extent you can as yet have no idea of, expressing itself in actions whose primary tendency will be to render initiation science completely impossible.'[352] At this time the wooden sculpture of Christ stood in a meadow in front of the de Jaager House, where it had been taken by helpers rescuing it from the flame-threatened joinery workshop.

*

IV
'The Story of Job'

The Fire, Illness and Death (1923-1924)

The night of the fire which robbed us of the Goetheanum, laid in her body already weakened by previous illnesses the seed that grew into a suffering that lasted for more than a year.

Rudolf Steiner[353]

*Miss Maryon fell ill in January 1923 while Dr Steiner was away.
I visited her in the studio, she had a pulmonary haemorrhage. This
was four weeks after the fire.*
Ita Wegman[354]

The devastating arson attack which transformed the wooden
Goetheanum to ash during the night of 1 January 1923 was the
work of destructive forces described by Rudolf Steiner in many
lectures. For years he had been telling members of the Anthroposophical Society of the reality of the incipient conflict focused
both on him and, still more, on the very essence of his spiritual-scientific and Christological mission, which it sought to
destroy. Few people had perceived as keenly, fearfully and specifically as Edith Maryon the manifest danger in which Rudolf
Steiner lived and in which the Goetheanum found itself, as witnessed by her clear-sighted appraisal of the situation in Munich
on 15 May 1922, seven months before the fire. Little suggests that
Steiner spoke to Maryon about this at length. Very probably she
herself experienced the powers at work through her own perceptions and with an esoterically developed capacity of feeling and
apprehension for Rudolf Steiner, her spiritual teacher and friend
whose 'Benedictus', in the first Mystery Play in 1910, spoke
already of an adversary 'who seeks to destroy the work / that is
my task / for the future of many human beings'.[355]

Six years before the fire, Edith Maryon had saved Rudolf
Steiner with great presence of mind ('my accident in the studio');
but by herself she was unable to protect his major architectural
work, the Dornach Goetheanum. After the Goetheanum fire
Rudolf Steiner wrote in his notebook:

> Thought was woven to thought
> The soul was consumed in creative joy

Feeling was breathed into forms
And so the spirit allied itself to art.
Will you plumb the pain
That destiny plunged us in?
Feeling went up in smoke and flame
Creative joy has found an end,
The eyes gaze upon ruins.[356]

*

Rudolf Steiner's refusal to place the—by then far-advanced—'Christ Group' in the Goetheanum for its supposed 'opening', meant that the sculpture survived the fire ('The time, and the members, were not fit for this; one must wait...'). However the fire had rendered the sculpture itself completely homeless—as the 'central creation' or 'crowning' of a building that no longer possessed any physical reality. The parts of the great Group placed, or rather thrown, upon a field near the building—something that Steiner had neither asked for nor endorsed—seemed symbolic of a situation that must have been devastating for Edith Maryon. The windows of her flat in the small house created and administered by herself and Rudolf Steiner, all looked out upon the site of the fire and the scene of destruction as, for so many years they had faced the building's double cupola and workshops. According to a notebook entry by Ita Wegman, at the end of January, four weeks after the Goetheanum had been destroyed, the latter found Edith Maryon in the studio suffering from a pulmonary haemorrhage.[357]

On 30 January, seemingly, Rudolf Steiner had not yet been informed of Maryon's serious illness. Shortly after his arrival in Stuttgart for renewed, night-long discussions with people in positions of responsibility in the Anthroposophical Society, he had written to her in Dornach:

My dear Edith Maryon

I can only write these few lines in haste—I got here safely but will perhaps only be able to arrive back on Friday at the studio since things here have no sign of getting sorted out.

Everything is hard work and the people do not gladly go along with me. I wish I were there.[358]

Three days later Edith Maryon recorded her will in writing in the presence of Ita Wegman and Sofie Bauer. Shortly after this, the next letter from Steiner arrived from Stuttgart, now with acknowledgment of her situation in Dornach:

My dear Edith Maryon

Only a few lines since I have so much to do. I hope you are not too unwell. I send my best thoughts. I hope to be there soon. But it is clear I can scarcely get there before Friday, since it is taking so long to sort things out here. The people make no progress.[359]

Letter from Rudolf Steiner to Edith Maryon, 6 February 1923.
Rudolf Steiner Archive, Dornach

Three days later, for her 51st birthday on 9 February 1923, Rudolf Steiner wrote the following lines for her in Dornach:

The human being's powers are of two kinds:
A stream of powers travels inwards;
This gives shape and inner rootedness;
A stream of powers travels outward:
This gives wellbeing and brightening of life's light;
So think yourself as a being light and bright
Afflicted by the formative powers of heavy bodily being.[360]

*

Rudolf Steiner's prescription for Edith Maryon. Ita Wegman Archive, Arlesheim

Immediately on his return from Stuttgart, Rudolf Steiner will have prescribed all details of the treatment for Edith Maryon, in close collaboration with her doctor, Ita Wegman. The records of Maryon's case history have not so far come to light, but very probably she suffered acute deterioration of pulmonary tuberculosis which later—in the final stages of her illness—also affected the larynx and intestinal tract. Rudolf Steiner prescribed specific medicines, a precise diet and daily rhythm, but also wrote a special therapeutic meditation for Maryon:

> Fear = latent lung irritation with heart vibration
> Dissatisfaction = becomes irritation of the lung apex
> Contentment = becomes healing in the lung apex
> Courage = makes heart and lungs healthy
> To accept circumstances with composure heals the workings
> of the digestion and regulates blood circulation.[361]

Edith Maryon was a patient soul who never complained about her situation; but being sundered from her work, and the destruction of the building, were immeasurably hard for her, as it was to witness the marked change in Rudolf Steiner following the fire, which she observed with increased concern and with deadly fear.[362] Edith Maryon wished to go on supporting Rudolf Steiner and his endeavours with all her strength—'Recovery is my dream', she wrote to him; and: 'Being in bed is no life.' But Rudolf Steiner put a humorous slant on this when he commented: 'Outer circumstances storm against a great and beautiful life in the spirit only as thoughts'[363]—and wrote in a notebook for her:

> One should not be fearful
> One should harbour thoughts of recovery
> One should have courage for health.[364]

*

At the beginning of February Rudolf Steiner could only stay in Dornach for four days before setting off again for Stuttgart for the next crisis meetings—talks about the failure of the Anthroposophical Society and (especially) about ways to renew and

regenerate it. For weeks and months, in endless meetings day
and night, Steiner waited for the members to wake up. For his
62nd birthday on 26 February, which he spent in Stuttgart, Edith
Maryon wrote to him from Dornach:

> Dear, respected teacher
>
> I am keeping calm and thinking as good thoughts as I can man-
> age. I send many thoughts for the meeting and hope for the best.
> Am waiting patiently for Friday and send my best birthday
> and other greetings.
>
> Edith Maryon[365]

The same day Steiner also received a letter from Sofie Bauer
about Maryon's condition:

> Dear Herr Doktor
>
> An attack of coughing brought up fresh [blood] again, though
> not so much as on the two other occasions. But overall Miss

Letter from Sofie Bauer to Rudolf Steiner, 26 February 1923.
Rudolf Steiner Archive, Dornach

Maryon does not seem weakened by this and we hope that despite it she continues to regain strength. Frau Dr Wegman was here today early on, and again prescribed absolute rest. The coughing this time came at 11.30 on Sunday.

To you Herr Doktor we send our warmest greetings and best wishes.

In gratitude, Sofie Bauer[366]

Despite her very weakened state, Edith Maryon continued to be deeply preoccupied by her teacher's efforts for the Society in Stuttgart. A few days previously, shortly after he had left Dornach on 23 February, she had written to him in another letter:

My dear teacher

So far no more has come. Frau Dr Wegman came yesterday and I sat in the large upholstered chair for 20 mins. and afterwards was very quiet and everything was well. The sunset was very beautiful. I hope the journey was also fine and that you arrived safely. [...]

My thoughts turn to Stuttgart a great deal, I very much hope that the people there will pull themselves together and create something worthwhile. The world needs it so much, and then one could find some hope again.

I send my very best greetings, also birthday thoughts and good wishes, and hope that you will soon return![367]

Rudolf Steiner was pleased about this news of her health. But he wrote to her in no uncertain terms—unsparingly, albeit very briefly—about what was happening in Stuttgart. In a letter written on his 62nd birthday he said among other things:

Here it cannot yet be predicted where things will lead. First of all we heard speeches from the committee people and the delegates from 9 or 10 in the morning until 11 at night. Most of them are fairly clueless. Probably much will still be very difficult. Really there is nothing much to be reported from this chaos.[368]

A month later, after many further discussions and disputes, he even wrote the following in a letter from Stuttgart:

> As to the Society all I have to say really is that I would prefer
> to have nothing more to do with it. Everything its committees
> do is repugnant to me. Warm thoughts for a good recovery.[369]

Für die Gesellschaft habe ich eigentlich nur zu sagen, dass ich am liebsten nichts mehr mit ihr zu tun haben möchte. Alles, was deren Vorstände tun, widert mich an. Herzliche Gedanken für gute Gesundung

Rudolf Steiner

*

Rudolf Steiner's birthday reply to Edith Maryon on 27 February 1923 was written in the midst of a delegates conference in Stuttgart with over 1000 participants. Despite Steiner's greatest personal efforts—which would continue through the whole of 1923—the raising of awareness and reorganization necessary succeeded to a very limited extent only. Steiner himself spoke in Stuttgart about the foundations needed for creating spiritual community, and left no doubt about the consequences of continuing inactivity on the part of leaders and representatives of anthroposophy. Indeed, on 26 February he first suggested that he himself might turn directly to members 'over the heads of the organization ... so that things might change'.[370] Apart from being honorary president, Rudolf Steiner had no official function within the Anthroposphical Society but acted as spiritual teacher in it. The Anthroposophical Society had been conceived in 1912/13 as a means to facilitate and protect the spiritual science that Rudolf Steiner represented, but in recent years, as Steiner had described in many letters to Maryon, it had scarcely managed to engage in the real collaboration needed to make anthroposophy an active force and influence within civilization. In the spring of 1923 it was still very much an open question whether a new beginning might still be possible in these hard-pressed times. But Edith Maryon, in her sickbed in the house on Dornach's Herzentalweg, was still hoping for this ('only my best wishes, hopes for Saturday and for things to go better in Stuttgart'[371]) although she was shaken by events in the Society and by the visible ruins outside her windows, as well as the inactivity forced upon her.

In Switzerland Steiner was tirelessly involved in the insurance consequences of the fire, and in April, in various cities, gave his lecture entitled 'What Was the Goetheanum's Aim, and What is the Purpose of Anthroposophy?', saying in Basel on 9 April in relation to the sculptural Group:

> A nine-metre-high sculptural Group in wood, in which Christ is portrayed as the Representative of Humanity between the temptations of Ahriman and Lucifer, was to sum up everything that lived in the forms of the Goetheanum and all that could ever have been said there or artistically presented. [...]
>
> [...] Anthroposophy is able to show how true spirit knowledge seeks the high-point of religious evolution, seeks Christ as the Representative of Humanity, the Christ God incarnated in the body of Jesus of Nazareth; it can show how we need this picture of the central point of all earth evolution in spirit knowledge, this picture of the secret of Golgotha.[372]

On Good Friday, 31 March—exactly three months after the fire—Rudolf Steiner had begun his great accounts of the cycle of the year as the earth's breathing process, and in doing so embarked upon lectures of a highly spiritual nature in the crisis year of 1923. It is not known whether Edith Maryon was able to attend any of his Easter lectures, but it seems unlikely. In a letter of 26 April to Steiner, she first mentions having briefly been to the studio—'I visited the studio, and all was in good order, apart from the air!'[373]

*

Die Angst ist eben chronisch,

aber die geht weg, wenn man

im Seelenland den Gemsenartigen

Astralleib ablegt —

Machtnix gute Prüfung

Das ist immer relativ nicht absolut —

Man sollte couragiert in die Welt blicken und

nicht Mücken durch ein Sieb

werfen wollen, um sie vom Staub

zu trennen.

'Conversation' between Edith Maryon and Rudolf Steiner. Rudolf Steiner Archive, Dornach

The letter of 26 April in which Maryon referred to visiting the studio was sent to Prague since Steiner had left Stuttgart that day to go there to give lectures, following an intensive pedagogical course for Swiss teachers at the Goetheanum. Before he left Stuttgart he had written her a few lines of farewell with a report on his activities:

> I hope your condition is good and that your recovery proceeds apace. One has to have trust in the inmost power of the soul, be courageous and hold to the positive. I send my best and heartfelt thoughts and also my warmest greetings.[374]

In Prague Rudolf Steiner gave public lectures on 'The Soul's Eternity in the Light of Anthroposophy' and 'Human Evolution and Human Schooling in the Light of Anthroposophy', as well as lectures to members on human evolution in relation to the higher hierarchies, and on the spiritual situation in the centuries following Christ.

Then, after five days, he travelled back to the city of the first Waldorf School to give a major lecture on the Logos and the renewal of mystery wisdom, and for educational and medical discussions. Then—over Whitsun—he was occupied with lectures and discussions in Dornach, and on 13 May travelled to Kristiania [Oslo] via Berlin. Three days before he got there (and a day after he had left Dornach), Edith Maryon sent a letter to await his arrival in Norway, in which she wrote, among other things:

> I hope you had a good journey and that you took the fur coat with you (it is still very cold here, I had to turn on the heating today). I very much hope that the cough is now completely better? My state of health remains the same. Since the sun is shining I will be in the studio for an hour. These days I have been thinking a lot about the story of Job since I have a very strong sense that the same will happen to us as to him—after so much suffering all and still more will be given back to us again: not the same beauty of the building and yet a different beauty. A second summertime is to come

to us after all. Don't laugh! I do believe a good time is coming, we need it so much and the world must have a Goetheanum again however little it deserves it and however little it
understands for the time being.[375]

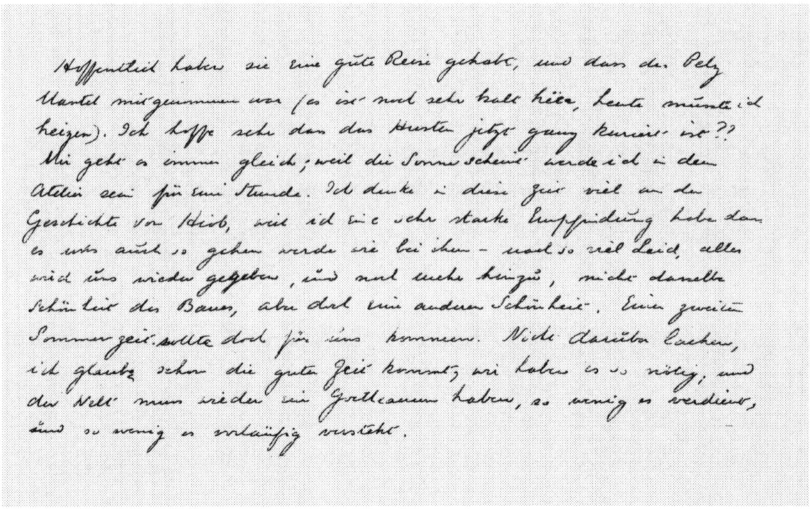

Despite her physical state, Edith Maryon continued to look forward to the future in acceptance of her personal and also their
shared destiny ('I have a very strong sense that the same will
happen to *us* as to him') and with an eye to the mystery centre of
the future, the future site of the Christ Group, its 'central' sculptural creation. But so far everything was still stagnating in the
Anthroposophical Society, and on 11 May Steiner had written to
her from Stuttgart:

> The AS continues to slumber on here and cannot be induced
> to wake up. Well, we will have to see what happens.[376]

In Edith Maryon's reply of 12 May, sent to Kristiania, Rudolf
Steiner read the following:

> I can really scarcely understand that the AS can still go on
> sleeping. If one has any strength at all one really should
> wake up now. Hopefully the Norwegians are less dreamy
> and you can experience something more hopeful there![377]

The founding of the Norwegian Anthroposophical Society was indeed hopeful, as were Rudolf Steiner's wide-ranging lectures on 'Human Nature, Human Destiny and World Evolution' and on 'Anthroposophy and Art', also in their Christological aspects; and likewise the esoteric lesson given in Kristiania on 20 May, the day before Rudolf Steiner's return to Berlin.

The following months of June and July, in Stuttgart and Dornach, were marked by Steiner's efforts to create a functioning Anthroposophical Society as the foundation for all future activities, including a second Goetheanum building. In the few spare moments, Steiner visited Maryon, sometimes taking her out for a walk ('It was glorious to see the sun again outside, I found courage because you were with me.'[378]) and continued working on the Christ statue. At the beginning of August he set off again for a trip to her homeland of England following more futile endeavours in Stuttgart ('I am well; but things are unbelievably awful in the Society. The impossibilities rear their heads from every quarter.'[379]). Nevertheless, on the day before his departure, Edith Maryon wrote to him:

> When you return, and before you have to go again, would it not be possible to celebrate a Michaelmas festival? You have spoken so much of this; would it be possible to make a beginning here now? By then, perhaps, I could participate.[380]

Wann sie wieder kommen und bevor sie wegfahren müssen wäre es nicht möglich ein Michaeli Fest zu feiern? Sie haben soviel davon gesprochen, wäre es möglich jetzt ein Anfang hier zu machen? Vielleicht bis dahin könnte ich auch dabei sein.

At Easter 1923 in Dornach, starting with his Good Friday lecture, Rudolf Steiner had first spoken of the need for a future Michael festival, further elaborating this theme especially in Kristiania and Berlin at the end of May.[381] Steiner had spoken of a 'festival of soul courage, of soul strength, of soul activity',[382] but had also emphasized the social relevance of such a festival—and on 21 May, in Norway, he had said: 'Truly, if people could decide to establish something that flows from worlds of spirit into the life of society, it would be of enormous significance for this social existence.'[383] A Michael festival of this kind, bearing in it the seeds of the future, was something that Rudolf Steiner had called a 'mighty impulse for the continuation of our civilization'.[384] In later lectures, however, he also urgently described the inner, spiritual-social conditions necessarily preceding the establishment of such a festival ('As surely as I will point to the need for this festival to emerge from the womb of the anthroposophic movement, so assuredly will I also hold this back as long as the strength is lacking to do so in a worthy fashion.'[385]). It lay in Edith Maryon's nature to follow up his stimulus in the summer of 1923. In her presence Rudolf Steiner had embarked on his lectures on Michael, in London in 1913. There lived in her the 'virtue of moral courage, of inner, spiritual courage' of which Steiner had spoken back then—that initiating selflessness with a social orientation that characterized all her work by the side of Rudolf Steiner to create a new, Christian mystery site, as well as her ongoing spiritual schooling path. Edith Maryon was physically frail and living close to death when she sent him her question shortly before his trip to England; nevertheless, prepared like few others, she was fully alive in these words: 'When you return, and before you have to go again, would it not be possible to celebrate a Michaelmas festival? You have spoken so much of this; would it be possible to make a beginning here now? By then, perhaps, I could participate.'

*

Many anthroposophists from Dornach had set off to attend Rudolf Steiner's major courses in England, from 4 August to 5 September, both the pedagogical lectures in Ilkley and also the 'summer school' at Penmaenmawr in Wales where Steiner would give lectures entitled 'Spiritual and Physical Evolution of the World and Humanity—Past, Present and Future from the

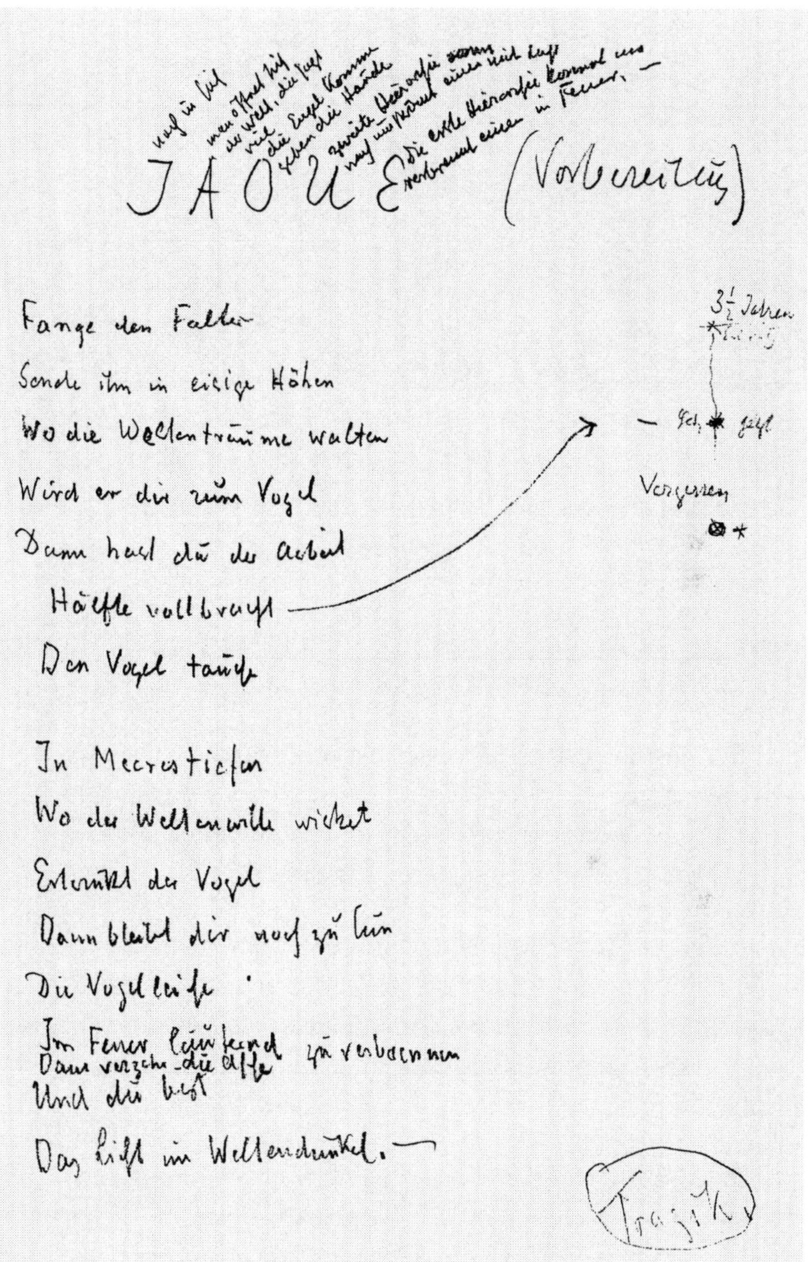

Rudolf Steiner: transcript of a mantram for Edith Maryon (from the esoteric lesson of 27 May 1923)

Edith Maryon: Instructions from Rudolf Steiner for meditative use of the mantram

Viewpoint of Anthroposophy'. But Edith Maryon had to stay behind, in a questioning, restless state of mind:

> It is growing ever quieter here, the only events are the post-
> man bringing a letter. I'm wondering what's happening in
> Ilkley, is all calm when you lecture? I hope nothing unpleas-
> ant has occurred. I am somewhat restless.[386]

She ended her letter to Steiner with the words, 'Please write to tell me you are well—the truth!',[387] and expressed concern, once again, that he was warmly enough dressed. On one occasion during these days she referred to what she herself was doing in Dornach:

> It is very hot here today, I read, paint [eurythmy] figures and
> sit in the garden; and think of the work in Ilkley. I hope it is
> not too strenuous? Is it possible to rest and have a little time
> for yourself?[388]

Rudolf Steiner soon replied from Ilkley to describe, in some-times humorous detail, how his journey had been,[389] and how his pedagogical lectures were going ('There are very few men at

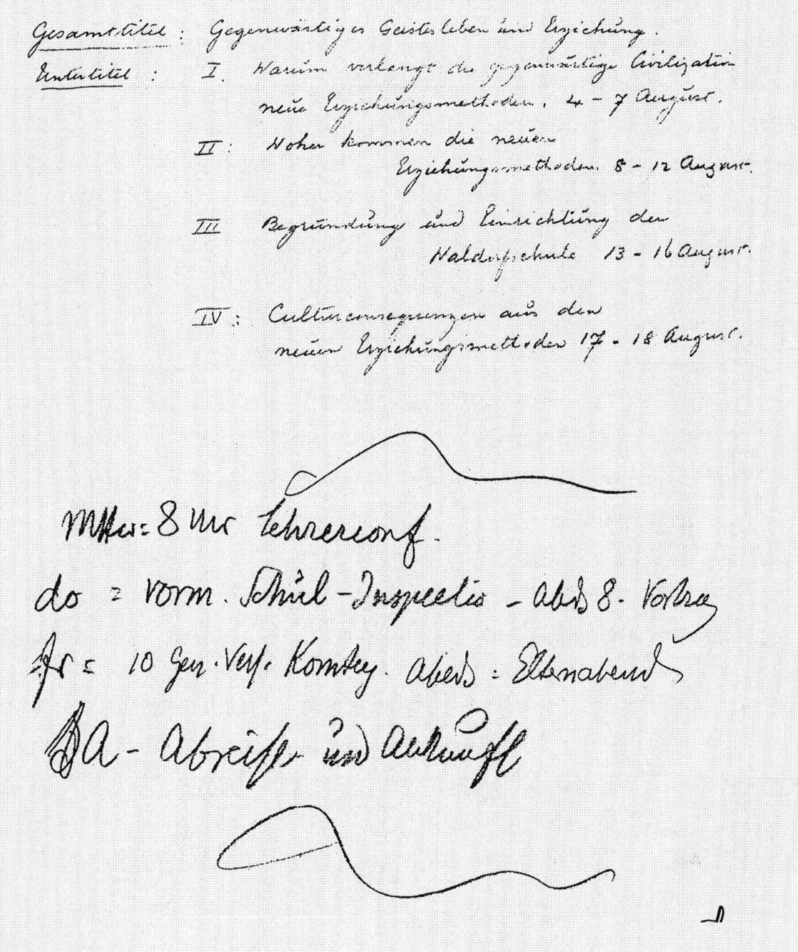

Programme of lectures in Ilkley (Edith Maryon) and Rudolf Steiner's appointments in Stuttgart

the lectures, mostly women. It is as if the men wish to withdraw from civilization';[390] 'Yesterday evening was the special lecture in Bingley. But this was an achievement since only an hour was allowed for both lecture and translation. And so I had to characterize the nature of human education and the Waldorf School in just half an hour'[391]). Weeks before his return, he soothed her anxieties about his journey back through a Germany where, only a few months later, Adolf Hitler would first attempt to seize power:

> Please do *not* worry that there might be any difficulties because of the sad news that is now coming from Germany. Care will be taken about the return journey, and to ensure there is no delay. So *please* do not be worried or anxious. But on the other hand what is happening [there] is unspeakably saddening. Unfortunately it was predictable; nobody wanted to believe me.[392]

In the middle of August, Edith Maryon's physician Ita Wegman also set off for the lectures and discussions in Penmaenmawr, which were of great importance to her;[393] but in her letters to Rudolf Steiner Edith Maryon repeated her suggestion about a Michael festival ('Is it possible to celebrate a Michaelmas festival? Or is it still too premature?'[394]) and concerned herself with the future of the abandoned and still ruined Swiss centre ('We ask why there should be a centre in Dornach when you are always working in the periphery? After this overlong period comes Stuttgart, as always and ever, Holland, Vienna, Stuttgart, Scandinavia and who knows what else! Probably America is next on the list'[395]); but nevertheless she cast a hopeful eye upon the initiatives in England:

> I just hope that something practical can grow from this, that somewhere in the world could be a little lovelier. The ugly news and tone from everywhere is so depressing and saddening.[396]

*

Edith Maryon waited many days in vain for post from Wales ('everything in Penmaenmawr seems to be veiled in mist, it is the fourth day but no news has arrived here'[397]) and in the quiet of Dornach she spent her time reading a selection of books that may have been suggested by Rudolf Steiner:

> I have read *Der Golem* ['The Golem'] by Meyrink and now I am reading *Der weisse Dominikaner* ['The White Dominican']. The double issue of *Anthroposophie* has also arrived. Then I am trying to read over my old notes from 1917-1919 etc, and sewing something, and lead a monastic life here. The windowsill in my room is now full of woodworm, Liedvogel had to remove it; every morning small piles of chewed wood stood there which the woodworm had left overnight.
>
> It is already very much autumn here, lovely sun but the feeling of things fading and dying is already apparent, and in the mornings the air is fresh and cool. You see what a small, quiet life one has to lead here!
>
> I often think, Is there a lecture today or not? Or is there a lecture going on all day long? One knows nothing!
>
> My health is very slowly getting a little better although the throat irritation persists unfortunately. If only that weren't so I could already be a bit more active, but for the time that's not possible.
>
> I hope your health is good? Not too much work and over-tiredness?[398]

But at last, in the middle of August, Rudolf Steiner's first letters from Penmaenmawr arrived in Herzentalweg; then on 23 August Steiner gave a more detailed description of the situation he found in Penmaenmawr and increasingly took a hand in shaping: a course whose facilitation and organization—in Steiner's later words—Edith Maryon had been substantially involved in:[399]

> Things go well here. My lectures are at 10.30 each morning.
> In these lectures I can speak in purely anthroposophic terms;

in Ilkley it was more about saying things to people about the pedagogy that didn't irritate them too much to begin with, so as to teach them about anthroposophy in a roundabout fashion. A group of our friends considers this the right thing. I myself have a different view. I know that our education will only be understood if people first gain anthroposophic ideas. That's why I am pleased really when events assume a character such as here in Penmaenmawr. Dunlop has made great efforts to instigate this character. [...] The lectures that can engage fully with esoteric themes are followed attentively.

Though the hotel is not exactly comfortable (though it is the 'best' one here) this is made up for by the fact that the spiritual memorials to ancient Druid culture make themselves apparent everywhere and this engenders a very esoteric atmosphere. And so I lack nothing except for my dear Dornach. I would always like to be there. (But there is no reason to be anxious.) I hope your health progresses well and I send my very warmest greetings.[400]

Envelope addressed by Rudolf Steiner, Penmaenmawr (August 1923).
Rudolf Steiner Archive, Dornach

Edith Maryon told Rudolf Steiner about her sporadic visits to the studio and directed her thoughts to his return ('Will you come straight back to Dornach—or visit that ghastly Stuttgart again? The last week of Penmaenmawr—how pleased I am! I hope London won't be extended!'[401]) and received further longer reports from Steiner from Wales, also for the first time with sketches he had made ('That is the view of the slate mountain from my window. Everything here is full of Druid memories, contrasting strangely with modernity'). Steiner again wrote to her about his own situation:

> My health is good; and slowly we have acquired some facilities in the hotel. Naturally the people here cannot immediately bring in electric light and suchlike. But it is really a very remarkable place. It was important to me to have stood physically before Druid memories. But I would be glad to be back in Dornach. The spiritual atmosphere here is such that, through thinking, Imaginations can easily inscribe themselves in the ether, as if one were drawing pictures in the air with a pen.[402]

Steiner's letter with his drawings and his news pleased Edith Maryon greatly. In her reply of 19 August she wrote:

> Sculpture studio, Goetheanum
> Dornach near Basel, 29 Aug. 1923
>
> Dear and respected teacher
>
> Such a wonderfully beautiful sky this evening. A blue ground, then gold of various shades below, up above countless white and golden little clouds, then later the gold became red gold, with a big fish, red with a long tail of pink cloudlets. Quiet, beautiful mood. The mountain walkers return, Steffen passes by sunk in a poetic dream. Your little sketch with the view from your window gave me great pleasure, but why do you not have a view of the sea? Usually the best rooms face that way. Is that part of the discomfort of the hotel that the best rooms have been allocated to others? Oh

how I wish I were in Penmaenmawr, to also feel this ancient
Druid atmosphere! But I am very pleased that you can have
these experiences, they must be extremely interesting and
valuable.

Thursday. A great wind and storm in the night so that it
was hard to sleep. I kept thinking about the strange Druid
experiences you are having there, and I hope to hear more
about this later.[403]

A day later, on 30 August 1923, Rudolf Steiner in Wales made a
another drawing for her, recording in detail the Druid circle he
had visited in the mountains and its geographical position. His
accompanying words included this:

Today is our penultimate day; and all has gone well. I just
want to say this too about the surroundings here: with a
few other people I went to one of the Druid altars by car; at
another place it is like this—from Penmaenmawr one sees
this view of the mountains: If one now follows the path…
on the other side of 'a' lies a plain up above on the summit;
up there are two fallen Druid circles that cars cannot get to.
There's a wonderful loneliness there. I went there on foot
with Wachsmuth. To stand at these sacred Druid shrines
where, so many years ago, people cultivated spiritual matters, was very significant for me. The path up there (about 1
¼ hours) was very beautiful, with the loveliest views of the
surrounding landscape.[404]

Edith Maryon replied again:

How interesting the picture of the double Druid circle
was—it looks just like the [Goetheanum] building, though
perhaps the number of pillars was different? I wait impatiently to hear much more about it, and am very envious of
Dr Wachsmuth.
I hope you weren't too tired after such a long and strenuous
walk—being a mountain climber is something new for you.[405]

Penmaenmawr, 30. August 1923

Meine liebe Edith Maryon!

Es ist heute der vorletzte Tag hier; und alles ist gut gegangen. Von der Umgebung möchte ich noch dieses sagen: Bei einem der Druidenaltäre war ich mit einigen andern mit einem Auto; an einem andern Orte ist es so: von Penm. aus sieht man etwa folgenden Bergaspect:

Geht man nun den Weg / so liegt auf der andern Seite von a eine Ebene oben auf dem Gipfel: da oben liegen [Dahin können Wagen nicht fahren. Es ist dort wunderbare Einsamkeit.] verfallene) zwei Druidencirkel. Ich ging dahin mit Wachsmuth zu Fuss. Das Stehen bei den Druidenheiligtümern, wo vor so vielen Jahren Leute die geistigen Angelegenheiten besorgt haben, war mir sehr bedeutsam. Der Weg hinauf (etwa 1½ Stunde) war sehr schön, voll der schönsten Ausblicke auf die Umgebung.

Nun kommt hier der letzte Vortrag. Dann nach der Abschiedabend. Dann geht es Samstag nach London. Von dort Abreise am 5. Sonntag ist vormittag Meeting

Letter from Rudolf Steiner to Edith Maryon, 30 August 1923

But of her own situation—and in marked contrast to Rudolf Steiner's mountain hike—Edith Maryon had to report:

> I am still housebound, the Day of Health has not yet dawned and I creep around like a snail, longing for a body to which I would not need pay any attention—scope to achieve something in this incarnation.[406]

A decade earlier, during their first conversation, Rudolf Steiner had told Edith Maryon that in this life she would be limited in the degree to which she could develop esoterically. Now the severely ailing artist longed for a body that would enable her to 'achieve something in this incarnation'.

*

In the autumn of 1923, Edith Maryon's health declined despite the efforts of Rudolf Steiner and Ita Wegman—she could scarcely get out of bed any more, and increasingly had to be nursed and cared for. Rudolf Steiner felt it ever more difficult to leave Dornach to meet his obligations, for instance to attend a conference of the Anthroposophical Society in Stuttgart, which he had to do just six days after his return from England.

Edith Maryon sent him best wishes for the conference, but given Steiner's previous experiences in Stuttgart she was sceptical about the outcome ('I hope the time in Stuttgart will not be too strenuous and horrible'[407]). In his account of the conference, in a letter to her, he wrote:

> The Stuttgart people have high hopes of this conference. But though they are mobilizing all their good will, the right outcome can scarcely ensue. This 'good will' is, you see,

not the spiritual power of will but the idea (illusion) that they have the will. These individuals have great abilities—this is clear for instance among the Waldorf teachers, who are even brilliant in many respects—yet they only have the 'idea of the will'. So they tell themselves, 'We have "good will" but just don't understand what we should do.' But what they ought to tell themselves is in truth this: 'We understand perfectly well what we should do, but we do not have the will to do it.' Yes, the truth can only be found behind the illusion.[408]

Following Stuttgart, Rudolf Steiner only had five days in Dornach—during which, still feeling echoes of the ancient Celtic mysteries, he made, among other things, a pastel drawing entitled 'Druid Stone'. Then he was at Basel railway station again, this time for a trip to Vienna for public and members' lectures in which he elaborated deepened perspectives of a future Michael festival and spoke about 'Anthroposophy and the Human Soul'. In the city where he had spent his youth and attended university, Steiner now gave intimate and subtle accounts characterizing the human being's future relationship with nature and her beings. Meanwhile Edith Maryon witnessed from her room the demolition of the concrete substructure of the destroyed Goetheanum, and wrote to him:

At 11 a.m. the first detonation took place—it was not so bad at all, though not without danger. I saw the splinters flying up, and several panes of glass in the joinery workshop windows suffered damage. At 4 p.m. they are going to continue. This time the windows will be left open.

My health is a bit better again. But I do not observe in myself the patience of which Miss Waller speaks, inwardly I wait impatiently for the time when I can move more freely again and will not have to concern myself forever with thoughts of health. I'd prefer never have to think about this subject.[409]

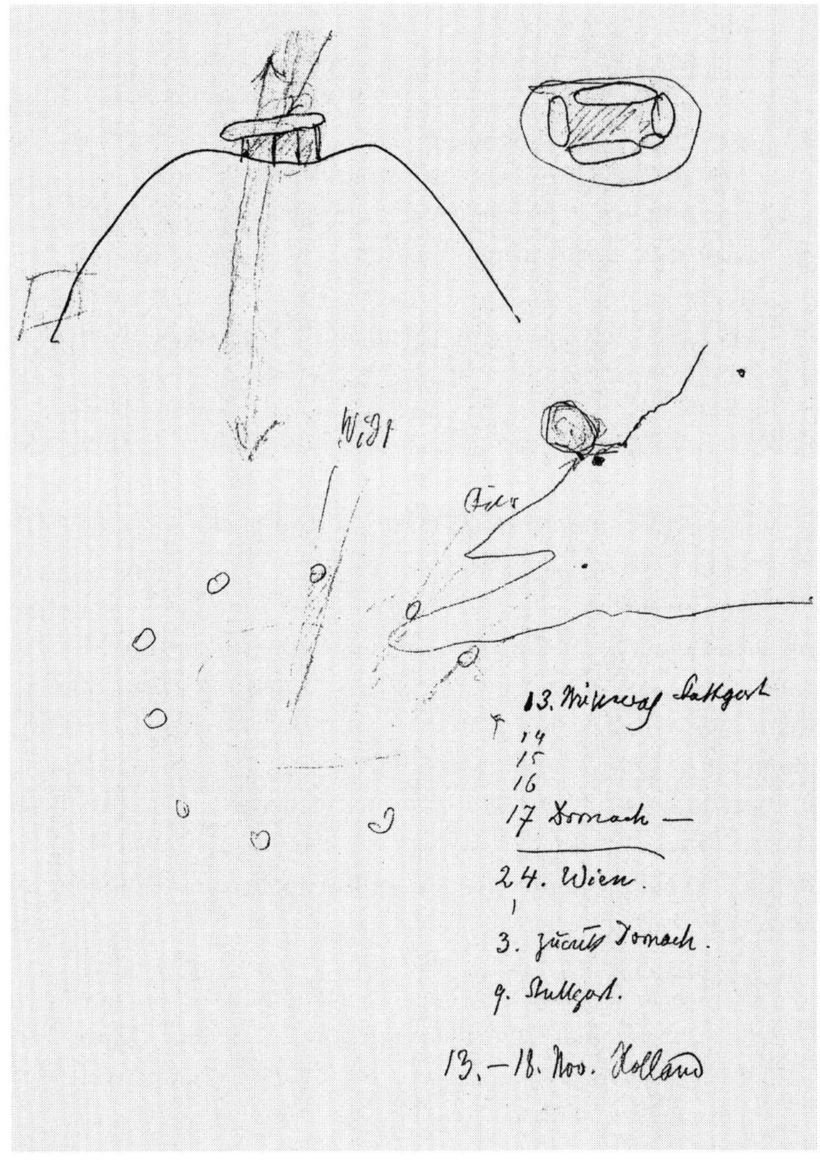

Sketch by Rudolf Steiner for Edith Maryon, with the schedule of his travels

In her letters in the next few days, she wrote further about the explosions:

> These explosions are continuing; with the 2nd one the rubble flew up vertically into the air, many pieces landed close to Brodbeckhaus. The windows of the joinery workshop are now cladded with boards. In Frau Doktor's room a pane of glass broke etc., but nothing of importance.
>
> I'm thinking of yesterday's lecture and hope that everything went well! And that one *sometimes* rests a little? I send all my good thoughts.
>
> [...] Everything here revolves around the explosions. Today there was an enormous one because the whole wall from East to North was blown up, along with the storeroom floor. All went well, the floor softly sank like the top of a cake and did not fragment into many pieces as was feared. All efforts are being made now to get the other half ready for Monday evening since otherwise they'll have to wait until Wednesday as the man in charge of the demolition will be away on Tuesday. Then most of the demolition will be finished apart from clearing a few other small areas.
>
> Kemper sprained his foot on the first day. Just after the first signal was given, Daffi ran towards the building with Markus, and he had to run after them and chase them away, and sprained his foot. He is still in bed. Curious that among all the women in the de Jaager House none made it their duty to keep the children away from danger. But after that experience there are stricter rules in place.[410]

After his lectures in Vienna and the more or less successful founding of the Austrian Anthroposophical Society ('All went well, except for the weighty fact that our Vienna friends too are asleep. But I'd rather relate that to you in person'[411]), Rudolf Steiner returned to Dornach on 5 October, where he was now able to stay until the middle of November with only brief interruptions.

The high studio in Dornach (left) and the demolition of the concrete substructure (October 1922)

Just two days after arriving there, in a lecture of 7 October, and with reference to a therapeutically oriented Easter Mystery Play that might be performed before the sculptural group, Rudolf Steiner for the first time pointed to the comprehensive context that this central sculpture was intended to create in the first Goetheanum—and indeed was able to open up for the future.[412] During these days, in collaboration with Ita Wegman, Rudolf Steiner also embarked on his work of establishing the foundations for an art of medicine in accord with the new mysteries, doing so every evening in the studio[413]—the place where the Christ sculpture stood, and the site of his collaboration of many years with Edith Maryon. The undated lines by Maryon, 'I am thinking of the studio and wishing I were there!'[414] may have been written during these weeks.

In mid-November, Rudolf Steiner set off on his last major trip of 1923. This took him to Holland for the—again arduous—founding of a national Society. Once again, on arriving there, Rudolf Steiner found a first letter waiting for him from Herzentalweg, which said:

> Dear, respected teacher
>
> I hope you arrived safely in The Hague with no adventures on the way, and that you are being allowed time to rest before

more work is demanded of you again! I do not understand
how anyone can demand a lecture immediately after such
a long journey, this always seems curiously inconsiderate!

Here things are improving, the chest pains have stopped,
the morning 'shower' was not too troublesome; it's just that
I am somewhat flat and tired. This morning I was so lazy, I
just slept, and I'm only writing now; then I will paint and
read a little, and think of the evening lecture. Please do not
forget to tell me when you will be returning, the Swiss time-
table doesn't list the trains from The Hague.

Once again Edith Maryon received detailed and unsparing messages ('All is going well; except that the Soc. is in an awful state
here too, disunity, insufficiency etc.[415]). In her replies Maryon
wrote to Steiner very openly and directly about her physical and
psychological state ('today is roughly like yesterday, I am still
tired and lazy and have a headache but I hope I can get up for
a little while tomorrow. I'm resting and I do very little so that
things can improve more quickly. [...] I try to be brave and to
make headway'[416]). In the last week of November, Rudolf Steiner
finally returned to Switzerland.

*

In Dornach, on 2 December, Steiner began his great lecture cycles
on the ancient mysteries to lay the ground for the mysteries of
the future. He was intently preoccupied also with the plans for
a second Goetheanum building and a complete refashioning of
the Anthroposophical Society founded upon national Societies
in other countries—a 'new' Anthroposophical Society of which
he himself would now become proactive president and director,
with the help of a few, suitable colleagues. As ever, and despite
all the work on his shoulders, Rudolf Steiner visited Edith Maryon's sickbed every day, reporting on the lectures she had missed,
bringing her esoteric exercises and mantras, and also reading to
her from the daily newspaper ('Her interest in the world was so
intense that Dr Steiner discussed world news with her every day
from the newspapers. It was always important to her to learn
how he judged the current world situation'[417]). He optimized her

medical treatment, cooked special meals and cheered Maryon up with drawings and verbal humoresques, in a strikingly original form of written communication: Maryon and Steiner often wrote remarks to each other on one and the same sheet—questions, replies and sayings. Even in Dornach, also, Maryon wrote letters to her dear and respected teacher:

> Things are very quiet here—I look at the clouds and think of the lecture, wishing I was sitting on my old chair in the joinery workshop. I so much wish I could recover quickly, I have lost too much time; but things so rarely go as I would wish! If only I got my health back I would be so very grateful for much. It would be easier for me if I could only see a purpose or reasons for why such a thing happens, for I'm sure

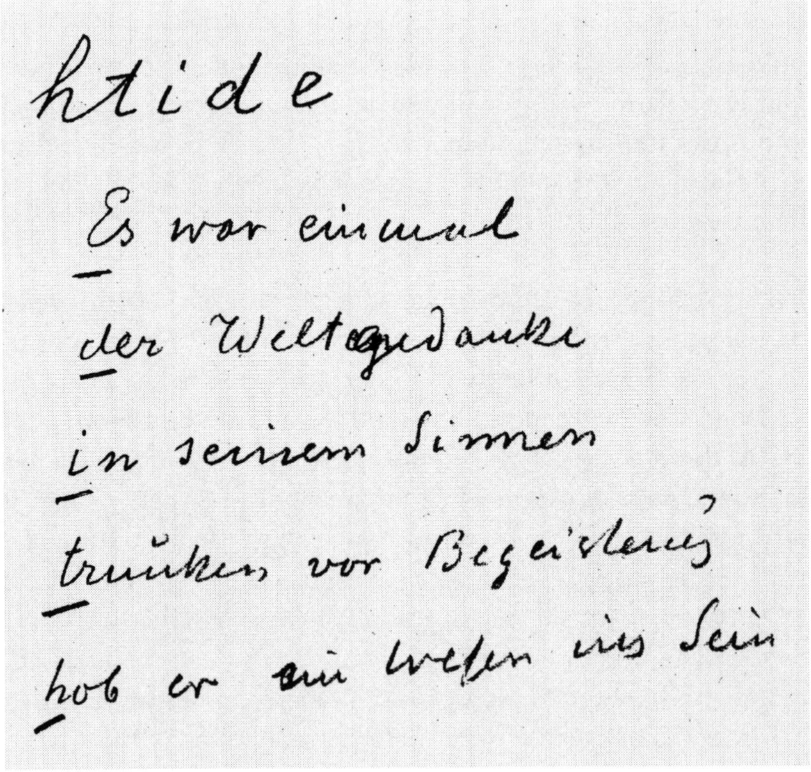

Verse for Edith Maryon based on her first name, written out by Rudolf Steiner. Ita Wegman Archive, Arlesheim

it does not happen without reason. I do not understand why so many stones fall on my path so that it becomes almost impossible to live. But I'm not complaining, only wishing to understand.[418]

Still figuring strongly before Maryon's inner eye were the studio she had guarded since 1914, and the work on the Christ Group, her thoughts and her 'practical sense' (Steiner) as ever preoccupied with many details of the work:

Dear respected teacher

Since it is not so cold today I think it will be enough tonight to leave the heating on behind the curtain in the studio and to turn off the heating in the middle of the studio. It ought not to get too hot since otherwise the upper part of the Christ figure will split. Please shut the door of the stove so that no sparks fly out.

I have a terrible longing to hear the lecture; and also to tidy up in the studio. I keep thinking of 'resting'; and was very sad today.

With warmest greeting
Edith Maryon[419]

*

By no later than mid-December Rudolf Steiner spoke with Edith Maryon about the forthcoming Christmas Foundation Meeting and the refounding of the Anthroposophical Society he intended. In his view Edith Maryon should be part of its future directorate, an 'esoteric executive'. But because of her situation and illness she herself saw no basis for this any longer. She did not, however, turn down Rudolf Steiner's request that she might at least take leadership of the Section for 'Visual and Sculptural Arts' in the new School of Spiritual Science. And so at the Christmas Foundation Meeting in the joinery workshop in Dornach on 28 December, Steiner was able to say the following:

[…] We will need a Section for the visual and sculptural arts. Now you know that Miss Maryon has stood by my side for

Sehr verehrter lieber Lehrer,

Ich denke, weil es heute nicht sehr kalt ist, für die Nacht genügt es hinter dem Vorhang im Atelier der Heizung ganz auf zu lassen, und der Heizung in der mitten im der Atelier zu schliessen. Es darf nicht zu heiss sein, weil sonst wird der oberen Teil der Christus Figur sich reissen. Bitte der Ofen Tür zu schliessen damit keine Funken heraus springen.

Ich sehne mich schrecklich der Vortrag zu hören; auch wieder Ordnung zu machen im Atelier. Ich denke immer an "aus-ruhen." und war sehr traurig heute.

Mit herzlichsten Grüssen
Edith Maryon

Letter from Edith Maryon to Rudolf Steiner. Rudolf Steiner Archive, Dornach

years precisely to support practice of the visual and sculptural arts for the Goetheanum. Sadly she cannot be here since she is suffering from what has been a very long illness, and cannot even make it over here to this gathering. But I hope that when she recovers after a while, she will be able to dedicate herself to the work I am speaking of here. What is to be done in the way of sculpture, and in the field of sculpture altogether, I will accomplish through the leader of this Section, Miss Maryon.[420]

A few weeks later, in a written account of the Christmas Foundation Meeting, Rudolf Steiner reformulated this as follows:

The visual and sculptural arts stood in the light of the Goetheanum's development. Through the key works that arose in this context a style developed that inevitably has many opponents still today. At present, of course, it can only imperfectly bring its intentions to expression. But it will become better understood as people come closer to anthroposophy in general. Miss E. Maryon has helped me in the development of this style in a way that means she must become the leader of the Section for sculptural art.[421]

'What she does, I have done'—'What is to be done in the way of sculpture, and in the field of sculpture altogether, I will accomplish through the leader of this Section, Miss Maryon.'

With the refounding of the Anthroposophical Society and the launch of the Dornach School for Spiritual Science, with its esoteric Michael School, Rudolf Steiner took another spiritual step forward, in absolutely Christian self-sacrifice[422] and with the clear intent to develop an influence upon civilization.[423] Edith Maryon was one of the few pupils and colleagues of Rudolf Steiner who were able to discern both the grandeur and the importance—but also the risk—of Rudolf Steiner's decision.

Rudolf Steiner

Only a few hundred metres away from the place where this was enacted, resting on her sickbed, she experienced the reality of the new beginning which Rudolf Steiner had so carefully and intentionally prepared:

> The mysteries themselves of course faded in the period when free human development had to come into its own. Now the time has arrived when the mysteries must be rediscovered. They must be rediscovered. One must be fully aware that today efforts must be made to rediscover the mysteries. It is in this awareness that the Christmas Foundation Meeting was held, for it is urgently necessary that a centre can be founded on earth where the mysteries can again be established. The Anthroposophical Society, as it develops, must become the path to the renewed mysteries. That, my dear friends, will also be your task: to help bring this about out of the right awareness.[424]

Even during the intense Christmas Foundation Meeting, which would ring in a new era in the Anthroposophical Society, one uncompromisingly founded on esotericism, Rudolf Steiner visited Edith Maryon every day and reported to her on everything that was happening: the mantric enactment of the laying of the foundation stone of the new Society, the meetings and discussions, and also his evening karma lectures on 'World History in the Light of Anthroposophy'. On the last day of this 'year of destiny' of 1923, and on the anniversary of the fateful fire, Rudolf Steiner spoke briefly again in the joinery workshop about the Christ Group, the statue 'in which the human being would have found a prompting to know himself as a cosmic being, interposed between the powers of the luciferic and the powers of the ahrimanic in inner, God-sustained balancing of his being'.[425] And, in further remarks about the spiritual orientation of the original building and its 'central creation', he continued:

> In Ephesus the statue of the gods; here at the Goetheanum the statue of the human being, the statue of the Representative

of Humanity, of Christ Jesus, to whom, identifying with him, we intended in all humility to knowingly dedicate ourselves entirely as, in their own way, one no longer wholly comprehensible to humanity, the pupils of Ephesus once dedicated themselves to Diana of Ephesus.[426]

Edith Maryon only lived another four, extraordinarily painful weeks after the Christmas Foundation Meeting. During this period she witnessed the collapse—or the actual poisoning—of Rudolf Steiner on 1 January (a realization of her continual deadly fears for his safety). From afar, and through Rudolf Steiner's communications with her, however, she also witnessed the (re)beginning of the esoteric Class Lessons in mid-February as well as the karma lectures that began a day later. According to Rudolf Steiner, Edith Maryon, despite her terminal physical condition, was filled during this time with thoughts about her future Section ('With intense inwardness she still made efforts on her sickbed to direct her thoughts to the way in which this Section should come about, the nature of its influence'[427]) and equally about the spiritual content of the Christmas Foundation Meeting and the Class Lessons, which she very probably experienced as the summit of her esoteric endeavours:

> Against the background of her grave suffering, her last weeks on earth were filled with the spiritual content of the Christmas Foundation Meeting and the Class Lessons of the School at the Goetheanum that it was possible to bring to her.[428]

When Rudolf Steiner set off again at the end of March for a longer trip to Prague, as always he left Maryon his address there, and noted his probable return dates via Stuttgart. He was going there to give karma lectures, public lectures and a Class Lesson, which he did in a beleaguered state ('How very different from before. His whole stance was deeply serious, almost sad. He was already gravely ill and we did not see it, did not wish to see it'[429]).

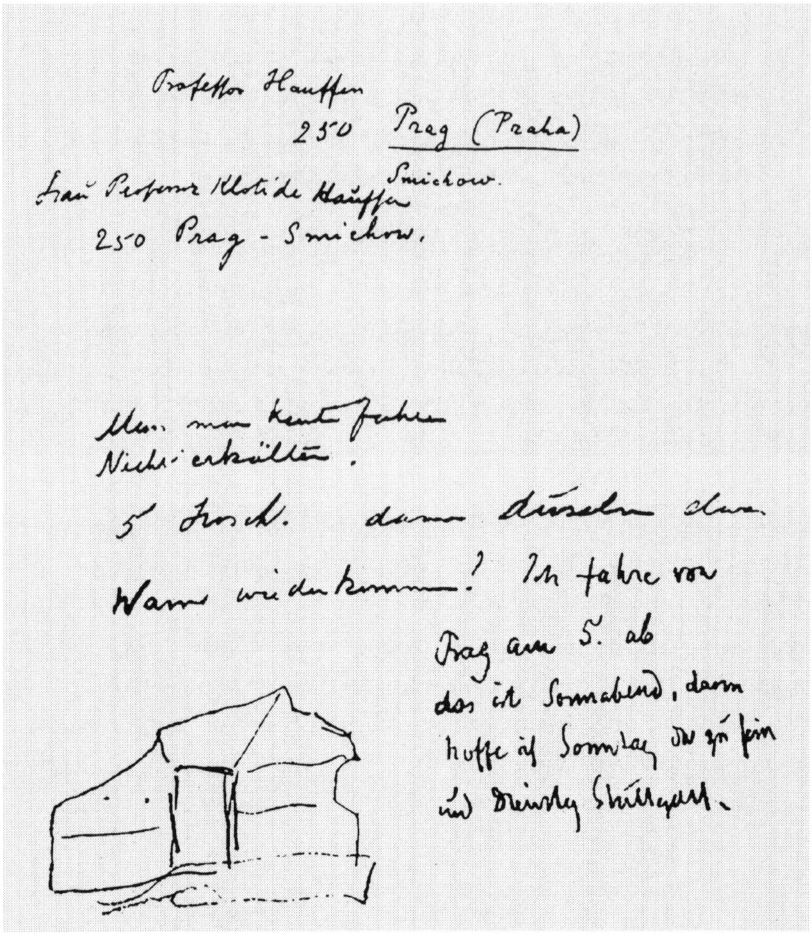

*Questions from Edith Maryon and replies from Rudolf Steiner about the trip
to Prague. Rudolf Steiner Archive, Dornach.*

Edith Maryon sent at least two letters to Prague that have not
survived, though his concerned letter to her has done:

250 Prague-Smichow, 27 March 1924, c/o Prof. Haufen

My dear Edith Maryon

From Prague I send my very warmest thoughts especially
for an improvement in your health. I do hope the distressing
conditions soon improve. I was very pleased when Frau Wegman told me on Thursday, by phone, that an improvement

that I myself witnessed on Wednesday has continued. My thoughts turn there often and I will be glad to get back. The journey went well. There was a lot to do in Stuttgart on Thursday but I left again already at 5 p.m. Then we arrived here on Friday morning, had a rehearsal at midday and a public lecture in the evening. But all went well. Still to come are: a lecture at 8 p.m. on Saturday (members), Sunday morning eurythmy at 11, 3 p.m. (members' gathering), Sunday evening at 8 (members' lecture); Monday 8 p.m., public lecture, Friday 8 p.m. public lecture, Saturday 7 p.m. members. Then I'd like to depart already on Saturday evening, and will no doubt arrive only a few minutes before the lecture scheduled for Sunday the 6th. I'm writing all this because I forgot to say it when I saw you last. Healthwise things are actually not bad for me. I hope all goes well. For today, so that these lines can be sent soon, my very warmest thoughts,
Rudolf Steiner

One can send letters here: c/o Prof. Hauffen, 250 Prague-Smichow, or also: Prague-Smichow, Stefanikova trida 56.[430]

Prag-Smichow, 1 April 1924
c/o Prof. Hauffen
Stefanikova trida 56

My dear Edith Maryon

I received the two letters with great pleasure and thank you very warmly for them. I am glad that the improvement which began before I left continued in the next few days. I hope things continue to go well and your health improves.

Here things go well although there is a great deal to be done. The Sunday was nearly all taken up from morning to evening with the gathering in which the Bohemian Anthroposophical Society was formed. But everything is proceeding as planned with lectures and eurythmy performances. I have already written to you about my time of arrival back in Dornach. But it seems as if I may only arrive very shortly

before the lecture. I will come as early as I can. I send my
very warmest thoughts for the strengthening of your health
And my very finest greetings
Rudolf Steiner[431]

*

The last weeks of Edith Maryon's life in March and April 1924 were
marked by intense pain and increasing difficulties with breathing—'she suffered unspeakably, especially in the last period'.[432]
The medicines prescribed, according to Rudolf Steiner, were no
longer effective—'but what was effective still was reading aloud
to her, either from the verses given for the Christmas Foundation
Meeting or also from the New Testament'.[433] In her room in Herzentalweg, Edith Maryon was preparing herself for her death, and
at the end of April asked for Christ's saying 'Come to me all you
who are weary and heavy laden' to be pinned to the side of her
bed. 'In Christo morimur—in Christ death becomes life.'

Steiner was in Stuttgart on 1 May, held up there with Society matters, when Ita Wegman phoned him to say that Edith
Maryon would very probably not survive the day. Brought back
by car in a hurry to Dornach in the night of 1/2 May, he found
there a further message from Wegman:

> Very respected, dear Herr Doktor, Miss Maryon died tonight
> at a quarter past midnight. She remained fully conscious to
> the end. Her last moments were less painful as I was able to
> reduce her breathing problems to a minimum with oxygen
> inhalations. Her last words were, 'I am so weak, I cannot
> wait any longer for him to come.' Then she grew very calm
> and death came softly and exaltedly a quarter of an hour
> later without struggle or pain. Please phone to tell me when
> you get here so that I can drive up there with you. I am glad
> that you are back. Always, Your Ita[434]

As Rudolf Steiner put it a few days later, Edith Maryon 'had been
led through the portal of death into the world of spirit in the
fullest clarity of thought, accompanied by her friend and faithful
physician Ita Wegman'.[435] Albert Steffen wrote of her deathbed:

Letter from Ita Wegman to Rudolf Steiner. Arlesheim, 2 May 1924

She lay in her narrow little room on a deathbed that was adorned only with a few branches, like the figure of a medieval saint.[436]

*

For the first time ever in the history of the Class Lessons, Rudolf Steiner began his esoteric presentation on the evening of 2 May with a great eulogy for a deceased colleague in the work of anthroposophy. He emphasized that Edith Maryon had stood 'foremost' among those 'who have pursued what this First Class has given with deep commitment and true inwardness'.[437]

On the evening of 3 May, in the joinery workshop, Rudolf Steiner interrupted his memorial address to members of the Anthroposophical Society for ten minutes in order to be present at the closing of the coffin before the corpse was taken to Basel ('Will you allow me to interrupt this address for ten to fifteen minutes for the closing of the coffin, and then to continue it afterwards'[438])—something that had likewise never happened before.

In his cremation address three days later, on 6 May, Rudolf Steiner described the life and work of Edith Maryon but also the advent of her illness and the efforts he and Ita Wegman had made to save her, saying in this context:

> The seed of Miss Maryon's illness was planted on the night of the Goetheanum fire. And she really could not be cured of what this seed instigated in her even through the most careful nursing. Such things are karmic. And while medicine of course can and must do much to counteract these karmic matters, nevertheless karma takes intransigent effect; and when even the most attentive care was unable to achieve its goal then one must indeed think of karma. While a person is still on the physical plane, we must think only of how they can be cured. And really everything that could have been done was done by the very self-sacrificing efforts of Dr Wegman.[439]

In his preparatory notes for the address in Basel for his colleague and friend Edith Maryon, Rudolf Steiner had written among other things:

> So many things do not come about
> because the people involved
> do not follow it through—she always followed it through.
> What *she did*, I could do! –

I have to wince when
resistance comes from certain
quarters—if I were required
to carry what is personal up
into the spiritual world =
this is often asked of me

You were the soul seeking in the spirit
You were able to suppress personality
That the work should be there: that was
your goal.[440]

Rudolf Steiner began and ended the address in Basel itself with a great, mantric verse—as he said, a 'last greeting' to Edith Maryon:

Whoever looks upon your karmic path,
poor in its joys,
beholds your noble spirit striving,
its warmth of soul:
to him a human being's sense for work and aims
appears in your earthly sojourn.

Whoever feels your still and quiet being,
its loving nature,
beholds the efforts of your soul
that never tire:
to him a human being's sense of heart
appears in your daily life.

Whoever stood before the gateway of your death
the all too near,
beholds the hard pathway of pain
softly endured:
to him a human being's sense of patient endurance
appears in your sickbed.

Whoever feels the beautiful works of your spirit,
seriously pursued
beholds your life devoted to

the spirit goal:
to him a human being's power of sacrifice
appears in the questing of your soul.

Whoever beholds in the spheres of spirit,
full of blessing,
your soul-life weaving in futurity,
its radiant light:
to him a human being's spiritual power
appears from your eternal being.

Whoever beholds from the sun's lofty heights,
their loving warmth,
your gaze shining down to us,
and giving us help:
to him a human being's power of blessing
appears from your spirit working.[441]

Wer da blickt
~~Ich blickt'~~ auf deinen Karmaweg
      Den freudearmen,
  Der
~~Ich~~ schaut dein edles Geistesstreben
      Das seelen — warme :
~~Und~~ ~~Ihm~~ erscheint eines Menschenwesens Wirkens~~sinn~~
      Aus deinem Erdenwandel —

  Wer da,
~~Ich~~ fühlt dein so stilles Sein
      Das liebevolle
  Der
~~Ich~~ schauet deiner Seele Mühen
      Das nie ermüdende
~~Und~~ ~~Ihm~~ erscheint eines Menschenwesens Herzenssinn
  Aus deinem Tagesleben. —

  Wer da stand
~~Ich stand'~~ vor deinem Todestore
      Dem allzunahen,
  Der
~~Ich~~ schaut den harten Schmerzensweg
      Den sanft ertragenen :
~~Und~~ ~~Ihm~~ erscheint eines Menschenwesens Duldersinn
      Von deinem Krankenlager.

  Wer empfindet
~~Ich bin beglückt von deinem~~ schönes Geisteswerk
      Der
      Dem ernst geführtest,
~~Ich~~ schaut dein Leben hingegeben
      Dem Geistes-Ziele :
      ~~Ihm~~ erscheint eines Menschenwesens Opfer~~kraft~~
      Aus deinem Seelenringen.

Wer da
~~Ich~~ schaut in Geistes – Sphären
Den
~~Ihr~~ segensvollen
Dein Seelenleben künftig weben
Das Licht – erstrahlende
Und ~~mir~~ Ihm erscheint eines Menschenwesens Geistes Kraft
Aus deinem Ewig – Sein.

Wer da
~~Ich~~ schauet aus Sonnenhöhen
Den
~~Aus~~ liebenswarmen
Deinen Blick zu uns herniedersprühen
Den hilfe – spendenden
~~Und~~ ~~mir~~ Ihm erscheint eines Menschenwesens Segenskraft
Wesens
Aus deinem ~~Sternenwesen~~
Geisteswirken, —

Notes and References

1   Hans Müller-Wiedemann, 'Zum Motto der Sozialethik' in, Richard Steel (ed.), *Das soziale Hauptgesetz—soziale Fragen im Spannungsfeld der Gegenwart*, Föhrenbühl 1994, p. 15.

2   GA 263/1, p. 220.

3   Ibid., p. 49.

4   Ibid., p. 203 f.

5   'And we must now also reckon with this karma, that precisely this special quality of Miss Maryon's will be lacking when the second Goetheanum is constructed.' GA 263/1, p. 225.

6   Ibid., p. 234.

7   These two first volumes from the Ita Wegman Archive for fundamental anthroposophic medical research appeared in the series of monographs, *Studien zu esoterischen Schülern* published in 2006 by the Verlag am Goetheanum, Dornach: *Michael Bauer. Ein esoterischer Schüler Rudolf Steiners* (volume 1) and *Marie Steiner-von Sivers. Aufbau und Zukunft des Werkes von Rudolf Steiner* (volume 2).

8   Cf. Rex Raab, *Edith Maryon. Bildhauerin und Mitarbeiterin Rudolf Steiners*, Dornach 1993.

9   Friedrich Rittelmeyer, *Meine Lebensbegegnung mit Rudolf Steiner*, Stuttgart 1983, p. 77.

10   Friedrich Rittelmeyer, quoted by Rex Raab in: *Edith Maryon…*, op. cit., p. 392.

11   Assja Turgenieff, *Was ist mit dem Goethenaumbau geschehen?*, Basel 1957.

12   Ibid., p. 26.

13   GA 263/1, p. 234.

14   Ibid., p. 23.

15   Cf. accounts by Diether Lauenstein about the biographical importance of the time around age 36, the second 'moon node': *Der Lebenslauf und seine Gesetze*, Stuttgart 1992, p. 66ff; and Florian Roder, *Die Mondknoten im Lebenslauf*, Stuttgart 2006.

16   Cf. comments by Andrew Welburn in: Rex Raab, *Edith Maryon…* op.cit., p. 56f.

[17] Cf. Rudolf Steiner's lecture to members of 1 January 1909 in GA 107.

[18] Cf. Rudolf Steiner, GA 146; Emil Bock, 'Das Fünfte Evangelium', in, Rudolf Steiner, *Studien zu seinem Lebensgang und Lebenswerk*, Stuttgart 1961, p. 223 ff; Hella Wiesberger, 'Aus der Akasha-Forschung. Das Fünfte Evangelium', in *Nachrichten der Rudolf Steiner-Nachlassverwaltung*, no. 8, 1962, p. 32 ff. and Peter Selg, *Rudolf Steiner and the Fifth Gospel*, Steinerbooks 2009.

[19] GA 118, p. 28.

[20] Cf. the chronological survey of Edith Maryon's life compiled by Konrad Donath ('only citations appear here which could be proven through archive material'; GA 263/I), in which it is stated: 'Studies in Italy. Further trip planned to Egypt. Reading of *Theosophy* by Rudolf Steiner. Interruption of stay in Italy and return to England.' (GA 263/I, p. 254).

[21] Cf. Rex Raab, *Edith Maryon...* op. cit., p. 87f.

[22] Harry Collison, who was to facilitate the meeting of Edith Maryon and Rudolf Steiner in Berlin in December 1912, explicitly stated, in two letters to Marie von Sivers at the beginning of December, that Edith Maryon had never been to Berlin before (cf. p. 21). If Maryon—an unknown English guest unable to speak German and not a member of the Theosophical Society—had wished to attend an internal branch lecture by Steiner in May 1912, a personal intervention and introduction would have been needed, to which (if it had happened) Collison would surely have referred in December. In her first two letters to Rudolf Steiner in October and November 1912, which she wrote at a point of crisis at the request of Dr Felkin (cf. p. 22), she made no mention of ever having attended a lecture by Steiner before. Nor does the tone of these letters point to the 'Master' experience she later described having already occurred in May 1912. The extant documents, by contrast, make it seem highly likely that Edith Maryon first heard Rudolf Steiner speak in December 1912 in Berlin, and also most probably spoke to him then (cf. p. 23). It is fully apparent that she was referring to *this* encounter in Berlin, which she had just had, when she wrote to him a few days (or weeks) later, in her letter from

Cologne of 1 January 1913 ('when I saw you in Berlin'; cf p. 27). In relation to Rex Raab's comment that Assja Turgenieff recalled that Edith Maryon had listened to the Berlin lecture of 14 May 1912 from the gallery, it should be noted that Turgenieff herself did not attend the lecture (though she was indeed present at the lecture in Berlin in December 1912); also that Raab misread one place in Maryon's handwritten letter to Steiner concerning her quest for an esoteric teacher whom she had found, in his person, in Berlin. She had written 'I was right *about* the Master', whereas Raab read 'I was right *above* the Master'. Raab then wrote in his biography of Maryon, 'We owe it to a note from the observant Assja Turgenieff that we can locate her [Maryon] on the gallery during Rudolf Steiner's Berlin lecture of 14 May 1912' then misquoted: ' "I knew immediately that I had at last found myself directly over the Master", she wrote [...] in a letter seven and a half months later.' (Raab, op. cit, p. 88).

[23] GA 143, p. 182.

[24] Ibid., p. 183.

[25] Ibid., p. 183ff.

[26] Ibid., p. 185.

[27] Five years later, in August 1917, in relation to ahrimanically distorted Christ depictions in art, Rudolf Steiner would say this: 'All of Ahriman's interest is focused on distracting human beings from the spirit, and directing them instead toward materiality—which is also a spiritual element but one concealed within the earth. Ahriman employs all kinds of cunning strategies to prevent human beings as far as possible from informing the person of Christ with any cosmic quality. Today already—this is not at all rare especially in texts on social democracy—we can discover a curious, ahrimanic image of Christ that is divested of all super-earthly spirituality, that is intended only to be purely human, not to speak of painters who have done everything possible to expel a cosmic quality from the Christ figure. Many years ago, here in Berlin, I saw an exhibition of Christ images, one next to another. I still have the exhibition catalogue, with my notes on this: one ahrimanic image of Christ after another! And how many wandering

apostles we find today who speak of Christ either in some official or unofficial capacity, not knowing that Ahriman is sitting on
their shoulders and misleading them into drawing *his* image of
the Christ impulse, rather than what actually does live and work
within it. This picture at work within the Christ impulse itself can
be portrayed in a way appropriate to our time solely through the
means provided by spiritual science. Because spiritual science
involves perceptions arising when one is outside the body, it is
able once again to behold the picture of Christ in his true form.'
(GA 176, p. 256f.) Two months later, on 29 October 1917, in Dornach, during an art-history lecture with slides entitled 'Trans-
formations of Views of Christ', Rudolf Steiner would refer again
not only to his—long-past—visit to the Berlin exhibition ('years
ago [...] I saw a whole collection of Christs in an exhibition, each
image more ghastly than the other!' GA 292, p. 336) but also to the
way depictions of Christ had changed since the early Christian
centuries: ('[...] One could also write a world history since the
Mystery of Golgotha by describing the way images people have
made of Christ have changed over time. This brings to expression everything that has actually occurred over the ages. And we
could trace this through into the present era.' Ibid).

28   GA 133, p. 106.

29   Ibid., p. 115f.

30   GA 263/I, p. 11.

31   Rudolf Steiner Archive, Dornach.

32   Letter from Harry Collison to Marie von Sivers, London 8 December 1912 (Rudolf Steiner Archive, Dornach).

33   Ibid.

34   Ibid. Harry Collison stressed also in a second letter to Marie von
Sivers of 6 December 1912 that Edith Maryon had never been to
Berlin before ('she has never been in Berlin').

35   Letter from Harry Collison to Rudolf Steiner, London 6 October
12 (Rudolf Steiner Archive, Dornach).

36   GA 263/I, p. 15.

37   Ibid.

38   GA 141, p. 105.

39 'A small shepherd's play was performed in the red "art room" at Motzstrasse. Mary and Joseph, not in costume, looking ordinary but friendly, sat before us on two chairs. Behind them, at the piano, the angel climbed on a chair when he needed to sing. The shepherds—two, I think—sat before them on the ground. Yet precisely through this simplicity a strong dramatic intensity issued from the play. The scene portrayed acquired a soul dimension and enriched night's world of pictures.' Assja Turgenieff, *Erinnerungen an Rudolf Steiner und die Arbeit am ersten Goetheanum*, Dornach 1972, p. 37.

40 GA 143, p. 215f.

41 Cf. for instance, Assja Turgenieff's account of her own conversation with Rudolf Steiner at this time, in Turgenieff, op. cit., p. 37.

42 Letter from Michael Bauer to Ludwig Sauter, 26 October 1905, quoted in Peter Selg: *Michael Bauer. Ein esoterischer Schüler Rudolf Steiners*, Dornach 2006, p. 54.

43 Cf. GA 142, p. 100ff.

44 Cf. GA 143, p. 225ff.

45 GA 263/I, p. 13.

46 Ibid., p. 14.

47 Ibid.

48 Ibid.

49 Ibid., p. 238.

50 Ibid., p. 15.

51 Ibid.

52 GA 152, p. 11.

53 Cf. Edith Maryon's reference in a letter to Rudolf Steiner of 30 March 1013 (GA 263/I, p. 15) to her conversation in The Hague with Steiner about spiritual accompaniment of her deceased friend Neville Meakin.

54 GA 152, p. 17.

55 Ibid., p. 33.

56 Ibid., p. 44.

57 Ibid., p. 46.

58 Ibid., p. 43.

59 GA 263/I, p. 16.

60   Ibid., p. 219.

61   Cf. the account by Andrei Belyi in *Verwandeln des Lebens. Erinnerungen an Rudolf Steiner*, Basel 1975, p. 235ff. for more on the personality and charisma of Sophie Stinde; also see the brief biography by Florian Roder in, Bodo von Plato (ed.), *Anthroposophie im 20. Jahrhundert. Ein Kulturimpuls in biografischen Porträts*, Dornach 2003, p. 798ff.

62   Quoted in Christoph Lindenberg, *Rudolf Steiner. Eine Chronik. 1861-1925*, Stuttgart 1988, p. 454f.

63   GA 263/I, p. 17.

64   Ibid.

65   Ibid., p. 18.

66   Ibid., p. 18f.

67   Ibid., p. 239.

68   GA 148, p. 161.

69   Ibid., p. 40.

70   Ibid., p.26.

71   Ibid., p. 73.

72   Ibid., p. 120.

73   Ibid.

74   Ibid., p. 207.

75   Cf. Peter Selg, *Rudolf Steiner und das Fünfte Evangelium*, Dornach 2005, p. 37ff.

76   GA 243, p. 233. Cf. Peter Selg, *Die Kultur der Selbstlosigkeit. Rudolf Steiner, das Fünfte Evangelium und das Zeitalter der Extreme*, Dornach 2006, p. 35ff.

77   Cf. Peter Selg, *Rudolf Steiner und das Fünfte Evangelium*, op. cit., p. 124.

78   The translation, in this volume, of early letters which Maryon wrote to Rudolf Steiner in German, which are housed in the Rudolf Steiner Archive, will try to retain a sense of some of the grammatical errors she made in the newly learned language to convey the original style of her correspondence with Steiner. Each such quotation from the letters has an end-note reference to the Collected Works (GA) in German in which these letters have appeared in an edited and corrected form (GA 263/I). In the Afterword to the

latter volume, Konrad Donat wrote: 'In her [Edith Maryon's] letters in German—she only began to learn German from 1913—only major deviations from German syntax and grammar have been corrected. It is remarkable how quickly she overcame her deficiencies in spoken and written German' (GA 263/I, p. 257).

79   GA 263/I, p. 19.

80   GA 263/I, p. 20.

81   Cf. Rex Raab, *Edith Maryon*... op. cit., p. 112.

82   GA 286, p. 70f.

83   Ibid., p. 72.

84   Already before she arrived in Dornach, Maryon had proposed collaborating on the St John's building itself because of her specific training in sculptural form. On 4 January 1914 she wrote (very probably to Thaddeus Rychter): 'I am sending you some pictures of my previous work, so that you can judge whether perhaps something more suitable [than woodcarving] could be found, either modelling or drawing work. But I am very willing to undertake the woodcarving work, without payment for the time being.' (Quoted in Rex Raab, *Edith Maryon*...op. cit., p. 112.)

85   Andrei Belyi, *Verwandeln des Lebens. Erinnerungen an Rudolf Steiner*, p. 50.

86   Assja Turgenieff, *Aus der Arbeit an der Gruppe*. Manuscript, 1928, p. 1 (Rudolf Steiner Archive).

87   Andrei Belyi, op. cit., p. 310.

88   Quoted in Rex Raab, op. cit., p. 345f.

89   'The form of "spiritual science" avowed by the writer of these lines has found some regard amongst his contemporaries, but especially since it has been possible to envisage building a dedicated site, a "School of Spiritual Science" (in Dornach, in the canton of Solothurn) where this spiritual science can be cultivated, attacks upon it have been coming from various sides.' (GA 35, p. 156.) With this opening sentence Rudolf Steiner launched a defence originally conceived in response to a lecture by Father Riggenbach published in the local daily newspaper for the Birseck, Birsig and Leimental region (Arlesheim 14 February 1914). Steiner replied in detail to this article in the same newspaper, but

then (after Riggenbach approached him in a friendly and human way), he developed the piece more generally, detaching it from its originating cause. Here Rudolf Steiner engaged among other things with accusations raised by the Church, writing in relation to anthroposophy's view of Christ: 'Why do Christians attack the doctrine of Christ enshrined in spiritual science? This contains *nothing*, really and truly nothing, of a denial of what Christianity has so far said about Christ. It offers only an enlargement, an elevation of the idea of Christ. One would have thought that those who authentically hold to Christ in their deepest hearts would rejoice at this. When, through the science of the spirit, the event of Golgotha is rigorously discerned in its world-encompassing significance, it is deprived of none of the acknowledgement and avowal that any Christian can bring to bear upon it.' (GA 35, p. 168.)

[90]   GA 263/I, p. 23.

[91]   Ibid.

[92]   Ibid., p. 24.

[93]   Ibid.

[94]   Ibid., p. 118.

[95]   Ibid., p. 24f.

[96]   Ibid., p. 231.

[97]   GA 192, p. 171.

[98]   Cf. Peter Selg, *Rudolf Steiner und das Fünfte Evangelium*, op. cit., p. 117 ff.

[99]   GA 263/I, p. 220 ff.

[100]   Ibid., p. 222.

[101]   Rudolf Steiner Archive, Dornach: note-page 6948.

[102]   GA 263/I, p. 232.

[103]   Ibid., p. 233.

[104]   Assja Turgenieff, op. cit., p. 69.

[105]   Friedrich Rittelmeyer, op. cit., p. 76f.

[106]   Ibid., p. 77.

[107]   Ibid.

[108]   Assja Turgenieff wrote: 'Only in obedience and reluctantly did she [Edith Maryon] put her own name to the small model, beside

that of Rudolf Steiner.' In 'Aus der Arbeit an der Gruppe'. Manuscript, 1928, p. 2, Rudolf Steiner Archive, Dornach.

[109] Friedrich Rittelmeyer, op. cit., p. 78.

[110] GA 158, p. 120.

[111] GA 159, p. 233.

[112] GA 162, p. 26.

[113] GA 159, p. 296.

[114] Ibid., p. 258.

[115] In a lecture given one year later (1918), Rudolf Steiner said this: 'Every thought that involves picturing a duality, let us say a good and evil principle, will never be able to illumine life. We can only illumine life if we represent it in terms of a triad, where one of these principles is a state of balance, and the two others the two poles between which the state of equilibrium continually swings back and forth. Thus the trinity of figures that we seek to depict in the Representative of Humanity and in Ahriman and Lucifer.' (GA 186, p. 112; cf. here also numerous further remarks by Steiner on this theme, not least in the lecture course *The Mission of Michael*, GA 194.)

[116] GA 159, p. 251.

[117] GA 272, p. 102.

[118] GA 165, p. 181.

[119] GA 254, p. 197.

[120] GA 157, p. 264f.

[121] In his address to the General Meeting on 21 October 1917. Cf. Rudolf Steiner, *Aufbaugedanken und Gesinnungsbildung*, Dornach 1942, or Ake Fant, Arne Klingborg, John Wilkes, *Die Holzplastik Rudolf Steiners in Dornach*, Dornach 1981, p. 21.

[122] GA 184, p. 314.

[123] GA 197, p. 107.

[124] GA 203, p. 251.

[125] GA 342, p. 36.

[126] GA 165, p. 181f.

[127] GA 157, p. 251.

[128] Ibid., p.253.

[129] In relation to the sculptural form of the figure of Lucifer, Steiner spoke among other things of the form of the forehead—by contrast to the ahrimanic accentuation of the lower jaw or the

'chewing and dental system'—and said, for instance, on 13 June 1915 in Elberfeld: 'The head of Lucifer is really such that one can say that a human head is reminiscent of it. You see, this head is shaped in such a way that the skull, the forehead especially, is grandiose in form. Whereas these upper parts are relatively immobile in us, everything is mobile in this being. Everything is soul expression. Just as we can move our hands and fingers, but not this region here, so this being can move everything up here. And you can tell from the sculptural work that everything there is mobile. But the lower part of the face recedes greatly on the other hand. One can say that the grandiose form of the skull arches over the receding face.' (GA 159, p. 293.) Elsewhere, in numerous accounts, also in ones in which he returned to the subject in later years, Rudolf Steiner referred to the special connection between Lucifer's speech and hearing organization, as was apparent in the sculptural Group ('They [modern people] do not know for instance that the whole organization issuing from the human being and radiating toward the head organization encompasses an inner, organic harmony between hearing and speaking. Hearing and speaking, in fact, belong together also organically, are bound up with a single organ complex, which modern physiology ignores. When I show you my wooden Group you will see from this tangibly presented physiology—though it does not seek to be this—how there appears from deep-lying anthroposophic foundations something that is very much a unity: breathing, speaking and hearing.' GA 343, p. 204; cf. also GA 348, p. 97f.) Already on 10 June 1915, in a first Berlin lecture on the sculptural Group, Steiner had said in relation to Lucifer and the evolution of the earth and humanity: 'Ear and larynx in the human being have only been divided from one another since Earth evolution began. On Old Moon they were a single organ. The small vocal folds on the larynx today, like small wings, were huge widenings which then went to form the lower auricle. Huge auricles existed there, while the upper ear, which now passes outward, was formed from the forehead. And what is today separate, so that when we speak and sing, this passes outward and we only listen with the ears, passed inward during the Moon period, and from there flowed into the music of the spheres. The whole human being was ear. This is because the ears were wings; and so you have ear, larynx and wing formations which move harmoniously and melodically with the reverberations of the world ether, and then give rise to the curious appearance of Lucifer; formations which draw in what is macrocosmic, for Lucifer only localized something that essentially is only cosmic.' (GA 157, p. 254.) Many years later, Rudolf Steiner would say in Dornach: 'We must succeed not only in looking at the human head with the ears on each side of it, with larynx, and stunted shoulder blades, but, by transforming natural form, we must succeed in having a single unity emerge from chest, head, wings, larynx and ears through the growth of the shoulder blades, through the interlacing of the larynx with the ears so that a luciferic figure appears' (GA 157, p. 254). Lucifer, as Steiner put it on 3 July 1918, again in Berlin, is an 'expanded' larynx ('We must think away from the human form what is most ahrimanic in the human being, thus think away the head, in place of which then the ears and auricles, the outer ear are substantially enlarged, spiritualized naturally and formed into wings, shaped into an organ which is, however, wrapped around its body, and the larynx likewise expanded—so that head, wings, ears form a single organ together. And the wings, the primary organ, are what appear as the figure of Lucifer.' GA 181, p. 315). The larynx determines Lucifer's whole form and itself possesses a connection to the ear: '[...] So we must picture this: Lucifer is a figure who absorbs the music of the spheres, draws it in to the organism of ear and wings; and without the individuality giving utterance, the cosmos, the music of the spheres itself speaks, once again through the same organ that, reconfigured in front into the larynx is thus another metamorphosis of the human form.' (Ibid.) As Steiner already described in Elberfeld in 1915, the being of Lucifer with his wings lives immersed 'in the harmony of the spheres'; Lucifer wings his way through space, 'through the waves of the harmony of the spheres' (GA 159, p. 293). Eight years later, on 7 October 1923, in a further elucidation, Steiner said in Dornach: 'In the luciferic realm there is an encircling, a moving around in waves so that [the wings] [of Lucifer], in their wave-shaped forms, feel their way toward everything that exists in the cosmos as mysterious, spiritual formations. And what is sensed in these wave motions passes through the ear structure into the inner being of Lucifer, and there reverberates onward. Through the ear structures the Lucifer being grasps what it senses through the wings, and through the larynx connected with them what weaves in the living forms becomes creative word. Thus if you perceive a luciferic being of this kind with its yellow-reddish formations of wings, ears and larynx, you find in this whole larynx bound up in an organic whole with wings and ears what acts within the cosmos by sensing, touching into, the mysteries of the cosmos through the wings, experiencing these cosmic mysteries through the ear structures that bear these effects further inward, and expressing these mysteries of the cosmos in the creative word' (GA 229, p. 52).

[130] GA 159, p. 249.

[131] Ibid., p. 292.

[132] GA 272, p. 100.

[133] GA 159, p. 248.

[134] Cf. Peter Selg, *Die Kultur der Selbstlosigkeit*, op. cit., p. 33f. Rudolf Steiner's Christ Group in Dornach was intended, *at one and the same time*, to depict the sheath-forces of the future manifestation of Christ *and* the historically incarnated Christ Jesus at the beginning of our era ('Yes, that is the Christ, this is how my eye of spirit beheld him in Palestine', said Steiner on 18 December 1920, in Dornach, to Willem Zeylmans van Emmichoven [in: M.J. Krück von Poturzyn (ed.), *Wir erlebten Rudolf Steiner. Erinnerungen seiner Schüler*, Stuttgart 1967, p. 255]; and in a text about the sculpture which Edith Maryon translated into English, Rudolf Steiner wrote: 'Those with a Christian sensibility will find in him [the Representative of Humanity] the embodiment of the figure of Jesus as he really appeared according to the means available to spiritual science. Depictions of Jesus all come from a later period, after all, and do not convey a picture that corresponds to the reality.' Rudolf Steiner Archive, Dornach; notebook page no. 5091).

[135] Speaking to Friedrich Rittelmeyer, Steiner emphasized that he had tried to depict Christ 'at the moment of temptation' (Friedrich Rittelmeyer, *Meine Lebensbegegnung mit Rudolf Steiner*, op. cit., p. 79). It seems of key importance here that the Christ being—in contrast to the corresponding stance of avoidance adopted by the Essenes (cf. GA 148)—here enters into a real encounter with the ahrimanic and luciferic powers. In his remarks on art in 1915, Rudolf Steiner repeatedly pointed out that formative principles of the luciferic-ahrimanic beings can be rediscovered in the central figure of Christ ('[…] In this central figure you will see that the whole left side tends upward toward Lucifer, and that the left part of the forehead is different from the right side, which tends toward Ahriman. The left half of the face follows the hand raised aloft, and the right half the hand extending downward. And this brings to expression the fact that a great inner mobility must inform the central figure than can exist in a human being.' GA 157, p. 242). Thus the motion of Christ's hands toward the adversarial powers—as intrinsic, soul-spiritual movement—affects the whole configuration of Christ's countenance ('And the Christ lifts his gaze and creases his forehead *as he raises his creased forehead to Lucifer*', GA 159, p. 259; author's emphasis): 'thus the head also had to be made somewhat asymmetric, since this figure is intended to show that the movements of the right hand, the left hand, the right arm and so on not only express the inner soul, but that in a being such as Christ who lives entirely within the soul, the form of the forehead and the whole of the rest of the figure are involved, far more so than could be true of a human being who makes this gesture' (GA 181, p. 317). On 30 March 1919, giving a slightly different emphasis, Rudolf Steiner said: 'You will have noticed that we have tried to depict this Representative of Humanity such that he must in fact appear in his entirety as otherwise only the features of the human face can appear. The features of the human countenance express the life of soul. We speak of physiognomy, we speak in respect of certain outward human expressions of gestures, and we know that this mobility expressed in physiognomy and gestures is connected with soul life. In the Representative of Humanity in our Group

we did not try to depict only a countenance possessing a physiognomy of expression such as a human face possesses between birth and death, but adhering to the same principle as that which forms the human face alone in nature, we tried to form the whole figure, making every part, every limb into an extended countenance in a sense.' (GA 190, p. 99.)

136   GA 161, p. 216f. According to Steiner in his lecture of 12 June 1921, Lucifer and Ahriman in the sculptural Group are in a state in which Christ has 'conquered' them. (GA 342, p. 37; see the rest of the text in this context.)

137   GA 229, p. 151.

138   Cf. also the lecture in Dornach on 3 April 1915 in which Rudolf Steiner pointed to the Christ being 'in his Jupiter glory', 'in his future glory, fettering Ahriman in the sub-earthly realm with chains of light so that he cannot reach the human being, and overcoming Lucifer so that he cannot lead the human soul upon his paths'. (GA 161, p. 228.)

139   GA 157, p. 255f.

140   GA 181, p. 314.

141   Ibid., p. 313.

142   GA 272, p. 99f.

143   GA 159, p. 248f.

144   Ibid., p. 295.

145   GA 272, p. 99.

146   GA 159, p. 295.

147   Ibid.

148   Ibid., p. 234.

149   Ibid., p. 259.

150   Ibid.

151   Cf. Peter Selg, *Marie Steiner-von Sivers. Aufbau und Zukunft des Werkes von Rudolf Steiner*, Dornach 2006, p. 121.

152   Cf. GA 255b, p. 87ff and note 240.

153   GA 180, p. 177.

154   GA 164, p. 228.

155   For instance, on 3 July 1918, in Berlin, Steiner said that he would be 'very pleased' if every observer of the central figure would

experience it as being Christ Jesus, but then immediately added: 'But the artistic conception is not that of depicting a Christ Jesus. The artistic idea rests purely in artistic form, in the configuring of forms while the other is a novelistic or programmatic thought about depicting a Christ Jesus figure. At least in the realm of sculpture, what is artistic lives in form itself.' (GA 181, p. 313.) Nine months previously, on 21 October 1917, at a General Meeting of the St John's Building Association in Dornach, Rudolf Steiner said: 'Whoever calls the Group a Christ Group must do so through their personal conviction, because it strikes them as such, so that they can regard and address the central figure as that of Christ. Here too it is not good to set something in stone in advance, to dictate what it must be. What appears before us here is initially the Representative of Humanity, spirit-pervaded, internalized humanity. Naturally some will immediately associate this internalized humanity with the Christ being, and will be right to do so. But it will not be good to emblemize the Group, define it narrowly as Christ Group and so forth. Leave it to each person who seeks to interpret this Group themselves to determine what name they wish to give it.' (GA 292, p. 416.) In response to the accusation made a few years later by the theologian Frohn-meyer (cf. note 250) that Steiner was indeed imposing upon his adherents and other visitors to the sculpture the idea that the central figure was none other than an image of Christ ('"This ideal human being...", said Steiner to the viewers present, "...must certainly be the true picture of Christ."'), Steiner remarked (Basel, 3 December 1920): 'Not a single one of thousands of visitors who came to see [the sculpture] will be able to say that I ever said those words. Enough witnesses in the room can testify that, weighing my words carefully, I never said anything other than this: "The figure here given form appears to me through spiritual vision as the one who walked the earth in Palestine. I cannot shape him in any other way than as he appears to me. I do not impose this perception upon anyone else." Never, my dear listeners, was said what appears here in quotation marks: "...must certainly be the true picture of Christ."' (GA 255b, p. 210.)

156   GA 194, p. 188.

157   GA 165, p. 182.

158   Assja Turgenieff, *Erinnerungen an Rudolf Steiner…* op. cit., p. 96.

159   Ibid.

160   Ibid., p. 97.

161   GA 263/I, p. 238.

162   Cf. Peter Selg, *Marie Steiner-von Sivers…* op. cit., p. 128.

163   Ibid., p. 30.

164   Rudolf Steiner Archive, Dornach (note-page 6948).

165   GA 263/I, p. 232.

166   263/I, p. 238.

167   Ibid., p. 234.

168   Assja Turgenieff, quoted in Rex Raab, *Edith Maryon…* op. cit., p. 204.

169   Ibid.

170   In a letter of 20 November 1925, Ita Wegman drew attention to the instruction by Rudolf Steiner 'that all correspondence should be sent to the secretary. Otherwise the unity of work could easily be disturbed.' (Ita Wegman Archive, Arlesheim; cf. also the following passage in a letter from Gertrud Goyert to Ita Wegman on 5 February 1935: 'Heartfelt thanks for your kind letter. I was very pleased to receive such detailed and kindly words from you, and I could well understand that Dr Steiner saw you as the secretary of the Society and wanted you to be in written communication with the members.' Ita Wegman Archive.) The widespread misunderstanding that Ita Wegman had been responsible for drafting executive committee (Vorstand) minutes (that is, had occupied the conventional post of a 'secretary') not only ignores Rudolf Steiner's understanding of an esoteric, initiating executive after the Christmas Foundation Meeting, but also Wegman's specific abilities (and weaknesses). This fundamental divergence of interpretation of the idea of 'secretary' seems vital to Wegman's view of her role, and, not least, forms the background to her—condemned—initiative to continue Rudolf Steiner's 'Leading Thoughts' for the whole Vorstand (cf. Emanuel Zeylmans van Emmichiven, *Wer war Ita Wegman. Eine Dokumentation*, 3 vols., Dornach 2000, p. 70ff.).

¹⁷¹ Quoted in Peter Selg, *'Ich bin für Fortschreiten.' Ita Wegman und die Medizinische Sektion*, Dornach 2004, p. 60.

¹⁷² GA 175, p. 19.

¹⁷³ Ibid., p. 29.

¹⁷⁴ Cf. Rudolf Steiner's comments in a lecture on 31 May 1908 in the Hamburg course on the Gospel of John (GA 103, p. 213); also Peter Selg, *Rudolf Steiner und das Fünfte Evangelium*, op. cit., p. 132; and Harald Giersch, *Rudolf Steiner über die Wiederkunft Christi*, Dornach 1991.

¹⁷⁵ GA 175, p. 32ff.

¹⁷⁶ Assja Turgenieff, 'Aus der Arbeit an der Gruppe', op. cit., p. 6.

¹⁷⁷ Lecture of 10 July 1915; GA 157, p. 264f.

¹⁷⁸ Cf. GA 292, p. 316ff.

¹⁷⁹ Assja Turgenieff, *Erinnerungen an Rudolf Steiner...* op. cit., p. 98.

¹⁸⁰ Assja Turgenieff, 'Aus der Arbeit an der Gruppe', op. cit., p. 6.

¹⁸¹ Assja Turgenieff, *Erinnerungen an Rudolf Steiner...* op. cit., p. 98f.

¹⁸² Ibid.

¹⁸³ Assja Turgenieff, 'Aus der Arbeit an der Gruppe', op. cit., p. 8.

¹⁸⁴ 'The time came when the model was finished. Freed of scaffolding, it was shown to the people in Dornach at Christmas 1917.' (Ibid., p. 3.) In her first, typed version of this passage, Turgenieff put an autumn date on this showing of the work, but then made a hand-written correction. Given that preparation of the wood began already in May 1917, and Rex Raab's comment that Steiner added the 'Rock Being' in a preparatory stage in autumn 1917 (cf. *Edith Maryon...* op. cit. p. 200f.), Turgenieff's dating of the showing seems improbable. We need to consider whether Assja Turgenieff's dating might be out by a year—thus that Rudolf Steiner showed the almost complete plastiline model at the end of 1916, before his departure for Berlin, and perhaps already at this point had begun to model the additional Rock Being in the Group (which Turgenieff told Wilkes dated from the winter of 1917/18). This could also have delayed his departure for Berlin. Comparing her notes and records, it is apparent that Assja Turgenieff sometimes confused annual dates. In 1928 she dated her visit to Edith Maryon with her sister Natasha, during which she saw

early stages of the Group, as 'Easter 1916', later amending this (in her published accounts) to Easter 1915, which was very probably correct.

185   'He seemed inwardly moved, attentive to what people bring to their encounter with the work, and his words resounded like answers to our unexpressed questions.' (Assja Turgenieff, 'Aus der Arbeit an der Gruppe', op. cit., p. 3.)

186   Assja Turgenieff, *Erinnerungen...*, op. cit., p. 97 (cf. also: 'I could not make them [Ahriman and Lucifer] exactly as they are—he said—for this distortion of the human, which they are in reality, is something people cannot yet be shown, since they would not endure it.' Assja Turgenieff, 'Aus der Arbeit an der Gruppe', p. 3).

187   Assja Turgenieff, 'Aus der Arbeit an der Gruppe', p. 3.

188   Ibid., p. 4f.

189   Assja Turgenieff, *Erinnerungen...* op. cit., p. 97.

190   It seems likely this was so from Assja Turgenieff's later account of the visit of the eurythmy group, where she writes: 'On one occasion Dr Steiner fetched Frau Doktor and a few eurythmists from a rehearsal to show them the model of the Group. "Herr Doktor, the Group is tipping to the right, it is not in balance" was the first reaction of Mieta Waller. She had the invaluable gift of saying what she thought, whether it was tactful or not. "You are right", he replied after pondering for a moment, "to balance it I will need to add something on the left." "Herr Doktor, you must tell us a fairytale about the Group," said Frau Doktor; and so he soon related to us the legend of the "New Isis".' (Assja Turgenieff, *Erinnerungen...* op. cit., p. 97.)

191   But Assja Turgenieff's formulation in her early manuscript would suggest that Marie Steiner-von Sivers's request was *not* made during this first visit: 'Frau Doktor, *as I was told*, wished to hear a fairytale about the Group, and in the evening, in the joinery workshop, Rudolf Steiner then told us the new Isis legend.' ('Aus der Arbeit an der Gruppe', p. 5. Author's emphasis.)

192   Quoted in Assja Turgenieff, *Erinnerungen...*, op. cit., p. 97.

193   GA 180, p. 176f.

194   GA 271, p. 91ff.

195 Ibid., p. 118f.

196 GA 181, p. 312.

197 Ibid., p. 318.

198 'Life must be engendered especially through treatment of the surface or plane: curving the plane and then curving the curve again—this special handling of the surface [of the sculpture], its double curvature, and how this draws life from the surface itself, is something we only see when actually working with these things. And so you will see that what we intended does not lie solely in what is represented but also in a certain artistic treatment of the whole. Achieving the ahrimanic, luciferic and in turn the human qualities was not a matter of mere novelistic imitation, but the fashioning had to enter right into our fingertips, had to inform the configuration of the sculpture's surfaces, had to enter fully and completely into artistic shaping.' GA 181, p. 317f.

199 GA 181, p. 314.

200 Ibid., p. 316.

201 Ibid., p. 316.

202 Cf. here also Steiner's above-quoted remark to Assja Turgenieff: 'I sought to bring soul into it everywhere,' he said. 'In stone, the ancients sculpted outwards out of impulses of wisdom. In Christian sculpture one has to engrave warmth into the living material of the wood.' (*Erinnerungen*... op. cit., p. 98f.) Edith Maryon's personal diaries from these years, which may have recorded numerous conversations with Steiner relating to the developing sculpture, have not so far been discovered.

203 GA 181, p. 312f.

204 GA 183, p. 9.

205 Ibid., p. 12.

206 On 21 September 1918, for instance, Steiner said among other things: 'If you [...] stand before another person, two people always emerge from him to meet you: one whose form is in danger of fossilizing, becoming dense and rigid and growing together with the earth, and the other who is in danger of repelling everything that tends to mineralization and self-hardening, thus becoming very soft, jelly-like and ultimately dissolving into the universe

as spiritual automaton. These two beings appear, really, to those
equipped with initiation science when they observe someone.
One is always anxious, as I might put it—forgive me, one has to
use the words that language offers and therefore many things
sound paradoxical when we are pointing to the realm of reality—
that the people whom one encounters could all become suddenly
like those curious figures you can sometimes see sculpted from
cliffs, riders on horses as if formed from the rock, or other figures
in the mountains, sleeping maidens and so on; that people themselves could become like this, uniting with the rocks of the earth
and living on only in mineralized form. Or that they could expel
what draws them toward mineralization and become jelly-like so
that the organs that have contracted could swell up, so that their
ears could become huge, could swell to encompass the larynx too,
and merge with wing-type organs growing out of the shoulders—
everything as soft as a jelly-fish but as if emerging from the person's own surging wave-form.' (GA 184, p. 176f.) In relation to the
form-language of the building and the sculpture he said shortly
afterwards in the same lecture: 'Look at the shapes of our building: everywhere straight lines pass over into curves, balance is
sought, everywhere the attempt is made to dissolve rigidity into
fluidity, everywhere rest is created within movement but stillness
in turn is brought into motion. This is the very spiritual nature
of our building. As human beings of the future we must seek to
create something in art and life by knowing this—that below is
Ahriman who seeks to make everything ossify, rigidify, and above
is Lucifer, who wishes everything to evaporate […]. And so our
building has become a state of equilibrium in the universe, one
wrested, raised from the realms of Ahriman and of Lucifer. All
this culminates in the central figure of our Group, in this Representative of Humanity in which everything of a luciferic and
ahrimanic nature is to be extinguished […] Regarding our Group
one can feel various things. One can feel at the centre the Representative of Humanity with his lines and planes and forms from
which everything luciferic and ahrimanic has been expunged. The
forms are still present but to the degree that these qualities can be

expunged in the human form, the luciferic and ahrimanic have been expunged.' (GA 184, p. 169ff.) Ten days later, in Dornach, Rudolf Steiner then accentuated the special importance of the central, rhythmic, mediating and balancing system in the configuring of the Christ sculpture ('the Representative of Humanity, who is, however, formed in such a way that the forces of breathing, of the trunk, heart activity and so forth, predominate', GA 183, p. 177; cf. Peter Selg, *Vom Logos menschlicher Physis. Die Entfaltung einer anthroposophischen Humanphysiologie im Werk Rudolf Steiners*. Vol. 2, Dornach 2006, p. 604ff., and Peter Selg, *Mysterium cordis. Studien zu einer sakramentalen Physiologie des Herzorgans. Aristoteles, Thomas von Aquin, Rudolf Steiner*, Dornach 2006, p. 112ff.).

[207] In his Dornach lecture of 10 November 1918, Rudolf Steiner said of the new edition of his *Philosophy of Freedom* published at the end of the war: 'The extent to which good can come from the terrible storms that await us will be entirely dependent upon whether people will or will not begin to gain understanding of things such as those I inaugurated with my *Philosophy of Freedom* and suchlike. Everyone does what they can, don't they, as it lies in their karma or their tendency. Of the things I myself have done I want to emphasize the production of thoughts that can give structure to the life of society and which, at the beginning of the 1890s, a quarter of a century ago now, I hoped would meet with a response. Today, again, I hope they can elicit a response now that the second edition has been published after a quarter of a century: perhaps they may meet with such response and resonance not only despite but because of the difficult times that are now beginning.' (GA 185a, p. 64f.)

[208] GA 263/I, p. 173.

[209] Ibid.

[210] GA 182, p. 84. In relation to various comments by Rudolf Steiner in these years about the culturally decisive task of Goetheanism and anthroposophy, see my survey 'Die geistesgeschichtliche Bedeuting der Anthroposophie', in Peter Selg, *Vom Logos menschlicher Physis*. Vol. 1, Chapter III: 'Erhöhung der Anthropologie durch Anthroposophie—die Dreligliederung des Menschen (1911-1919)', p. 253ff.

211 GA 263/I, p. 29.

212 Ibid., p. 51.

213 Cf. Rex Raab, op. cit., p. 322ff.

214 GA 263/I, p. 233.

215 Ibid., p. 27.

216 Ibid., p. 28.

217 GA 263/I, p. 29.

218 Ibid., p. 29f.

219 See notes 247 and 250.

220 GA 263/I, p. 30.

221 Ibid., p. 31.

222 Ibid., p. 31f.

223 Ibid., p. 33.

224 Ibid.

225 Ibid.

226 Cf. Peter Selg, *Die Kultur der Selbstlosigkeit. Rudolf Steiner, das Fünfte Evangelium und das Zeitalter der Extreme*, Dornach 2006.

227 Michael Bauer, *Gesammelte Werke*, Vol. 4, Stuttgart 1990, p. 68. Cf. also Christoph Rau, *Michael Bauer. Sein Leben und seine Begegnung with Friedrich Rittelmeyer*, Dornach 1995, p. 92ff. and Peter Selg, *Michael Bauer. Ein esoterischer Schüler Rudolf Steiners*, Dornach 2006, p. 80f.

228 GA 263/I, p. 34.

229 Ibid.

230 Ibid., p. 36.

231 Ibid., p. 37.

232 Ibid., p. 37f.

233 Thus on 14 September 1919, Edith Maryon wrote to Rudolf Steiner as follows about her impressions of reading the translation by Elisabeth Bowen-Wedgewood: 'The second translation of chapters 1 and 2 of your book has finally arrived, but I find it endlessly difficult to form a judgement about it. First of all I read the two chapters purely from the standpoint of an English book, and found that it is well written in perfectly good, modern English, the images entirely in keeping with English, no trace of it being a translation from German (unlike my poor endeavour!). Only here

and there did I find a sentence that seemed to me to be too modern 'slang', but this is probably not felt as misplaced in England today. It flows well and holds the reader's interest. I could imagine that, if properly published, it would even become a popular book. The translator is also already a practised and well-known writer; she has much influence in these circles and could greatly help the book to be published by the Nat. Lab. Press. Then I read it in comparison with the original. And it turns out that the 2 translators have allowed themselves much freedom with the sentence structure and—in my opinion—without good reason except in 1 or 2 places. I mean they have made 2 or 3 sentences from one, or one from 2 etc. This happens on average two or more times on every page. But this could be quickly corrected and restored. I think it would be desirable because it gives a different nuance. Then three-quarters of the words in bold are normally printed in their version, so that the accentuated word has only the same value as the others. It seems to me also they have often translated too freely, that is, they have tried to understand the meaning and then to reproduce it freely in their own way. So it is a bit like seeing a blue painting and making it into a green one in memory! It is the same with the paragraphs, they make entirely new ones, arbitrarily. Finally I compared chapter 1 in the two versions, and find the other one reads more easily overall, which is very understandable as one of the translators has written so much already, while I have not at all! I find my sentences often more awkward but perhaps more faithful to the original in some respects, others are actually like the other version, and some better (is that immodest?). But ultimately I find that the best thing would be to use the other translation since the people [who did it] have a following in England and I have none, and they must work there and will have more interest in it if they can create their own tools. The only thing I would insist on is that the emphases on particular words are also emphasized in English, and that an arbitrary sentence structure should not be introduced.' GA 263/I, p. 39f.

234 GA 194, p. 186. In the context of another lecture, Rudolf Steiner said of the real state of balance of the Christ being or the Christ

sculpture: 'We can […] distinguish what lies above a certain level in the human being, in a sense, and what lies below a certain level. That is to say, I explain to almost every person I think can have some understanding of this, every person who comes to view the wooden sculptural Group in Dornach: "Christ in the centre as Representative of Humanity, Ahriman and Lucifer on either side"—so that the human being we have before us can only be imagined by picturing everything in him as a state of balance. On the one hand is the supersensible, on the other the subsensible. The human being really always only embodies the state of balance between the supersensible and the subsensible.' (GA 324a, p. 152.) In the Christ figure, as Steiner says in another passage, 'a synthesis of everything sensory and supersensible is placed before us'. (GA 342, p. 37.)

[235]   GA 194, p. 186.

[236]   The forms of the Goetheanum and the path that could be followed within it from West to East were, as Steiner put it already on 28 June 1914 in Dornach, a direct expression of the 'path of the ordinary self to the higher self'. GA 286, p. 159.

[237]   GA 298, p. 42.

[238]   Cf. here also, for instance, Eugen Kolisko, *Vom therapeutischen Charakter der Waldorfschule* (ed. by Peter Selg), Dornach 2002.

[239]   GA 333, p. 101.

[240]   GA 263/I, p. 41.

[241]   Rudolf Steiner, *Aufbaugedanken und Gesinnungsbildung*, Dornach 1942, p. 40. See Erich Zimmer, *Rudolf Steiner als Architekt von Wohn- und Zweckbauten*, Stuttgart 1985, in relation to the artistic and architectural history and form of the dwellings, and the collaboration on this between Steiner and Maryon.

[242]   GA 263/I, p. 44.

[243]   Elisabeth Vreede (1879-1943) had become acquainted with Edith Maryon no later than 1913/14 in Berlin, where Vreede likewise lived at 17 Motzstrasse. She was writing her doctoral thesis and, at Steiner's request, giving basic courses in science. Vreede then came to Dornach for two years and lived with Edith Maryon before returning temporarily to Berlin in 1916 to work there on

behalf of prisoners of war. Various biographies and memoirs refer to Elisabeth Vreede—who after the war would compile an archive of Steiner's lectures and writings in the joinery workshop, and in 1923/24, with Maryon, would join the esoteric Vorstand envisaged by Steiner—as Edith Maryon's 'friend'. Vreede's commemorative words for Maryon, on 30 March 1943 in Arlesheim (three weeks after the death of Ita Wegman and only five months before her own passing) have not survived but very probably were among the most important accounts of Maryon's life's work and character. (For the context of this Arlesheim memoir of Maryon by Vreede, see Madeleine van Deventer/Elisabeth Knottenbelt (eds), *Elisabeth Vreede. Ein Lebensbild*, Arlesheim 1976, p. 11f.)

[244] GA 263/I, p. 43/46.

[245] Ibid., p. 49.

[246] Ibid., p. 51.

[247] For more on this see in particular the documentary volume of lectures by Steiner with extensive Introduction and commentary edited by Alexander Lüscher and Ulla Trapp, *Die Anthroposophie und ihre Gegner*, GA 255b, Dornach 2003, and also the account by Lorenzo Ravagli, *Unter Hammer und Hakenkreuz. Der völkisch-nationalsozialistische Widerstand gegen die Anthroposophie*, Stuttgart 2004. From 1919, Stuttgart, and Württemberg altogether, was one of the chief centres of agitation against the public profile of anthroposophy, with aggressive attacks upon it from, among others, the nationalist 'Württemberg Citizens Party', and commentaries published by Traub, Professor of Theology in Tübingen (*Rudolf Steiner als Philosoph und Theosoph*, Tübingen 1919).

[248] GA 263/I, p. 46.

[249] Ibid., p. 47.

[250] Cf. J. Frohnmeyer, *Die theosophische Bewegung, ihre Geschichte, Darstellung und Beurteilung*, Stuttgart 1920. Rudolf Steiner first referred in his public lecture in Basel on 3 December 1920, and then again four weeks later in a public lecture in Stuttgart (cf. 255b, p. 209f. and 289f.) to comments on the sculpture by the Protestant theologian and missionary Frohnmeyer ('Currently a nine-metre high statue of the ideal human being is being carved

in Dornach: above with "luciferic" features and below with animal characteristics').

251 GA 263/I, p. 52.

252 Ibid., p. 51.

253 Ibid., p. 53.

254 Ibid.

255 'The full nature of humanity is to be depicted in this Group. The human being is in reality what must seek balance between what wishes to go beyond the human and what draws the human being down to earth, between the luciferic and the ahrimanic. *In terms of physiology, physical nature,* the luciferic principle is in fact the force in us that induces fever, the pleuritic tendency, that induces temperature in us, warmth conditions that dissolve us and make us scatter abroad in the world; while the ahrimanic is the force that ossifies and calcifies us. *In terms of soul,* the human being is what must seek balance between enraptured mysticism, between theory, between everything that strives upward toward insubstantiality, albeit light-illumined, and what draws us down to the pedantic, philistine, materialistic, intellectual level. *In terms of spirit,* the human being must maintain balance between what continually lulls us asleep and induces us always, as it were, to surrender ourselves to the cosmos—the luciferic—and what continually awakens us, what electrifies us with a power that will not let us sleep—the ahrimanic. We do not understand the human being if we cannot place him in the centre between the luciferic and the ahrimanic.' (GA 199, p. 152; author's emphasis.)

256 Cf. Peter Selg, *Marie Steiner-von Sivers...* op. cit., p. 160.

257 Assja Turgenieff, *Erinnerungen...,* op. cit., p. 99.

258 Assja Turgenieff, 'Aus der Arbeit an der Gruppe', p. 7.

259 Assja Turgenieff, *Was ist mit dem Goetheanumbau geschehen?* Basel 1957, p. 26.

260 GA 200, p. 133.

261 GA 263/I, p. 182.

262 GA 24, p. 12.

263 Ibid., p. 51.

264 Hans Müller-Weidemann, 'Zum Motto der Sozialethik', in: Rich-

ard Steel (ed.), *Das soziale Hauptgesetz—soziale Fragen im Spannungsfeld der Gegenwart*, p. 15.

265   Cf. also Maryon's memorial relief for deceased members of the Anthroposophical Society such as Sophie Stinde, Olga von Sivers and Maude Künstler, her plaque for a memorial to the war dead, or her relief for the boy Theo Faiss who suffered a fatal accident in Dornach (in Rex Raab, *Edith Maryon…*, op. cit., p. 246ff.).

266   GA 202, p. 256. In this context, however, Rudolf Steiner also said: 'Outward earth existence, in so far as it is an outcome of former eras, will pass away, and those who believe they can perpetuate old habits of thought and will are hoping in vain. What must emerge is a new discernment and a new will in all spheres. We must acquaint ourselves with the idea of the demise of a culture, of a civilization; but we must look into the human heart, into the spirit that dwells in the human being. We must have trust in this human heart and this human spirit that live in us, so that through all that we can do within the ruins of the old civilization, new forms arise, truly new forms.' GA 202, p. 254, author's emphasis; cf. also my study *Die Wärme-Meditation*, Dornach 2006, p. 58ff. in relation to the perspectives developed by Steiner in these lectures—with which Edith Maryon was quite clearly deeply conversant—on a new Creation emerging from the will and morality of the human being.

267   See Willem Zeylmans van Emmichoven's account of his visit to the studio on 18 December 1920 in M.J. Krück von Poturzyn (ed.), *Wir erlebten Rudolf Steiner. Erinnerungen seiner Schüler*, p. 253.

268   GA 263/I, p. 56.

269   Ibid., p. 58.

270   Ibid., p. 58f.

271   Ita Wegman Archive, Arlesheim.

272   In his preparatory notebook entries for the course, Rudolf Steiner wrote, among other things: 'Scepticism cannot figure in these lectures. The founding thought is that the threefolding impulse fulfils the most essential demands of the present. 1. One must speak out of love for the work, and out of love of human beings.—Imponderables.—2. One must see through the super-

stitions that the economic question could be resolved on its own. 3. Today one must recognize firstly the lack of a sense for spiritual productivity and secondly the lack of interest in the needs of others.' (GA 338, p. 269.) In his biography of Rudolf Steiner, Christoph Lindenberg wrote of this course for speakers: 'Around 50 speakers took part in this course, and in the following weeks they gave around 200 lectures. In 1923, Steiner commented on this campaign in very drastic terms: "I gave this speakers' course before a horde was let loose on the German public. Just look at the reverberations of what this cavalcade caused! All the ramifications of this in the public domain. The grotesqueness of what resulted sometimes exceeded everything."' (*Rudolf Steiner. Eine Chronik. 1861-1925*, p. 454f.)

273   GA 263/I, p. 59.

274   Ibid., p. 60.

275   Ibid., p. 62.

276   In relation to the intensifying and in some respects initially culminating attacks, cf. Steiner's reply to them in his public lectures in Stuttgart on 4 January and 25 May 1921 (GA 255b) as well as the essay by the historian Karl Heyer in June 1921, 'On the Opponents to Threefolding' (in *Die Drei*, Year 1, no. 3, p. 3776ff.). On 18 January 1921, in an internal meeting in Stuttgart, Steiner spoke of the real 'destructive will' of his opponents. Three months later, in Dornach, he referred explicitly to the threat hanging over the Goetheanum building ('There is the greatest desire in the world to take this from us!' GA 204, p. 107), and said in this context: 'The campaign of opposing forces will grow ever fiercer [...]. And it is not possible to say, as yet, that this opposition has reached its peak. Such opposition is still far from reaching its peak. [...] Humanity is strongly possessed by the powers of evil, by love of evil. And those who do not pay heed today to this love of evil, to this ever increasing and intensifying love of evil in the battle waged against anthroposophic spiritual science, will not be able to form a sense, an awareness of the opposing forces and powers that are still to manifest. For years I have been speaking of this ever-intensifying opposition. [...] But the deciding thing for us is the strength to

stand firm upon a ground we have recognized to be right and true. Every possible attempt will be made to undermine this ground, you can be quite sure of that. [...] It is up to us to do as much work as can possibly be done; and if the ground is to be taken from under us so that we fall into the opening rift, nevertheless the work we have done must be of a kind to find its spiritual way through the world. You see, these are the death throes of a world going under; but even in its death throes it can hit out wildly like a madman, and such blows can kill one.' (GA 204, p. 105ff.)

[277] GA 263/I, p. 63.

[278] GA 263/I, p. 63f.

[279] Thus at a general meeting of the Goetheanum Association at the end of June, Rudolf Steiner found that a sum of 390,000 Swiss francs was lacking for further work and completion of the building, whereupon he repeated his concern at 'how little the so-called "practical person" today is fully equal to his tasks'. In this context Steiner said of the situation of the anthroposophic movement and Society, 'It is self-evident that work of an ideal and spiritual nature suffers from this fact, and cannot reach the level it ought to.' (Quoted in Christoph Lindenberg, *Rudolf Steiner. Eine Chronik. 1861-1925*, op. cit., p. 462.)

[280] Sofie Bauer, quoted in Rex Raab, *Edith Maryon...* op. cit., p. 346.

[281] GA 263/I, p. 63.

[282] Ibid., p. 64.

[283] GA 263/I, p. 66.

[284] Ibid., p. 68.

[285] Ibid.

[286] Ibid., p. 69.

[287] Ibid., p. 71.

[288] Ibid., p. 71f.

[289] GA 268, p. 273.

[290] GA 263/I, p. 73f.

[291] Ibid.

[292] Fifteen months later, on 28 February 1923 in Stuttgart, Rudolf Steiner would say that the anthroposophic movement could by no means be destroyed by its opponents, adding by way of expla-

nation: 'It cannot be [destroyed]. The greatest danger from our opponents is for the Anthroposophical Society, *if you like, for me personally and so forth.* But no harm can come to the anthroposophic movement, at most it can be delayed by its adversaries.' (GA 257, p. 142.) Cf. note 276 ('but in its death throes it can hit out wildly like a madman, and such blows can kill one').

293 GA 263/I, p. 74.

294 Ibid., p. 76.

295 Ibid.

296 Ibid.

297 Ibid., p. 182.

298 GA 303, p. 330.

299 Ibid., p. 322.

300 Ibid., p. 323.

301 Quoted by Willem Zeylmans van Emmichoven, in, M.J. Krück von Poturzyn (ed.), *Wir erlebten Rudolf Steiner...* op. cit., p. 255.

302 GA 263/I, p. 78.

303 Ibid., p. 79.

304 Ibid., p. 80.

305 Ibid., p. 85f.

306 Ibid., p. 82.

307 Ibid., p. 84.

308 Ibid.

309 Ibid., p. 85.

310 Ibid., p. 79.

311 Ibid., p. 86.

312 Ita Wegman Archive, Arlesheim.

313 Cf. GA 210.

314 GA 263/I, p. 87.

315 Ibid., p.88.

316 Ibid., p. 98f.

317 GA 211, p. 189.

318 Ibid., p. 193.

319 Quoted in Christoph Lindenberg, *Rudolf Steiner. Eine Chronik...,* op. cit., p. 484.

320 GA 263/I, p. 92.

[321] Ibid., p. 93.

[322] Ibid., p. 94.

[323] For more on Munich as an early hotbed of nationalist and Nazi activity cf. among other publications the book by David Clay Large, *Where Ghosts Walked: Munich's Road to the Third Reich*, W.W. Norton 1996. There were also fierce attacks on Steiner in Munich from 1918 onwards by Otto Zimmermann, a Jesuit priest there, who published invectives in the journal *Stimmen der Zeit* ['Voices of the Time'].

[324] GA 263/I, p. 95.

[325] 'I told the Stuttgart executive committee about the danger for Rudolf Steiner and proposed setting up security protection for him. But the committee rejected this; they were embarrassed about discussing such a thing with Steiner and told me that if I thought this necessary I should raise the matter with him myself. After a lecture at the Sieglehaus in Stuttgart, I presented my concern to him in the cloakroom, with some embarrassment. Rudolf Steiner said, in perfectly friendly manner, "So you think they want to bump me off?" Me: "Indeed, yes, I am convinced of it." Rudolf Steiner, calmly: "Yes, that is very probable." At the same time his eyes altered with indescribable speed.' (Hans Büchenbacher, 'Munich 1922', in, Erika Beltle/Kurz Vierl (eds.), *Erinnerungen an Rudolf Steiner*, Stuttgart 1979, p. 323.

[326] Ibid., p. 234.

[327] Ibid., p. 236.

[328] GA 263/I, p. 95.

[329] Ibid., p. 96.

[330] Ibid., p. 97.

[331] Annemarie Dubach-Donath, *Die Kunst der Eurythmie—Erinnerungen*, Dornach 1983, p. 124.

[332] Shortly after Rudolf Steiner's departure Edith Maryon—referring among other things to Eugen Kolisko's controversial lecture at the Vienna medical association (cf. Peter Selg, *Anfänge anthroposophischer Heilkunst*, Dornach 2000, p. 149ff.)—wrote to Rudolf Steiner: 'I am waiting impatiently for someone to write to us here with news of the trip and a report on the situation (relating to the

Congress) since I hope that all the newspaper reports of Dr Kolisko's lecture may have been somewhat exaggerated, and that we have not been so greatly harmed as might at first have appeared. I would also really like to know if one can sense anything in Vienna of the hostile attacks that have occurred in Germany, or whether we remain spared this there? It would be very fine indeed if the Austrians were to show themselves to be more dignified and reasonable than, sadly, the Germans have done. Then one could have greater hope for the future of the central powers. [...] I hope you are well and the first lecture went well? Did a great many people attend? I wish I also could be there. Here all is quiet, difficult and boring, also fearful, one does not know what might happen and would like to hear and experience everything that is going on! Please take great care.' (GA 263/I, p. 97f.) Six days later, Maryon received a first, confident and optimistic letter from Steiner; on 12 June he wrote again from Vienna: 'My dear Edith Maryon, Since the first letter no letter has arrived here from the studio. Here all continues well, and no continuing echoes of the Kolisko prelude. But this does nevertheless rumble under the surface, though is not yet appearing outwardly. One has to be pleased at the reception but should not succumb to any illusions. What we must seek to realize can only slowly come about but we must also pay heed to the moment. I will be very glad to be able to be back in the studio, but this can only happen on Saturday now since a quantity of work remains here for me to do that I could not get done during the strenuous days of lecturing; Tomorrow, Tuesday, I am still here, then in Horn on Wednesday and can only depart on Thursday. But after that there will be no further delays. Warmest greetings from Rudolf Steiner.' (GA 263/I, p. 101f.)

333　Cf. Peter Selg, *Marie Steiner-von Sivers. Aufbau und Zukunft des Werkes von Rudolf Steiner*, Dornach 2006. The reminiscence of Willem Zeylmans van Emmichoven—who on 17 December 1920 received an appointment with Steiner for a discussion the next day, but only got past Maryon with great difficulty to see Steiner—shows the lengths to which Maryon went to protect him from the endless requests for discussions and advice from members of the

Anthroposophical Society. Van Emmichoven wrote: 'The next day I arrived punctually in the vestibule of the studio, where a lady was at work carving a wooden sculpture. She asked me in very friendly fashion what I wanted. "I have an appointment with Dr Steiner." "Herr Dr Steiner is not seeing anyone today." "But please, he himself arranged this." "No, he is not seeing anyone today." This was too much for me. "Please be so good as to tell him I am here." Before any further refusal came, the door opened and a lady appeared, who turned out to be Dutch, and said: "Do come in, Herr Doktor is expecting you." And so I went in.' (Willem Zeylmans van Emmichoven in, M.J. Krück von Poturzyn [ed.], *Wir erlebten Rudolf Steiner*... op. cit., p. 253.)

[334] For more on the personality and biography of Sofie Bauer (1882-1958) see the obituary by Maria Kleiner in *Mitteilungen aus der anthroposophischen Arbeit in Deutschland*, 1959, issue no. 47. Sofie Bauer, the daughter of teachers in Göppingen, belonged to Edith Maryon's closer circle of acquaintances in Dornach, along with the Stuttgart painter Maria Kleiner (1888-1966) and Elisabeth Vreede (cf. note 243). With Maria Kleiner, Irma Kucerova and Marie Kalähne, Sofie Bauer nursed Maryon at the end of her life. On 31 December 1922, Sofie Bauer was the first to detect an altered smell in the Goetheanum and to alert the night-watchman, who then discovered the fire. With Rudolf Steiner and Edith Maryon she spent part of the night of the fire in a small hut close to the joinery workshop ('Sofie Bauer wanted to turn on the heating in the hut, and brought hot tea. Miss Maryon waved her away so as not to disturb Dr Steiner, who sat by the window and gazed into the flames. But he turned round and said to Miss Maryon, "Let her, after all, if she is so kind as to do this!"' Quoted in Maria Kleiner, 'Nachruf auf Sofie Bauer', p. 47). After Edith Maryon's death, and Rudolf Steiner's own illness, Sofie Bauer and Maria Kleiner took shared responsibility for the safety of the food eaten by Steiner, not leaving the joinery workshop during the seven months of Steiner's illness, 'in other words they were in the vestibule [of the studio] day and night and had to sample everything that came from the kitchen before Dr Steiner received it. They both fulfilled

their tasks faithfully and responsibly. It was in the nature of the two of them that they never disclosed the words, "Sofie Bauer and Maria Kleiner have never disappointed me." Rudolf Steiner's thanks to them was apparent in the arrangements he made for his cremation: the Vorstand travelled in the first car, and Sofie Bauer and Maria Kleiner in the second.' (Margot Rössler, 'Nachruf auf Maria Kleiner', in: *Mitteilungen aus der anthroposophischen Arbeit in Deutschland*, Easter 1967, p. 59.) Both Sofie Bauer and Maria Kleiner, who were very dedicated to Wegman, worked for many years after Rudolf Steiner's death at Ita Wegman's clinic in Arlesheim before they returned to southern Germany in the thirties, dying decades later in Murrhardt and Stuttgart.

[335] Letter from Edith Maryon to Sofie Bauer, 19 September 1922, Rudolf Steiner Archive, Dornach.

[336] GA 263/I, p. 224.

[337] GA 214, p. 194f.

[338] GA 211, p. 177f.

[339] GA 36, p. 332.

[340] GA 263/I, p. 104.

[341] Ibid., p. 106.

[342] GA 300b, p. 147.

[343] Cf. especially GA 218, p. 67ff, where Rudolf Steiner spoke of the temporal rhythm and the form configurations of ahrimanic-luciferic influences.

[344] Letter from Edith Maryon to Sofie Bauer, 15 November 1922. Rudolf Steiner Archive, Dornach.

[345] GA 218, p. 157.

[346] GA 263/I, p. 183.

[347] Rudolf Steiner, *Die verborgenen Seiten des Menschendaseins und der Christus-Impuls*, Dornach 1939, p. 33.

[348] Assja Turgenieff, *Erinnerungen an Rudolf Steiner*... op. cit., p. 103.

[349] 'Miss Maryon came running over from her flat to the joinery workshop and telephoned Dr Steiner. He came immediately [...].' (Notebook entry; Ita Wegman Archive, Arlesheim.)

[350] Assja Turgenieff, *Erinnerungen an Rudolf Steiner*..., op. cit., p. 106.

[351] Cf. Peter Selg, *Marie Steiner-von Sivers*... op. cit., p. 171.

352   London, 30 August 1922; GA 214, p. 194.

353   GA 260a, p. 230.

354   Ita Wegman, notebook entry. Ita Wegman Archive, Arlesheim.

355   GA 14, p. 71f.

356   GA 268, p. 261.

357   At the end of 1923, speaking possibly of this situation but very probably of further haemorrhages, Maryon wrote to Steiner (in an undated letter): 'Dear and respected teacher, since Tuesday, unfortunately, I have not been well. I believe that a small vein in my windpipe has burst, I have had several haemorrhages [though] not a great deal [of blood] at any one time. Frau Dr Wegman does not think it is dangerous, but wants to discuss it with you. I am very sorry indeed to be so stupid. Now I'm lying in bed and hope to be better in a few days. I feel very sad not to be able to get on with the work, I've had too much bad luck this year—not me alone though. I wish you would arrive here today. I did not telephone yesterday since the telephone [connection] is so bad, one hears almost nothing; now I am going to get Bauer to phone.' (GA 263/I, p. 166.)

358   GA 263/I, p. 115.

359   Ibid.

360   Ibid., p. 184.

361   Quoted in Rex Raab, *Edith Maryon*...op. cit., p. 352.

362   For more on Rudolf Steiner's physical condition (and the altered appearance of his movements) after the Goetheanum fire, see Peter Selg, *Marie Steiner-von Sivers*...op. cit., p. 195. In a reminiscence of the year 1924, Ludwig Polzer-Hoditz wrote: 'The work achieved by Rudolf Steiner that year was quite overwhelming, although he often felt very unwell and one could observe his suffering and weariness. When I was with him on one occasion in the studio during this period, he told me how difficult it was to convey the "striding" of the figure of the Representative of Humanity.' ('Erinnerungen an Rudolf Steiner', in Peter Tradowsky [ed.], Ludwig Polzer-Hoditz: *Erinnerungen an Rudolf Steiner*, Dornach 1985, p. 198f.)

363   Quoted in Rex Raab, *Edith Maryon*...op. cit., p. 353.

364 Rudolf Steiner Archive, Dornach (note-page 5880).

365 GA 263/I, p. 115.

366 Rudolf Steiner Archive, Dornach.

367 GA 263/I, p. 116.

368 Ibid.

369 GA 263, p. 117.

370 GA 259, p. 379.

371 GA 263/I, p. 117.

372 GA 84, p. 42f.

373 GA 263/I, p. 119.

374 Ibid., p. 118.

375 GA 263/I, p. 120.

376 Ibid., p. 121.

377 Ibid.

378 Letter from Edith Maryon to Rudolf Steiner (undated). Rudolf Steiner Archive, Dornach (not included in GA 263/I).

379 GA 263/I, p. 126.

380 Ibid., p. 127.

381 Cf. here especially the lectures of 21 May 1923 (Kristiania; GA 226) and 23 May 1923 (Berlin; GA 224). For more on the whole theme of the 'Michael festival' see for instance the studies by Manfred Schmidt-Brabant, *Michael-Gedanken und Drachenkräfte. Anregungen zu einem künftigen Michael-Fest*, Dornach 1992, and Gunhild Kacer: 'Das Michael-Thema im Lebensgang Rudolf Steiners' in: *Mitteilungen aus der anthroposophischen Arbeit in Deutschland*, Michaelmas 2000, p. 169-178. An extensive documentary study of the Michael teaching in Rudolf Steiner's whole opus is currently being prepared by the Ita Wegman Archive for fundamental research in anthroposophic medicine, as a continuation of Ita Wegman's early publication *Aus Michaels Wirken* (Stuttgart 1929).

382 GA 223, p. 86.

383 GA 226, p. 116.

384 GA 224, p. 214.

385 GA 217a, p. 152.

386 GA 263/I, p. 129.

387 Ibid.

388 Ibid., p. 132.

389 On 25 August 1923, Steiner wrote to Maryon from Ilkley: 'My dear Edith Maryon, things are well; let me tell you about my delayed arrival. We—Frau Dr, Mr Pyle, Dr Wachsmuth and I—were travelling according to plan from Stuttgart to Oldenzaal, the border station with Holland. There I was summoned forth because the customs wanted to inspect our registered luggage. So I went through the station barrier and was asked for our passports. But the man retained the passport of Frau Doktor, who had stayed in the train, and said he had to see her in person and would therefore bring the passport back to the train. So I got back in the train with only my passport. By the time of departure Frau Doktor's passport had still not come. I put on my overcoat—please note that I had not travelled without it—and went to look for the passport. But the train departed! Frau Doktor, Mr Pyle and Dr Wachsmuth were in the train while I was left in Oldenzaal. I soon discovered what had happened to the passport—which was in fact in the train, so all was well, except that I had been left behind. So I quickly got someone to phone the next stop to ask the others to get out there and say I would come with the next train—to Almelo. The next train was already there. I got in and then met Frau Doktor, Mr Pyle and Dr Wachsmuth in Almelo. Now all four of us had to wait in Almelo— we found good rooms; there was a wedding going on at the hotel, the people were shouting, dancing, a terrible hoo-hah. Next day we travelled on to Hook of Holland and thence to Harwich, and from there straight to Ilkley, arriving there on Saturday 24 hours late. It didn't matter that we arrived late except that we didn't go through London. I will therefore have to rely on the snuff arriving by post instead. So our journey was fraught with adventure. Many thanks for the letter, which I found here when I arrived. I am pleased to see that things are not going too badly there, and I hope that they will continue to improve. This evening I am due to give the first lecture. Despite the romance of the journey I am feeling sufficiently rested today. Here one is already in the North of England, from where I send my warmest greetings—Rudolf Steiner' (GA 263/I, p. 129f.). Edith Maryon's reply to this anecdote included the words: 'I can't

understand how both gentlemen had so little presence of mind that they both comfortably journeyed on instead of one of them getting out at the right moment. *That surely would not have happened if it had been me.'* (GA 263/I, p. 140; author's emphasis.)

390 GA 263/I, p. 131.

391 Ibid., p. 134f.

392 Ibid., p. 136.

393 Cf. Emanuel Zeylmans van Emmichoven, *Wer war Ita Wegman. Eine Dokumentation*, volume I, Dornach 2000, p. 144ff.

394 Ibid., p. 137.

395 Ibid., p.140.

396 Ibid., p. 140.

397 Ibid., p. 141.

398 Ibid., p. 141f.

399 'If it has been possible in recent years to give lectures in Stratford, Oxford, London and Penmaenmawr, and to further the cause of anthroposophy and eurythmy, so Edith Maryon's quiet work of mediating between the Goetheanum and the English-speaking world must be seen as the prime mover in this' (GA 263/I, p. 233).

400 GA 263/I, p. 143f.

401 Ibid., p. 145.

402 Ibid., p. 148.

403 Ibid., p. 150.

404 Ibid., p. 154.

405 Ibid., p. 156.

406 Ibid., p. 156.

407 Ibid., p. 157.

408 Ibid., p. 158.

409 Ibid., p. 159f.

410 Ibid., p. 160f and 162.

411 Ibid., p. 163.

412 On 7 October 1923 in Dornach, towards the end of a wide-ranging lecture on the Easter mystery, and turning ever more insistently to the sculptural Group to speak of the potential reality of an Easter Mystery Play to be performed in front of it, Rudolf Steiner said: 'A kind of Mystery Play set precisely before this sculpture

and within this architectural reality should unfold, whose chief protagonists are the human being and Raphael, Raphael with the staff of Mercury, Raphael with all that is related to the staff of Mercury. In the living realm of art everything, everything makes demands on us, and fundamentally there is no sculpture and no architecture which, if it is inwardly a cosmic truth, would not require and demand what occurs artistically within a room possessing this architecture, this sculpture. And at Eastertide this architecture and this sculpture would require a Mystery Play: the human being, instructed by Raphael to the degree that ahrimanic and luciferic forces can render the human being sick and to the degree that, through the power of Raphael one can be guided to understand, to recognize the healing principle, the great cosmic therapy, that lives in the Christ principle. And if all this could be achieved entirely—for all this lay as potential in the Goetheanum —then for instance, among many other things it would be established that everything that can flow into the human being from ahrimanic and luciferic influences would undergo a certain crowning and culmination precisely at Eastertide.' (GA 229, p. 53f.)

[413] Cf. Emanuel Zeylmans van Emmichoven, *Wer war Ita Wegman*, op. cit., vol. 1, p. 155ff.

[414] Letter from Edith Maryon to Rudolf Steiner (undated), Rudolf Steiner Archive, Dornach (not in GA 263/I). A notebook entry by Wegman from April 1925 suggests that Wegman (like Marie Steiner-von Sivers [see below]) had trouble with the close connection between Steiner and Maryon: 'Some months after the fire / the karmic connections / that lay between Dr and myself / were revealed to me./ Karma existed of course / always between us / karma action hindered / by Miss von Sivers / by Miss Maryon […].' (Ita Wegman Archive.) As described, Rudolf Steiner only began his intensive collaboration with Ita Wegman *after* Edith Maryon had fallen ill (in autumn 1923); in December 1922, still, Steiner had sent a message to Ita Wegman relating to the medical staff of the Clinical-Therapeutic Institute (and thus to a core concern of Wegman) via Edith Maryon, writing on 5 December:

'And so I am asking, though do not exert yourself, to tell Frau Dr Wegman at once *by telephone* that I would consider it best to ask Dr Knauer to come to Arlesheim for a few days. He should see things there for himself, for now he definitely wishes to go. But I think the demands on him would be too great since he has to support his mother and sister. I'm writing this because I have too little time to write to Frau Dr Wegman myself—it will be enough to tell her this by phone.' (GA 163/I, p. 109; cf. also in regard to the destiny connection between Ita Wegman and Edith Maryon the views of Emanuel Zeylmans van Emmichoven in, *Wer war Ita Wegman*, op. cit., vol. I, p. 269f.) As regards Marie Steiner-von Sivers's view of Rudolf Steiner's close connection with Edith Maryon, Elisabeth Vreede recorded the following in an unpublished manuscript ('Short history of the first weeks after R.[udolf] St.[einer]'s death', October 1934) concerning the return of the Vorstand from Steiner's cremation and the discussions that began about the studio: 'On the return journey Frau Dr W[egman] said she hoped that we will often come together for meetings in Dr Steiner's studio. Frau Dr St.[einer] said she had planned to ask the Vorstand to leave her the studio for the purpose of cataloguing Dr Steiner's literary estate. [...] At Dr Wegman's objection that they should retain the studio as a shared memorial, she said that the studio had no good memories for her anyway, that Dr Steiner had always been there with Miss Maryon, and she cried out most emotively, "I had to tolerate what no woman ever had to tolerate!" This small-minded outbreak of jealousy at this very moment was horrifying for me.' (Manuscript p. 3, Archive at the Goetheanum.) Rex Raab's well-meaning assumption that the relationship between Marie Steiner-von Sivers and Edith Maryon had been 'good' (*Edith Maryon*, op. cit., p. 224, cf. also Raab's 'deduction' there) very probably does not by any means stand up to scrutiny of the complicated relationships involved. There is much to suggest rather—as Elisabeth Vreede's memoir shows—that the discussions about the studio and Ita Wegman also indirectly related to Edith Maryon. Until his death, Marie Steiner-von Sivers wholly and unreservedly accepted and affirmed Rudolf Steiner's wishes and work intentions (cf. Peter Selg, *Marie Steiner-von Sivers... op.cit.*). But after 30 March 1925, quite clearly, breakdowns and conflicts occurred that were the expression of huge emotional strains and unresolved relationships.

415 GA 263/I, p. 165.

416 Ibid., p. 165f.

417 Sofie Bauer, quoted in Rex Raab, op. cit., p. 324.

418 Letter from Edith Maryon to Rudolf Steiner (undated). Rudolf Steiner Archive, Dornach (not in GA 263/I).

419 GA 263/I, p. 167.

420 GA 260, p. 144f.

421 GA 260a, p. 110.

422 Cf. Sergei Prokofieff, *'Menschen mögen es hören'. Das Mysterium der Weihnachtstagung*, Stuttgart 2002.

423 See in this connection my exploration of this influence for the field of medicine: *'Die Medizin muss Ernst machen mit dem geistigen Leben.' Rudolf Steiners Hochschulkurse for junge Mediziner*, Dornach 2006 (especially Chapters 1 and 2).

424 GA 233a, p. 134f.

425 GA 233, p. 143.

426 GA 233, p. 144f.

427 GA 263/I, p. 235.

428 Ibid., p. 240.

429 Julie Klima, 'Erinnerungen an Rudolf Steiner', in: Peter Tradowsky (ed.): *Ludwig Polzer-Hoditz: Erinnerungen an Rudolf Steiner*, p. 310.

430 GA 263/I, p. 168.

431 Ibid., p. 169.

432 Ibid., p. 239f.

433 Ibid., p. 235.

434 Quoted in Rex Raab, *Edith Maryon...*, op. cit., p. 372.

435 GA 263/I, p. 240.

436 Ibid., p. 371.

437 Ibid., p. 217.

438 GA 261, p. 297.

439 GA 263/I, p. 225.

440   Rudolf Steiner Archive, Dornach (note-page 1417).

441   GA 263/I, p. 229f. After repeating these lines at the end of his
       address, Rudolf Steiner said in conclusion: 'And so, you soul so
       faithfully devoted to our cause, pass onward! We wish to look
       upward to you. We know that you look down upon us, we know
       that we remain united with you through all cycles of eternity. We
       live onward with you as you live the life that conquers death for
       as long as we are here, and when we are no longer here, we will
       continue to live with you at one, at one, at one.' (GA 261, p. 316.)

Bibliography

Volumes in the Collected Works (GA) by Rudolf Steiner directly referred to or cited in the text and notes. English titles are given where published translations are available.

GA 14	*Four Mystery Dramas*
GA 24	*Renewal of the Social Organism*
GA 35	*Philosophie und Anthroposophie: Gesammelte Aufsätze 1904-1923*
GA 36	*Der Goetheeanumgedanke inmitten der Kulturkrisis der Gegenwart: Gesammelte Aufsätze aus der Wochenschrift 'Das Goetheanum' 1921–1925*
GA 84	*The Aims of Anthroposophy*
GA 118	*The Christ Impulse*
GA 133	*Earthly and Cosmic Man*
GA 141	*Between Death and Rebirth*
GA 142	*The Bhagavad Gita and the West*
GA 143	*Erfahrungen des Übersinnlichen. Die drei Wege der Seele zu Christus*
GA 148	*The Fifth Gospel*
GA 152	*Approaching the Mystery of Golgotha*
GA 157	*Destinies of Individuals and Nations*
GA 158	*Our Connection with the Elemental World*
GA 159	*Das Geheimnis des Todes. Wesen und Bedeutung Mitteleuropas und die europäischen Volksgeister*
GA 161	*Artistic Sensitivity as a Spiritual Approach to Knowing Life and the World*
GA 162	*Kunst- und Lebensfragen im Lichte der Geisteswissenschaft*
GA 164	*Der Wert des Denkens für eine den Menschen befriedigende Erkenntnis. Das Verhältnis der Geisteswissenschaft zu Naturwissenschaft*
GA 165	*Unifying Humanity Spiritually*
GA 175	*Building Stones for an Understanding of the Mystery of Golgotha*

GA 176   *The Karma of Materialism / Aspects of Human Evolution*

GA 180   *Ancient Myths and the New Isis Mystery*

GA 181   *Dying Earth and Living Cosmos*

GA 182   *Death as Metamorphosis of Life*

GA 183   *Human Evolution*

GA 184   *Eternal and Transient Elements in Human Life*

GA 185a   *Entwicklungsgeschichtliche Unterlagen zur Bildung eines sozialen Urteils*

GA 186   *The Challenge of the Times*

GA 190   *Conscious Society*

GA 192   *Geisteswissenschaftliche Behandlung sozialer und pädagogischer Fragen*

GA 194   *Michael's Mission*

GA 197   *Polarities in the Evolution of Mankind*

GA 199   *Spiritual Science as a Foundation for Social Forms*

GA 200   *The New Spirituality and the Christ-Experience of the Twentieth Century*

GA 203   *Der Mensch in Zusammenhang mit dem Kosmos 3: Die Verantwortung des Menschen für die Weltentwickelung durch seinen geistigen Zusammenhang mit dem Erdplaneten und der Sternenwelt*

GA 204   *Materialism and the Task of Anthroposophy*

GA 211   *The Sun Mystery and the Mystery of Death and Resurrection*

GA 214   *The Mystery of the Trinity*

GA 217a   *Youth and the Etheric Heart*

GA 218   *Spirit as Sculptor of the Human Organism*

GA 223   *The Cycle of the Year as Breathing Process of the Earth / Michaelmas and the Soul Forces of Man*

GA 224   *Die menschliche Seele in ihrem Zusammenhang mit göttlich-geistigen Individualitäten. Die Verinnerlichung der Jahresfeste*

GA 226   *Man's Being, His Destiny, and World Evolution*

GA 229   *Das Miterleben des Jahreslaufes in vier kosmischen Imaginationen*

GA 233a   *Rosicrucianism and the Modern Initiation*

GA 243   *True and False Paths in Spiritual Research*

GA 254   *The Occult Movement in the Nineteenth Century*

GA 255b   *Die Anthroposophie und ihre Gegner 1919–1921*

GA 257   *Awakening to Community*

GA 259   *Das Schicksalsjahr 1923 in der Geschichte der Anthroposo-phischen Gesellschaft: Vom Goetheanumbrand zur Weihnacht-stagung*

GA 260   *The Christmas Conference for the Founding of the General Anthroposophical Society 1923/1924*

GA 260a   *Die Konstitution der Allgemeinen Anthroposophischen Gesellschaft und der Freien Hochschule für Geisteswissenschaft. Der Wiederauf-bau des Goetheanum*

GA 261   *Our Dead*

GA 263   *Rudolf Steiner—Edith Maryon: Briefwechsel. Briefe—Sprüche—Skizzen, 1912–1924*

GA 268   *Mantric Sayings*

GA 271   *Art and Knowledge of Art*

GA 272   *Anthroposophy in the Light of Goethe's Faust*

GA 286   *Architecture as a Synthesis of the Arts*

GA 292   *Art History as a Reflection of Inner Spiritual Impulses*

GA 298   *Rudolf Steiner in the Waldorf School*

GA 300b   *Faculty Meetings, Vol. 2*

GA 303   *Soul Economy*

GA 324a   *The Fourth Dimension*

GA 333   *Freedom of Thought and Societal Forces*

GA 338   *Communicating Anthroposophy*

GA 342   *First Steps in Christian Religious Renewal*

GA 343   *Vorträge und Kurse über christlich-religiöses Wirken, Bd.2 Spirituelles Erkennen—Religiöses Empfinden—Kultisches Handeln*

For English-language titles contact Rudolf Steiner Press, UK (www.rudolfsteinerpress.com) or SteinerBooks, USA (www.steinerbooks.org).

A note from the publisher

For more than a quarter of a century, **Temple Lodge Publishing** has made available new thought, ideas and research in the field of spiritual science.

Anthroposophy, as founded by Rudolf Steiner (1861-1925), is commonly known today through its practical applications, principally in education (Steiner-Waldorf schools) and agriculture (biodynamic food and wine). But behind this outer activity stands the core discipline of spiritual science, which continues to be developed and updated. True science can never be static and anthroposophy is living knowledge.

Our list features some of the best contemporary spiritual-scientific work available today, as well as introductory titles. So, visit us online at **www.templelodge.com** and join our emailing list for news on new titles.

If you feel like supporting our work, you can do so by buying our books or making a direct donation (we are a non-profit/ charitable organisation).

office@templelodge.com

TEMPLE LODGE

For the finest books of Science and Spirit